MASH Angels

Tales of an Air-Evac Helicopter Pilot in the Korean War

T0150235

RICHARD C. KIRKLAND

Burford Books

Printed in the United States of America.

10   9   8   7   6   5   4   3   2   1

Cataloging in Publication Data is available from the Library of Congress.

MASH Angels

Dedication

To my wife Maria,
for her continued encouragement and inspiration

Chapter 1

The Worthless Contraption

"Bogies twelve o'clock. Drop your tanks," came the calm voice of Captain Dick Bong in my earphones. Normally Bong didn't talk much during a dogfight—he was too busy blowing Zeros out of the sky. But on this flight he was leading the squadron, so it was his job to call for external-fuel-tank drop when an enemy engagement was imminent.

By the time I had switched the fuel-selector valve and punched the salvo switch, he'd added, "Okay, let's go get 'em, Captive." (Captive was our call sign. The Army Air Corps 9th Fighter Squadron of the 49th Fighter Group in World War II were "The Flying Knights.")

When I felt my tanks drop away, I rammed the twin throttles of my P-38 fighter to full power and followed Bong as he winged over and dove on a formation of Japanese Zeros. They were about 3,000 feet below and flying toward us. I could tell they hadn't seen us yet because they were holding course directly toward us, which they wouldn't intentionally do with P-38s because of our superior fire power.

Bong fired first since he was in the lead, and his initial burst caught a Zero head on. It exploded in flames then snapped into a wild tumble, shedding flaming pieces as it hurtled into its death plunge. The rest of the Japanese formation scattered in all directions with our fighters in hot pursuit like hounds after a fox. Within seconds we were entangled in a giant aerial melee of swarming P-38s and Zeros.

I took a snap shot at a Zero as it zipped past, then rolled into a bank for a deflection shot at another. Before I could get a lead on him fireballs came flying past my canopy. I glanced over my shoulder to see black engine cowling and blinking wing guns: I had a Zero right on my tail and he had me in his sights! I rolled into a split S and dove away. He followed, but fortunately for me, he had to break off because one of my squadron-mates came swooping down on him.

When I pulled out of the dive and looked around, there was no one on my tail, but I could hear the pitched radio chatter that went something like this:

"Blue Three, look out! Two o'clock! Two o'clock!"

"I got 'em, I got em'!"

"Red Leader, there's a couple heading for that cloud."

"Blue Four, you're trailing smoke!"

"I took a hit in my left engine."

"Bill! You got one on your tail!"

"Sonofabitch! Get 'im off!"

"I'll get 'im—!"

"I got one! Look at that bastard burn!"

"I see him, John. That's a confirmed."

"Red Leader, I'm gettin' outta here, I lost an engine!"

"Who's calling Red Leader?"

"It's Red Four! Red Four!"

"Red Three, cover Red Four!"

"Roger, I got him in sight."

To be involved in an aerial dogfight between opposing fighters in World War II had to be one of the most terrifying, yet exhilarating, experiences in the business of warfare. Although this form of combat originated in World War I, the airplane of that day was little more than a motorized kite compared to the powerful, heavily armed fighters of WWII. The basic rules of engagement were the same, but we flew at speeds and altitudes never dreamed of by those first air knights. The result, however, was the same: it was an aerial duel to the death; the winner went home to fame, the loser went down in flame.

The big winner that November day in 1943 was Captain Dick Bong, who scored two kills, his 20th and 21st. He eventually shot down 40 Japanese aircraft and became America's all-time Ace of Aces. His record will stand forever, since that type of aerial combat is history.

The loser that day on our side was Lt. George Haniotis. He was on the losing end of an aerial duel. But he managed to keep his mortally wounded fighter in the air until he was out to sea and away from the Japanese base, then had to parachute out.

We covered him until he landed in the water and got into his one-man rubber lifeboat. There was nothing more we could do. The dog-fight was over. The Zeros that survived had gone home. We also had to go home since we barely had enough fuel remaining to get there. We swooped down over Haniotis. He waved. Then we climbed back up to cruising altitude and set course for the long flight back to our base at Dobodura, on the Island of New Guinea.

Normally, on a successful mission where we had downed enemy aircraft, there would be lots of spirited radio chatter on the flight home. This time it was quiet on that long flight. The vision of our squadron-mate waving goodbye from his tiny boat in that vast expanse of the Bismarck Sea burned vividly in our thoughts. We all knew there was little chance he could survive. We were right.

I had a number of memory-searing incidents involving the loss of squadron-mates during the course of flying 103 combat missions in World War II. All of which I remember vividly. But if we fast-forward ten years, the one that came back to me in crystal-clear focus on a cold winter day during the Korean War was that of George Haniotis.

I was the pilot of a Sikorsky helicopter hovering over the wind-swept waves of the Yellow Sea where a downed jet pilot struggled for life in the freezing water directly below. When I looked down at him, I could see Haniotis waving from his tiny boat. There hadn't been anyone to rescue Haniotis. But now there was someone to rescue this fighter pilot: me, and my helicopter. And I did that. But getting there and getting that job done wasn't easy. The helicopter pilots of the Korean War were indeed pioneers, flying primitive helicopters with no armor, no instruments, no lights and no guns. And it was particularly difficult for me because I was a misplaced fighter pilot flying a helicopter! To tell that story I need to start back at the end of WWII…

● ● ●

I had decided to stay in the Army Air Force after the war because the new jet fighters were just coming out and, like most fighter pilots, I wanted to fly them.

Mass confusion reigned as our giant war machine was dismantled in wholesale slaughter fashion. Military and political leaders were aware of the burgeoning communist threat, but we had just fought the most devastating and costly war in history, so no one wanted to hear about a communist threat. And you couldn't blame them. Millions of servicemen were discharged and millions of war machines were disposed of as we reduced our defenses to peacetime status—while the communists geared up for world domination.

As I waited for an assignment to jet fighters, I was sent here and there, finally ending up at McChord Army Air Base in Tacoma, Washington, in a sort of catch-all squadron with an assortment of leftover war birds. Our official mission was air and sea search and rescue, or whatever else command could think of.

The colonel in charge of this assortment had spent the war in a fat cat job so he didn't have a lot of medals to wear. That must have given him some kind of complex because he wasn't very friendly toward me or any of the other combat returnees. Every time I submitted an application to jet fighters, he would disapprove it.

When a Sikorsky R-5 helicopter was assigned to our base for rescue work, they scheduled a flight demonstration the day it arrived. I'd never seen one and wasn't very interested, but all pilots were required to attend. So we gathered in a group out on the flight ramp and stood around waiting impatiently for it to show.

Before I saw it, I heard this totally alien sound. Not like the deep crack of a fighter engine, or even like the roar of the new jets. It was a whirling, beating sound. When it appeared over the tree line at the far end of the airfield, it looked like some kind of gangly bird right out of prehistoric times. It had spindly legs on a fat body and a tail like an elongated ice cream cone with a small propeller at the tip. The front end looked like the discarded greenhouse from a Heinkel 111 and the whole cluster of heterogeneous parts dangled beneath a whirling, multiblade windmill.

As it labored toward us, the big windmill on top beat the air desperately, sending shock waves bouncing off the metal hangars where our group of disbelieving pilots stood gaping. I saw it, but didn't believe it. There were no wings! No aerodynamic surfaces! No stabilizers! It shouldn't fly. But it did, thrashing its way across the airfield just a few feet above the ramp. When it moved up near us the swirling blast of air from the windmill sent service caps sailing in all directions.

"Look at that crazy thing!" one of the pilots exclaimed. "I can't believe it!"

I couldn't believe it either. Yet I watched, fascinated, as the helicopter hovered over the ramp in one spot for several minutes. Then, turning sideways, it moved slowly out across the flight ramp, stopped, reversed itself, and moved back in the opposite direction, coming to a halt directly in front of us. Hovering there, it slowly rotated 360 degrees, then, as though saving its greatest feat till last, began to move backwards—to the astonishment of every pilot watching.

I will always remember the disturbing ambivalence I experienced as I watched the helicopter perform. It was homely and awkward looking, without a single pleasing aerodynamic feature. It was an ugly duckling if I'd ever seen one. Yet, it was uniquely graceful. And there was something fascinating about the way it hovered there, defying the laws of gravity—and seemingly of aerodynamics.

When the R-5 landed, it touched down like a feather in front of our gawking group. After a moment, the engine sputtered and died and all of the strange grinding noises began to subside as the long, fabric-covered windmill blades gradually slowed, drooped down, and wobbled to a stop.

A small door in the nose section opened and the helicopter pilot, wearing a bright red baseball cap with a gold bar pinned to the front, stepped out and reported to the colonel who was standing there with a scowl on his face.

"Is that special issue head gear for heeleocopter drivers?" he snarled, glaring at the red cap.

The pilot tried to explain that a ball cap was the most practical headgear for the helicopter because it flies at low altitude and you don't need an oxygen mask.

The colonel waved off his explanation and said, "On this military installation, lieutenant, you will wear regulation head gear."

The helicopter pilot snatched the ball cap from his head and muttered, "Yes, sir."

"Lieutenant, I want you to do whatever is necessary to put that thing in storage. It won't be needed around here until our rescue mission is fully integrated. I want it pickled, and parked in the back of the hangar, out of the way of our real aircraft."

"But...sir."

The colonel turned on his heel, as some of the pilots and ground crew had begun to move toward the helicopter for a closer look. "That's all, gentlemen!" he snapped. "The formation is dismissed. You may return to your duty stations." Obediently, though reluctantly, the curious ground crewmen dispersed and the pilots followed the colonel off the flight ramp, in order of rank, for the most part.

As the procession exited, I slipped into the hangar through a side door, walked back through the interior and out onto the ramp. I didn't know why beyond that I simply wanted to have a closer look at it. As I approached the helicopter, the pilot, with one hand still clutching the red ball cap, slowly raised the other hand to the side of his machine, as though in a gesture of defense.

I grinned and said, "That guy isn't what he appears, lieutenant. Actually, he's a baboon we dress up to look like a colonel." I could see by the way the helicopter pilot looked at me that didn't know what to make of it all. I introduced myself and said, "How about explaining to me how this flying machine works?"

After some coaxing he calmed down and gave me my first lesson on how a rotary-wing aircraft functions. "The basic aerodynamic principles are the same as an airplane." Pausing, he glanced back over his shoulder, as though to insure the colonel had not returned. Then looking up at the windmill. "Those rotor blades serve the same function as the wing on an aircraft except that the aircraft wing is fixed to the fuselage, whereas my wing turns. And for the same purpose: to create lift. A fixed wing is pulled through the air with a propeller to create lift and thus sustain flight. My wing is whirled thought the air, with the same result." He gave me a little grin and added, "There's nothing magic about it. Just plain ole aerodynamics like any bird or airplane."

"Birds and airplanes all have tails for stability and directional control. How do you do it with a bird that doesn't have a tail?"

"Oh, but it does! The tail rotor. That little prop at the end of the tail cone provides for stability and directional control, the same as a tail on an airplane. The angle of attack on that airfoil is changed through application of the rudder pedals, thus countering engine torque, while providing directional control."

"So that's how you do it. Then the little prop in the back doesn't push?"

"No."

I peeked into the cockpit. "There are some strange-looking levers in there. How do you control the attitude?"

"Let me show you," he said, opening the side door. "The attitude is controlled with this lever here in the center of the cockpit. It's similar to the stick on an airplane. We call it cyclic control. Upon application, it changes the pitch on the main rotor blades selectively during the cycle of rotation, thus tipping the rotor plane in whatever direction you've selected. Like an aircraft—when you push forward, the nose goes down; pull back and the nose comes up."

"Okay, I follow that. But how do you go straight up...uh, how do you hover?"

He reached across the cockpit and grasped another lever. "This is called the collective pitch stick and when you move it up or down, it changes the angle of attack on all of the rotor blades simultaneously and you go straight up or down."

"Okay. So now you got one hand on that stick...the...uh, collective, and the other on the azimuth and your feet on the rudders, how do work the throttle?"

"That's easy," he said smiling. "There is a motorcycle-type twist throttle on the collective stick."

I shook my head. "You gotta be busier than a one-armed paper hanger to fly this thing."

"Well, yeah...you're busy all right. But it's not all that bad once you get the hang of it."

I shook my head. How did you ever happen to get stuck flying these things?"

"Well, I joined the Army Air Corps to be a fighter pilot and somehow I ended up in helicopters. But you know how it goes in the good ole Army."

"Yeah, I know how it goes in the good ole Army! Your first choice was good, but I don't know about this."

"Well, I'll tell ya, I wanted to be a fighter pilot all right, but now I wouldn't trade you places for all the tea in China. I love it, and I'll tell you something else: this machine, the helicopter, will someday play a major role in aviation, particularly in saving lives."

"Think so, huh?"

"Yes. Despite the general impression that it's just a novelty with no real mission, I can tell you it has some remarkable capabilities. I wish I could show you."

"Well, why not?"

The color drained from the pilot's face. "Uh...well, you know, the colonel."

"Didn't he tell you to do whatever is necessary to get it ready for storage?"

"Yeah...he did."

"So, getting it ready could include a test hop to adjust the...uh, azimuth?"

About that time the line chief and two helpers arrived on the scene. "Sir, I'm supposed to help you get this...ah, machine, into hangar storage," the sergeant said courteously.

"This thing's gotta have a test hop before it goes in the hangar, Sarge," I said.

The pilot looked at me, then said, "Uh, yes...I need to make a...quick test flight."

The line chief, a senior sergeant whom I knew from our days in the same fighter squadron, looked at me suspiciously then said to the pilot, "Yes, sir. How long will it take?"

"Not long," he said, opening the door to the front cockpit and motioning for me to climb in.

I started to get in, but noticed there was no parachute. "Lieutenant, there's no chute up here. I'll have to go get one."

"Another of the great features of the helicopter: no parachute necessary."

I looked at him incredulously. I'd never flown without a parachute. "What if it shoots craps?"

"If we have a problem...shoots craps, we simply land. And we can land anywhere: on a road, in a backyard, in a pea patch. Wherever. The helicopter doesn't need a runway to land on, so in essence, it takes its own landing field right with it."

I looked at him skeptically. "What happens to the windmill if the engine quits?" I asked, jabbing my thumb upward at the rotor blades.

"If that happens, we just windmill down," he explained confidently. "We call it autorotation. It's just as good as a parachute."

I glanced at the sergeant, who was standing there with his arms folded and the hint of a smile on his face. All my instincts said don't do it, but for whatever reason, I had to fly this crazy machine. I climbed into the front seat and strapped myself in...tight.

The sound of the starter reminded me of a model-A Ford I once owned. Finally, the engine coughed, belched a cloud of black smoke and roared to life.

After a short warm-up, the engine began to labor and the windmill started to move. Slowly at first, then it increased in revolutions until its resolution was a blur above the helicopter. Simultaneously, the sounds and vibrations of many dynamics filled the cockpit.

I heard the pilot call the tower for takeoff clearance and over the intercom: "Here we go!"

Without acceleration of speed or sound, the whirling, tremulous machine simply lifted itself up off the earth. And a new dimension was added to my fascination for flying—the third dimension: vertical flight.

There was indeed, a freedom of movement, a thrilling release from the surly bonds of earth that was even more sensational than conventional flight. In a passing thought, I wondered how John Gillispie Magee might have worded "High Flight," if he could have flown a helicopter.

I was vaguely aware the pilot was explaining his application of the controls, but the dominance of my attention was on the esoteric sensations I was experiencing as the helicopter hovered over its omnidirectional course. And what a strange, unique contrast in sight and sound to that which I was so familiar. Absent was the acceleration for take-off: the rising crescendo of sound, the wind roar over the canopy. The helicopter had just lifted itself up into the air space, where it defied gravity and moved with boundless freedom, similar to that which a hummingbird must enjoy.

Hovering, it sidled out across the flight ramp, past the line of hangars. Applying rudder pedal, the pilot swung the tail around to where the nose had been. Then he moved forward again, slowly out across the grass beyond the runways and over a small creek that ran along the perimeter of the airfield. I glanced down into the clear water and saw a rainbow trout dash under a rock. I had wondered if there were any fish in that creek. Now I knew. There was at least one.

When we reached the edge of the tree line, he pulled up on the collective pitch lever and the helicopter lifted over the tall evergreens, its landing wheels skimming along the top branches. As we passed over the village that bordered the air base, a woman wearing a bright orange dress looked up from where she was hanging clothes in her backyard. I could see the surprised look on her face. How clearly and easily I could see detail that would only be a fleeting blur from a fighter. Then I caught another movement below: a covey of quail fluttered into a thicket and a cottontail rabbit dashed in the opposite direction. I felt as though

I was suspended on a moving skyhook that featured a grand panoramic view of the passing parade of life below!

When the helicopter began to lose its forward speed, it triggered an instinctive warning in me: approaching stall speed...Watch it!...Going to stall! But it didn't. The helicopter gave a little extra shudder and came to a stop in midair. And it hovered there, above the treetops, in one cubicle of air space, all forward speed gone. "Try that in a fixed-wing airplane!" I heard the pilot say over the intercom.

Then the helicopter began to sink: down it went through the tree-tops. I could see branches waving and dancing all around from the wind of the rotor blades. I grabbed onto the structure of the cockpit in antici-pation of the imminent crash. But the helicopter didn't crash. Its decent gradually slowed and stopped as it came to a hover. Then the wheels gently settled into a carpet of green grass on the bank of a sparkling brook in a grove of evergreens.

When we landed back on the flight ramp at McChord a few minutes later and all the machinery had ground to a stop, I crawled out of the front cockpit of the Sikorsky R-5 helicopter and stood silently staring at it while strange, ambivalent thoughts ricocheted around in my head. Flying was the love of my life. And the ultimate in flying was an agile, swift, fighter plane. I knew that; everyone knew that. So what was this? How did this strange machine fit into the picture? It was ugly. It was noisy. It was tremulous...yet it was fascinating. The freedom of movement...the sensation of vertical ascent and descent...hovering in midair...landing in a meadow...?

I heard a voice say, "Isn't that some way to fly?"

I turned and looked into the helicopter pilot's beaming face. "Yeah, it is," I muttered, shaking my head. "It was some kind of experience." Then, as though to myself, "But it was very disturbing."

"Why was it disturbing?" he asked.

I glanced back at the helicopter, as though it might answer my question, because I didn't have an answer. All I knew was that I'd just had a unique experience that left me exhilarated, yet confused, and with a strange anxiety. Christ! I was a fighter pilot, and a good one...and one way or another I was going to be a jet fighter pilot! So what was this…what…?

"Lieutenant Kirkland," interrupted the line chief. "The colonel wants to see you in his office immediately."

I pulled my eyes from the helicopter and looked at the line chief accusingly. "Sarge, did you squeal on me?"

"Naw, lieutenant, wasn't me. I don't know who ratted on you."

When I stepped into the headquarters orderly room a few minutes later, the colonel's adjutant, a wormy little captain, looked at me with a smirk on his face and I knew I was in trouble. Sure enough, a few minutes later as I stood at attention on the carpet in front of the colonel's desk, his opening salvo was: "Kirkland, who the hell do you think you are?"

"Well…."

"You think just because you got a couple hero badges you can get away with anything, don't you?"

"No, sir."

"Let me tell you something, lieutenant, in case you didn't know it. The war is over and the days of you fighter jocks cutting a wide swath is over, too. We are back to the regular Army days and back to proper discipline. Do you understand me, lieutenant?"

"Yes, sir."

"I ordered that contraption put in the hangar and that didn't exempt the great you."

"I—"

"Shut up!"

"Yes, sir."

As the colonel glared at me, I could tell from the look on his face that wheels were grinding. Sure enough, a little cat smile eased out and he leaned back in his chair. "You know I just came up with the perfect solution for a smartass like you, Kirkland. You and that worthless contraption were made for each other. We got a requisition for a pilot to heeleocopter school. Guess who I'm gonna volunteer for that?"

I looked at the colonel's smirking face and said, "Thank you, sir, that would be just fine." After the words were out of my mouth, I couldn't believe I'd said them.

He got a strange look on his face, as though he couldn't believe it either.

"Is that all, sir?" I finally croaked.

He nodded.

I flipped a salute, did a smart about-face and walked out of his office with a sense of satisfaction, but also with the terrible feeling that my dream of flying jet fighters had just gone up in smoke.

Why had I said that? I didn't want to fly helicopters. I wanted to fly jets! All my training and experience was in fighters and that is where I should go: to jet school, not helicopter school! Yet, the flight in the helicopter had stirred a powerful emotion that I couldn't deny. So, with mixed feelings, I gathered up my wife and kids and drove off down the road to the USAF Helicopter School at Waco, Texas.

● ● ●

My attitude wasn't the best when I reported in at Connally Air Force Base for helicopter training. But I had only myself to blame, so I resolved to make the best of it. I just assumed that flying the helicopter would be a breeze for a hotshot fighter pilot. I was wrong.

I learned quickly that flying an airplane and flying a helicopter require two different breeds of cat. In fact it was downright frustrating at first, but after I got over the initial shock to my ego, I discovered why that first flight at McChord Field had fascinated me so. Helicopter flying offers a challenge and a thrill that can't be matched in an airplane. Although the early models were difficult to fly and quite primitive by today's standards, it was a whole new sensation to ascend vertically, hover like a bird, and do all those other things a fixed-wing pilot like me never dreamed of.

I also discovered that the history of the helicopter is every bit as interesting as that of the airplane. There were many imaginative pioneers who struggled with the challenge of vertical flight beginning with

Leonardo Da Vinci in the fifteenth century. He was the first to imagine a vertical-lift machine that would carry passengers, but his efforts were limited to drawings. Gustave de Ponton d'Amecourt, a Frenchman, actually built a vertical-lift machine in the late nineteenth century that he called a "Helicoptere." It was from the Greek words *heliko* and *petron* meaning spiral and wing. Gustave's machine didn't fly very well but the name stuck.

Like the airplane, the first controlled helicopter flights did not come until the twentieth century and even then they were quite primitive with limited performance. Wilbur Wright set the tone in 1909 when he said, "Like all novices we began with the helicopter [in childhood] but soon saw that it had no future and dropped it. The helicopter does with great labor only what the balloon does without labor, and is no more fitted than the balloon for rapid horizontal flight. If its engine stops it must fall with deathly violence for it can neither float like the balloon nor glide like the aeroplane. The helicopter is much easier to design than the aeroplane but is worthless when done."[1]

But then Wilbur and the aviation world didn't know about autorotation in 1909. That's a feature developed later that allows the helicopter, if the engine fails, to windmill down and land like a feather.

A number of pioneers designed and flew helicopters in the early part of the twentieth century, but historians generally agree that Igor Sikorsky's VS 300 was America's first practical helicopter. Sikorsky, a highly successful aircraft designer who had immigrated from Russia to the United States, built and flew his helicopter in 1939. Sikorsky is reported to have made this statement: "The development of a helicopter is so important to the future of aviation and society, that it becomes our inherent responsibility to understand and pursue it. Admittedly, it is radical, but the helicopter concept is wholly rational and like no other vehicle it will operate without regard to prepared landing surfaces. Therefore it will free us of the serious handicap of airport limitations imposed by fixed-wing aircraft. Now the helicopter is not competitive with the airplane. It is complementary, and I envision it will bring into the world a whole new means of saving lives."[2]

As it turned out, Sikorsky was not only the first American to design, build and fly a practical helicopter, his belief that its greatest benefit to the aviation world would be in lifesaving was right on target. But it didn't come easy. Sikorsky and others of the WWII era designed and built helicopters that could lift off vertically, hover, fly modest distances and land without an airport, which gave them a unique capability. But at that time the aviation world was in its budding romance with the new jets and continued to consider the helicopter a novelty and a poor competitor with fixed-wing aircraft.

In the years following WWII, American helicopter pioneers like Sikorsky, Frank Piasecki, Larry Bell, Stanley Hiller, Charlie Kaman and others continued their research and development, making progress in improving performance and reliability. But the helicopter remained a second cousin to the aviation world since its true value in both commercial and military aviation was unrecognized.

What changed that? The Korean War.

Today, the jet-powered helicopter, which enjoys all the technological advantages of any other flying machine, is highly efficient in a variety of vital missions in both military and civil aviation. But as Igor Sikorsky predicted, it performs nothing so well as saving lives. Whether it's snatching a downed pilot from the clutches of terrorists, a shipwrecked sailor from a raging sea, a mother and child from a flooded rooftop, or an injured motorist from a highway accident, the helicopter excels in saving lives. And today few major hospitals are without emergency medical service via helicopter. That lineage comes directly from the MASH "chopper" of the Korean War.

My part in that historic episode was precipitated by a twist of fate. When the Korean War broke out, I was involved in "Operation Greenhouse," which was testing atomic bombs on Eniwetok Atoll in the Marshall Islands. This was a highly classified project requiring isolation on a tiny atoll in the middle of the Pacific Ocean. So I knew little of what was going on in the Korean War until the atomic bomb project was completed and I returned to the States.

It was good to get home to my wife and family after more than a year's separation. The bad news came a short time later when I got my shipping orders for Korea. Needless to say, I was pissed. I had suspected that it might happen because the Air Force needed experienced fighter pilots to combat the Russian MiGs in Korea. And whereas I wasn't crazy about another combat tour, at least I would be doing what I knew best.

Wrong. I was going to Korea as a helicopter pilot!

I couldn't believe it. What was the Air Force thinking? It didn't make any sense. I was an experienced fighter pilot and logic would dictate I be assigned as one. Besides, what could the Air Force possibly do with a helicopter in a shooting war? I had come to love flying the whirlybird, but it was not a combat vehicle. In fact, it didn't even have guns! What were you supposed to do when the bad guys started shooting? And what in the world was a MASH?

Well, I reluctantly went to Korea and found out the answers to all the above.

[1,2] Data from the records of the Helicopter Foundation International, Alexandria, Va.

Chapter 2

Assignment to Korea

The roar of the engines and the vibrations in the aluminum seat of the C-47, a "Gooney bird," hadn't changed much since WWII and the old bird was just as uncomfortable, noisy and cold as ever. This one, flying over the Sea of Japan on November 17, 1952, on its way to Korea, had cargo piled on the cabin floor between the two rows of bucket seats that were filled to capacity with GIs in combat gear who had probably also ridden many a mile in a Gooney.

"I got an extra parka. Wanna put it on?" shouted the sergeant next to me as I sat shivering in a summer blouse. Shouting was necessary for communications in a Gooney bird as there was no insulation or sound-proofing in the passengers' cabin.

"I sure would, Sarge," I shouted back through chattering teeth.

"Don't they give you pilots winter gear?" he asked as he opened his duffel bag, extracted a fur-lined parka and handed it to me.

"Yeah, but it wasn't winter where I came from," I replied and quickly pulled on the parka.

"Well, it's winter where you're going, capt'n."

"You been in Korea?" I asked, as feeling began to return to my frozen body.

"I been there. And I hate goin' back. It's a shithole if there ever was one," the sergeant said, leaning back against the canvas seat straps and pulling the hood of his parka down over his face.

So now I had firsthand confirmation of what I'd already heard about my new assignment. But there wasn't much I could do about it. When I had arrived in Japan a few days earlier from the U.S. and reported to headquarters, 3rd Air Rescue Group, Johnson Air Force Base, Japan, I told the colonel I wasn't happy about my assignment. He was sympathetic, but said there was a shortage of Air Force pilots because they hadn't trained enough since WWII and there was a desperate shortage of helicopter pilots in Korea, so I was needed. To be needed is supposed to make you feel warm and fuzzy. It didn't.

When we landed at Seoul, Korea, designated K-16, I gave the sergeant back his parka and crawled out of the Gooney bird in a pretty depressed frame of mind. And when I looked at the surroundings, I got even more depressed. It reminded me of the devastation I'd seen in WWII with the addition of a cold drabness that made it seem even worse.

"See what I mean?" muttered the sergeant as we walked across the ramp to the broken-down building that served as a terminal. I just nodded.

Inside the terminal was as bad as outside and almost as cold. You could see through the cracks in the board walls. The floor was strewn with gear, duffel bags and GIs standing around in groups talking and smoking. I asked the dispatch sergeant where the helicopter rescue unit was. He shrugged and said he didn't have a clue. Fortunately, one of the MATS (Military Air Transport Service) pilots who had flown the Gooney overheard and said, "They're in that cluster of tents directly across the runway."

"Thanks. How can I get over there?"

"Just walk across the runway. They're pretty loose around here," he replied.

"Better watch out for jets takin' off," informed the uninformed clerk.

"I'll be sure and watch out," I replied sarcastically, picked up my B-4 bag (a zippered travel bag) and walked out of the terminal and across the runway to a cluster of GI tents with a couple of rusted metal Quonset huts on one end. The place looked deserted but I could see smoke coming out of a chimney pipe from one of the Quonsets. It was surrounded by sandbags and had a sign on the door that read: "Rescue Operations."

When I opened the door, the first thing I saw was a black, potbel-lied stove in the center of the room, which I made a beeline for.

"They're supposed to issue you winter clothes in Japan," said a tousle-headed captain sitting at a cluttered, homemade table on one side of the Quonset.

"The supply honcho told me they don't issue winter gear until De-cember 12, that's when winter officially starts," I said dropping my B-4 bag and holding my hands over the stove.

"That figures. You Kirkland?"

I nodded.

"Welcome to Korea."

I nodded again.

"I'm Bill Ryan, operations officer and that guy with the Van Dyke is Sergeant Mills, our operations clerk." Across the tent and behind a 2-by-4 railing, the sergeant, a small, skinny guy with a scraggly beard, looked up from the ancient typewriter he was pecking on. "They got you assigned to tent number four, captain. That's Kim's tent and he's the best house boy we got," advised Mills.

"That's good to know, sergeant," I replied without much enthusi-asm. "I'm not sure I know what a house boy is supposed to do."

"Oh, he does all kinds of things for ya, like gettin' yer laundry done, guarding your footlocker when yer out on the circuit, and stuff like that."

"Guarding my footlocker?" I asked, glancing at Ryan.

Ryan was of medium build with dark hair and eyes and a friendly face. He sort of nodded as though to support the sergeant's claim. "Yeah. Things are a bit rough here in the Seoul area," he explained. "The city is in shambles since both the commies and our troops have fought over it four times in the past couple of years. The Koreans are a proud people but many of 'em are homeless and starving. A few get desperate and turn to stealing anything they can lay their hands on. We hire as many as we can as house boys and guards, and pay them enough to keep 'em from starving to death."

I guess nothing changes in the business of war, I thought.

"You checked out in the H-5?" asked Ryan.

"Yeah."

"Good. That will be your first duty assignment."

"What will I be doing?"

"Medevac and pilot pickup."

"And what will be my second assignment?"

"You checked out in the H-19?"

"Yeah."

"Medevac and pilot pickup," repeated Ryan. "We do a lot of that around here. The only difference is where you do it. That determines what bird you fly. We operate in elements. Each one consists of eight to ten pilots and medics and a couple H-5s or H-19s. The elements are rotated every two or three weeks between the different tactical locations around Korea."

"Sounds like a traveling medicine show."

"I guess you could say that. But the neighborhood where you put on your show can be a rough in some places. Like two of our locations are over a hundred miles behind enemy lines in North Korea."

"Excuse me?" I said, looking at the captain incredulously. "Did you say behind enemy lines?"

Ryan nodded, pulled a cigarette from a package on the cluttered table and fired it. "Yeah. A couple of small islands off the North Korean coast. Living conditions there are a bit primitive," he said, the cigarette smoke tumbling out as he spoke. "But the good news is that after you complete a circuit you get a week in Japan. We're the only combat unit in Korea that gets R and R [Rest and Recuperation] every eight weeks."

I had to admit that was a bright spot in a dark sky. In the South Pacific during WWII, combat crews only got R and R once every 16 weeks. But the rest of what Ryan said made no sense. "Captain Ryan, I'm curious. Just what kind of combat are you talking about with an aircraft that doesn't have a damn gun on it?"

"It's the kind where the bad guys get to shoot at you but you don't get to shoot back," Ryan replied, grinning.

I shook my head, but couldn't help returning the grin. "That's kinda what I figured. But I kept saying to myself that doesn't make any sense so there's gotta be something I don't understand and when I get to Korea they will explain their secret way of flying unarmed helicopters into enemy territory without getting shot down."

"Sorry, no secrets. At least not that I know of. But we have developed some tactics that allow us to fly our missions with reduced risk."

"Could I ask what that means?"

"Your element commander will brief you on our tactics. But what it means is that we are able to save a lot of lives on a daily basis. We pluck downed aircrew out of North Korea and the Yellow Sea, and pull wounded GIs right off the battlefield."

"That sounds very humanitarian. But unless this war is different than the one I fought, I can't imagine how you're doing it."

"No, it's the same. War is war, even if they do call this one a police action...and we do get our ass shot off on occasion. But you'd be surprised at what we accomplish."

I had the feeling that Ryan was telling it straight, but I was having trouble accepting it. My problem, besides believing I shouldn't be there, was that I was skeptical of the whole operation. I'd been flying the helicopter long enough to know that it had unique capabilities and was much improved over the earlier models, but it was still relatively primitive and therefore operationally limited. It was slow, had no instrument flight capability and could only be flown during daylight hours as it had no night-flying equipment. It also had no protective armor and no guns. It simply wasn't suited for combat.

"So the mission is to rescue crews that have been shot down, and evacuate wounded from the battlefield?"

"Yeah. We do some other things too, but that's primarily our mission."

I shook my head, fished out a cigarette and fired it. "Well, at least my old fighter squadron buddies should appreciate that kind of service."

"Your fighter squadron buddies?"

"My old WWII squadron is over here flying jets."

"You were a fighter pilot?"

"Yeah." I could see from the look on Ryan's face what his next question was going to be. "And don't ask me what I'm doing here in a helicopter outfit," I grumbled.

He sort of shrugged, got up from the table and said, "Okay. What say we get you settled and then I'll fill you in on details. Our CO, Major Woods, is at a meeting at headquarters and won't be back till tomorrow. But there's a good friend of yours here and I promised to let him know as soon as you checked in."

"A good friend of mine?"

"Yeah. Major Al Lovelady."

"Ace Lovelady?"

"I didn't know he was an ace."

I smiled. "He sure is. In my book anyway," I replied.

It was great news to hear that my good friend and previous commander was there. I had served under Al Lovelady during the atomic bomb tests on Eniwetok Atoll and knew him to be a sharp officer and a super person. That's why I always called him ace even though he hadn't flown fighters in WWII. I was confident he would have some answers for me, if anyone did. My morale took an upturn.

Ryan pulled a winter parka out of a dilapidated metal wall locker and handed it to me. "This will keep you from freezing until we can get you some winter clothes."

I thanked him kindly and we walked out of the operations Quonset and down a pathway that detoured around a series of sandbagged slit trenches. "You get bombed much?" I asked.

"Not a lot. But when we do, it's almost always in the middle of the night by Bed-Check Charlie. It's a real pain in the ass to get out of the sack and crawl into a slit trench, particularly now that winter's coming on."

I'd crawled into a lot of slit trenches in the middle of the night because of Bed-Check Charlie, but at least in the Southwest Pacific it was always warm, even in the winter.

"Your Bed-Check Charlie ever hit anything?" I asked.

"Aw, once in a while. But he's just a damn nuisance for the most part." It sounded to me like Bed-check Charlie's MO hadn't changed much.

Tent number four that Ryan took me to was in a group of about a dozen pyramidal tents. They were classic GI, but I was surprised to see a wooden floor and a door that had a small piece of Plexiglas you could peek through. Inside there was a potbellied stove in the center and four GI cots, one in each corner with a footlocker and a small homemade wooden table. A bare lightbulb hung on one of the tent poles.

"All the comforts of home," I said, throwing my B-4 bag on the one empty bed.

"Well, it's better here at K-16 than some of our locations. This is home base, but you're not here much because you spend most of the time on the circuit. The other three pilots who bunk here are out now, but you'll get a chance to meet them at element change time."

"How often do you change elements?"

"It depends on what kind of action is going on and the weather. But generally every two or three weeks."

"So we live out of a B-4 bag?"

"Yep. Your footlocker stays here."

"You got any idea when I'll get my footlocker?"

"I hope you don't need it right away because you're not gonna see it for a couple months."

"That figures."

When I shipped my footlocker in WWII, they said I'd get it in 30 days. I didn't get it till two years after the war was over. But they had told me at the POE (Port of Embarkation) in San Francisco that things had improved since that war and this time I'd get it in a two to three weeks. I should have known better.

"There is a small PX over at UN headquarters in Seoul. You can get a few things there."

"I doubt they have painting stuff."

"Painting stuff? What'a you gonna paint?"

"Pictures."

Ryan looked at me curiously.

"I'm gonna paint pictures of beautiful Korea," I explained with a straight face. Then added, "Like I painted pictures of beautiful New Guinea."

"Well, sometimes when things are slow you do have some spare time. But you're right, they probably don't have painting stuff at the PX," said Ryan opening up the lid of the stove. "Normally Kim would have the place all nice and warm for you but we didn't know when you were coming. I'll show you how to fire up the stove and then we'll go on over to Major Lovelady's tent. He's anxious to see you."

After Ryan fired the stove, we left the tent and headed between the row of tents. "Lovelady is in charge of all our aircraft maintenance and support and if it weren't for him, we'd be in deeper trouble than we already are," said Ryan as we walked. I wanted to ask what that meant, but decided against it.

It was good to see Ace Lovelady again and we had a warm reunion. I had some questions to ask him but I decided to wait until we were in private, so our first conversation was light with some reminiscing about our days together on the "rock" at Eniwetok Atoll.

"When they set off that big bomb, which was the initial hydrogen bomb test, it sure enough looked like the whole world was going up in smoke," said Lovelady as the three of us sat on homemade stools around the stove in his tent. "Ya see, Bill," said Lovelady to Ryan. "We had set off some regular atomic bombs, about the size they dropped on Japan, and they were awesome to see. But when they set off that big one it made the others look like a firecracker compared to a thousand-pound bomb."

"Well, didn't you guys get some radio active or somethin'?" asked Ryan seriously.

"Oh sure. We got a shot of nuclear radiation all right, but it didn't affect, affect, affect us none, did it, Ace?" replied Lovelady, grinning. He always called me Ace too. Al was a tall, handsome man and although his hair had grayed and receded early, he had a youthful face and a very expressive smile, particularly when he was joking.

"Naw, it didn't affect, affect, affect me none either," I replied.

We laughed and Lovelady said, "Hey guys, this calls for a little celebration. I got a bottle of Jack Daniel's I been saving for an occasion like this and it looks like Ole Sol is about through for the day."

Ryan got up and peeked out through the little Plexiglas window in the wooden door of the tent. "Yep, she's down. Let's get to celebrating."

"Our party time doesn't start till the sun goes down. That's when we're off flight alert," explained Lovelady, pulling the bottle out of his footlocker.

"As you know, our birds aren't equipped for night flying," added Ryan, glancing at me.

"Yeah, I know. And they're not equipped for a lot of other stuff," I grumbled.

Lovelady and Ryan exchanged glances. "You brief him yet?" asked Lovelady.

"Oh, we had a little discussion, but no details."

"Well Ace, since you're no stranger to combat operations, that part won't hold any big surprises. But the flying you're gonna be doin will be...uh, somewhat different," said Lovelady, pouring some of the Tennessee bourbon into a canteen cup and handing it to me. "By the way, how come you were assigned to—"

"Don't ask," I interrupted. "At least until I've had a shot of the Jack."

Lovelady grinned. "Okay. All I got for mix is Korean H_2O. But it's all right because the alcohol kills the bugs."

"Yeah. It's the only time I drink the water," agreed Ryan.

Sitting on the homemade stools there in the semidarkness, we touched cups and drank. Then Ryan and I dug out cigarettes and fired them while Lovelady fogged up a big black cigar. This was back in the days before we knew that tobacco smoking was on a par with a real overdose of nuclear radiation. "We got a generator for light in the tents, but the damn thing shot craps," muttered Ryan through the cloud of smoke we had created.

"That brings back some memories. I remember one time in New Guinea our generator blew up and we couldn't fix it so we traded one of our P-38s to another outfit for a new generator."

"You're kidding," said Ryan incredulously.

"Don't you guys swap stuff with other outfits?"

"Yeah. But not whole airplanes."

"Well, it was an ole dog that was too beat up to fly combat anymore so we were glad to get rid of it."

"But...?"

"Don't tell me you don't have any ole dogs."

"We got any ole dogs, Al?" asked Ryan.

Lovelady smiled and removed the cigar from the corner of his mouth. "Yeah, we got dogs, but not from being old. They're dogs from taking a hell of a beating."

"So you're getting a lot of battle damage?" I asked.

"Yeah. We get battle damage. But operating conditions is the real culprit. The Korean weather varies from insufferable heat in the summer to subzero winters and knee-deep mud in the spring—with our birds right out in it. Another problem, and it's probably the worst is having to do out-of-envelope flying [exceeding performance limitations of the aircraft]."

"That doesn't surprise me. In fact I can't imagine how the hell you're operating at all."

"Actually, Ace, we're doing pretty well, considering."

"How are you doing well if you got all those problems with the helicopters?"

Lovelady took a puff of his cigar. "We're accomplishing the mission, despite having to overstress the airframe and overspeed our engines, not to mention beating up the rotor blades," Lovelady muttered in the darkness, then snapped his Zippo open, lit a candle and placed it on his footlocker. It gave off enough light so we could at least see each other. He glanced across at Ryan. "You want to give him your slant on it, Bill?"

Ryan shifted on his stool and said, "Well, as I mentioned earlier, we've developed some tactics that have reduced the mechanical problem somewhat, but often our mission demands still exceed the limitations of our birds. We're having to go places and do stuff that's beyond design limits. But we're doing it anyway and accomplishing a mission far beyond what anyone imagined the chopper could do. And that means the helicopters are taking a beating."

"Then you better change the mission," I said.

"It ain't that easy," muttered Ryan.

"Ace," said Lovelady, "You remember the story you told me once about being boxed in by a swarm of Zeros and to get away you had to dive at full throttle, overspeeding the P-38 so badly it nearly shook to pieces?"

How could I forget? "Yeah, but you're not engaging enemy aircraft with helicopters."

"No, but the principle is the same. You do what has to be done when you're trying to save a fellow pilot's life, or snatch a shot-up GI off the battlefield while some son of a gun is shooting at you." Son of a gun was the worst swear word I ever heard Al Lovelady use.

I could relate to that all right. In the early days of WWII we had that problem. Our fighters were flying missions beyond their capability, stretching endurance and engaging superior enemy aircraft—and taking a beating. But we persevered and did what had to be done. Then, when we were equipped with aircraft that matched the enemy's performance and had the range to attack him wherever he was, we kicked ass.

As admitted, I knew little of the Korean helicopter mission before I arrived there. But I did know that our fighter aircraft had the same handicap in the early days of Korea as we did in WWII. Again, America had been unprepared at the outset of the Korean War and the Russian-built MiGs were superior to our F-51 and P-80 fighters. But that changed as our pilots gained experience and received better-performing jets. The pilots flying the new F-86 Sabre jets against the MIGs in Korea about the time of my arrival were starting to kick ass.

But the helicopter was a different story. Since it was all but unknown on the battlefield before Korea, there was no way to judge its relative performance. From what I was being told, it was having a tough row to hoe, but it was performing the mission. My skepticism was hard to disguise and Lovelady removed his cigar and said, "Ace, the helicopters we have in Korea, the Sikorsky H-5 and H-19 and the Army Bell H-13, are the best technology to be had in rotary-wing aircraft in this year of our lord, nineteen hundred and fifty-two. But the best in this case is marginal, relative to the mission we've taken on. Ya gotta remember this is opening curtain for the helicopter—its first big show on the battlefield. By comparison, the mission of fixed-wing fighter aircraft was well defined in WWII and they played a major role in winning that war, as you well know. As such, they have enjoyed significant technological improvement, particularly with the advent of the jet engine. On the other hand, the helicopter saw little application in WWII and that put it on the back burner afterward. So it has not enjoyed the performance advancements that fixed-wing aircraft have. They are well into the jet age. We are not. We're still basically flying first-generation technology with internal-combustion engines. However, despite all that, our helicopters are doin' a job that's never been done before and our crews are doing whatever has to be done to accomplish the mission. We're making the rules, improvising as we go, and in my opinion, doing it amazingly well, considering the obstacles."

I grinned at him. "By golly, Ace, that was quite a speech."

"It sure was," agreed Ryan.

"Amazing what a little Jack Daniel's will do for the tongue," he said with one of his great smiles as he put the cigar back in the corner of his mouth.

I laughed. "Well, I can't disagree with what you said. In all honesty, I still can't imagine how you're doing it. But I guess I'll find out."

"Yep, that you will," said Ryan.

The roar of an aircraft taking off from the K-16 airstrip filled the tent for a moment. When the sound faded, Ryan said, "I assigned you to Captain Enderton's element, Richard. He and his guys will rotate to the

8055 MASH next week so that will be your first duty tour. You'll like Enderton, he's a good troop. He calls his element the 'Tiger Element.'"

"From a Flying Knight, to a Tiger," I muttered.

"A what?"

"We called ourselves The Flying Knights in my ole fighter squadron. Uh, tell me about this MASH. What is it?" I asked.

"You don't know what a MASH is?" said Lovelady.

"Not a clue."

"It's an acronym for Mobile Army Surgical Hospital."

"Is that the same as a field hospital?"

"Well, sort of, except it's been revamped and configured to be more efficient and highly mobile. And of course, a new addition that sort of happened is called 'the chopper.'"

"And that's our part of the act?"

"Yep. Actually, flying for the MASH is pretty good duty. They even have a mess hall."

"They have a mess hall?"

"Yeah."

I glanced at Ryan, then back at Lovelady. "Well, what about it? What's so special about that? I mean, that's where you eat in the military, isn't it?"

Ryan and Lovelady exchanged glances. "Uh...not all our element locations have a mess hall," admitted Ryan.

I laughed. "You guys are putting me on...aren't you?"

They both shook their head.

I rolled my eyes. "So where there is no mess hall, what do we eat?"

"C-rations."

"C-rations? Jesus, I joined the Air Force to stay out of the infantry. Gimme another shot of that jack, would ya?"

"Sure, Ace," said Lovelady.

"Good idea," said Ryan holding out his canteen cup for a refill. "We got our own mess hall here at K-16 and it's tolerable. Before that we had to go across the Haun River to a motor outfit and their chow was so bad one of our guys got ptomaine poison and almost died. Ours is closed right now on account of the generator being down. But it should be back in operation before you go out on the circuit. Our problem is that we're so far down on the logistical priority list, we only get what's left over."

They had told me at headquarters in Japan that the Korean helicopter detachment was one the most decorated combat units in Korea, and had been awarded both a U.S. and Korean Presidential Unit citations. If that was true, it didn't make sense that the unit would be low on the logistical priority list. "Why is that?" I asked.

"Well, it's understandable in a way," replied Ryan. "Ya see, when the Korean War started, there was only a half dozen helicopters in the whole command and they were almost an afterthought in the operational picture. I doubt any of the brass ever thought the helicopter would come to play much of a role on the battlefield. So it will take some time before perceptions change."

It still didn't make sense, but I shrugged and said. "Well, tell me more about how this MASH outfit works."

Ryan was quick to answer. "It works damn good, considering. The MASH was only activated at the outset of the Korean War so they are kinda in the same boat we are—making the rules as they go and improvising. But they've done a bang-up job under really bad conditions. They work in tents right on the edge of the battlefield, taking fire and all that goes with it. And when the commies go on the offensive, the MASH has to run for its life. Then, when our troops go on the offensive, it's move again in the other direction, while trying to patch up wounded GIs."

"And we're there with them?"

"You got it. We live with them, eat with them, work with them and when they move, we and our birds go right with 'em."

"It's tough duty for those MASH folks, particularly the nurses," added Lovelady.

"Nurses? They got nurses on the battlefield?"

"They sure do and those gals do a great job, considering the conditions under which they have to live and work."

"Yeah, I would guess so. We had nurses in the South Pacific at the field hospitals, but they were mostly in the rear areas, out of the combat zone."

"Yep, the MASH is a different breed of cat and so is our chopper. We work together as a team. A great team that is writing history, and you can bank on that," proclaimed Lovelady with a flourish of his cigar.

"You're in really good form tonight, Al," said Ryan.

"It's been awhile since I heard him, but you're right, Bill, he is in good form," I agreed with a chuckle.

"Compliments, gentlemen, will get you everywhere and it just happens I'm in a position to get us a good meal at the headquarters mess. What say we adjourn to yonder facility?"

"Hot diggedy dog!" blurted Ryan and tossed off the remainder of his drink. "Let's go."

In consideration of my blank look, Lovelady explained: "I got a buddy over at UN headquarters and he invites Bill and me over once in a while to have dinner at their mess. And this is one of those nights, and you're included."

"Is that good?" I asked.

"You bet it's good. A couple of generals eat there, so they have good chop," said Ryan.

"Well now, I have to admit I never got invited to dine with no general in WWII," I admitted.

"We aim to please, Ace," said Lovelady.

And so went the introduction of my assignment to Korea. Looking back, even after a half century, I can still remember that Lovelady's and Ryan's encouragement made me feel a little better about being there. But I still harbored some serious resentment and concerns. I knew that surviving WWII had been just good fortune for the most part, and in that war I was doing what I was qualified to do in the best fighter of the day. Now, I was in another war, not doing what I was best qualified to do, and in a primitive flying machine with no means of defense. I simply could not imagine with any degree of confidence how this was all going to work out.

It would be an unforgettable experience, to say the least.

Chapter 3

8055 MASH

T he helicopter unit's designation was Detachment 1 of the 3rd Air Rescue Squadron and they had a supply section that did issue me a full set of winter gear, even if it wasn't official winter yet. That helped with my disposition since it turned brutally cold a few days later, just in time for the beginning of my first duty tour at the 8055 MASH.

Including me, eight members of Captain Enderton's element—four pilots and four medics—were loaded into the back of a two-and-a-half-ton GI truck and driven up the valley northeast of Seoul to the town of Uijongbu (pronounced we-jon-boo). It probably had been a quaint little Korean village before the war. It was now a dreary, war-ravaged cluster of shacks with makeshift repairs using war-wreckage parts and pieces. It appeared deserted other than a column or two of smoke drifting up from within the rubble.

The truck drove on through the rubble and up the road another mile or two, where we came to the 8055 MASH. It was a drab, austere tent city that looked almost as dreary and depressing as Uijongbu.

The main line of resistance (MLR) was a short distance up the road where the Chinese and North Korean forces faced the UN forces on a battle line that generally ran along the 38th parallel. That was the dividing line between North and South Korea which had been established after WWII. So after fighting up and down the length of Korea for two years and killing tens of thousands of soldiers and civilians, the war was right back where it started. And the fighting was just as deadly and vicious as it was in the beginning, even though "peace talks" were now ongoing.

Our element relieved the helicopter crew on duty at the MASH and they got to ride the bouncing, freezing truck back to K-16. From there they would go on by truck or Gooney bird to the next rescue location to replace that crew, which would rotate to another location, and so on until all the rescue stations had been changed. There were seven sites strategically located to provide the best possible coverage for battlefield medevac, air-sea rescue and behind-the-line aircrew recovery. The rationale for rotating the helicopter crews was to balance out the hardship duty at the more primitive and higher risk stations. It worked, but we lived the life of battlefield gypsies.

The MASH tent city was staked into the frozen Korean earth along the banks of the frozen Imjin Gang River, a stone's throw from a bombed-out railroad bridge. The valley lay between two stark, rocky mountain ridges that were nearly void of trees or foliage. The valley was also stark and rocky, with a war-torn village here and there. I didn't see many inhabitants anywhere. Most were probably huddled somewhere in the rubble trying to keep from freezing to death.

Some of the scarred pillars of the railroad bridge still stood, but the main section lay in the frozen riverbed in big chunks of broken concrete and twisted steel. Part of the mutilated track jutted up out of the wreckage like a tortured sentinel. The destroyed bridge with the stark mountain ridges in the background told a story in itself and was the subject of an oil painting I subsequently did after my footlocker finally arrived.

The living quarters were the usual, GI pyramidal tents, but the 8055 had been in this location for awhile so they too had put in wooden floors and doors. That, and the potbellied stoves kept us from freezing to death in a canvas tent at subzero temperatures. Since generators were critical to the function of the MASH, they had a priority on repair and replacement so we had electric lights most of the time.

The hospital was a cluster of tents spread around a large one that was made up of a series of smaller tents lashed together to form one big U-shaped enclosure. Patient receiving was on one end and post-op and outpatient on the other. The personnel's living section was off to one side, and administrative and logistics on the opposite side. The heliport, where we positioned two H-5 Sikorsky helicopters, was about 50 yards out from the central compound.

The four pilots—Captains Charles Enderton and I, and Lieutenants Jeff Drake and Jerry Pouhlin—were quartered in one of the men's tents. Our tent was set up similar to the one at K-16: no frills. However, being gypsies, we lived out of our B-4 bags anyway. It was an Air Force standard-issue folding fabric bag with zippers and side pockets and was about the size of an average suitcase, but you could cram a lot of stuff into it. We each slept on an Army cot with a GI air mattress and "mummy" sleeping bag. It was two down-filled bags, one inside the other, and a necessity for survival on a Korean winter sleep-out.

All our rescue missions in Korea were flown with a medical technician aboard the helicopter. They pulled alert and rotated the same as the pilots. There were four of them at the MASH and they were similarly billeted in the enlisted men's quarters, which was down the hill from the officers' area. This was before unisex facilities, so the nurses' tent area was on the opposite side of the compound.

As it happened, the battlefield was on one of its rare quiet spells the afternoon of our arrival, so Enderton said to me, "Do you partake of alcoholic beverages, Richard?"

"I have been known to do so," I admitted.

"Good. It's recommended as a therapeutic against combat fatigue," he replied with a grin.

I liked Enderton from the outset. He was muscular, solid as a rock, and wore his hair cut short, which made him look like a tough prize fighter. In reality he was softhearted and considerate, although he could be a tough commander when necessary.

"Back in the big war, our ole flight surgeon would hand us a full two-ounce shot of bourbon whisky after a combat mission," I admitted.

"No foolin'?" piped up Drake, from where he lay on his cot in one corner of the tent. Drake was just the opposite of Enderton in that he was tall and slender and wore his hair in 1920s style: parted right down the middle. Drake almost always appeared as though he didn't have a care in the world.

"The Air Force gave you free whisky?" asked Pouhlin. He was tall and handsome with a mop of dark hair, an infectious smile and a great sense of humor. He was easygoing and could always come up with his version of the solution to a problem.

"It was the Army Air Corps in those days," I said.

"Ah yes. Boys of the wild blue yonder. But you know, that's a great idea. I'm gonna suggest it to Major Woods," said Pouhlin. "Free booze after every combat mission."

"Yeah. On days we fly four or five missions we could be stoned by sundown," put in Drake.

"Hey, man, what's wrong with that?" said Pouhlin.

Enderton rolled his eyes. "Anyway, I got my hands on a couple bottles of good English gin the last time I was in Tokyo, so we're gonna have a happy hour tonight and Richard will get a chance to meet the MASH folks."

"That sounds good to me," I said.

That evening I met some of the 8055 doctors and nurses. They were an interesting group with a variety of personalities, but with one common denominator: they didn't like being there any more than I did, but with few exceptions, they were dedicated to the MASH function of saving as many lives as possible despite the adverse conditions and obstacles that faced them daily. As I would subsequently discover, some coped better than others with the challenge.

The temperature was below freezing, so the happy hour attendees were dressed in winter clothes with boots and parkas. But with a tent full of live bodies and our potbellied stove on full power, it was comfortable. There was pretty much standing room only and we used our homemade map table as a bar. Everybody knew to bring their own canteen cups and Drake went out and got a bucket of icicles so we had gin on the icicles or gin mixed with canned grapefruit juice and icicles. It made for a pretty lively party.

One of the surgeons I met that evening had been there for almost a year and only had a short time remaining before going home. I remember that in the course of our conversation something came up about the old Army field hospital. I asked him what he thought was the difference between the Korean MASH and the field hospital of WWII.

"The difference is that you earn your big pay at the Korean MASH," he replied with a smile. That brought snickers and guffawing from the surgeons standing in the group. "I'll answer your question," he said, turning serious. "This is a bloody, vicious war that has already been fought from one end of Korea to the other. And MASH has been right there with the troops like a pack of camp followers. We've implemented whatever surgical procedures were necessary and used our own initiative to improvise under extremely adverse battlefield conditions… while we dodged enemy fire and drug our butts from one shithole to another." He paused a moment, then added, "But we've been uniquely successful because of our mobility, innovative methods, and a new priority system of treating critical wounded based on that thing-a-ma-gig you fly captain: the chopper."

"Right on, Doc!" said Pouhlin.

"Then the helicopter has played a major role in your success?" I asked.

"No question about that. It has added a whole new dimension to battlefield lifesaving capability. With the chopper, a seriously wounded GI can be under a skilled surgeon's care within minutes instead of hours, and that has cut the mortality rate dramatically," said the captain, who then took a big slug of his gin on icicles.

So there it was again. The same thing Ryan and Lovelady had said to me. And now I'd heard it from the horse's mouth, so to speak. About that time I was distracted from the conversation when Enderton pulled me aside to introduce Alice Smith, one of the MASH nurses. She was a large-framed girl with a mop of blond hair, a pretty face and big hazel eyes.

"Alice is the greatest and if you need anything at the 8055, this is the gal to see," claimed Enderton with his arm around her waist.

Alice gave me a warm smile and said, "Welcome, Richard. Charles exaggerates, but I do admit to a bit of partiality to chopper pilots. So if I can be of assistance, just whistle."

We all laughed and Enderton launched into a story about something Alice had done for him. He was interrupted by Pouhlin, who introduced me to another of the MASH surgeons. And so it went until all the gin was gone, then we trooped over to the mess tent and had dinner. I'm not sure how good the food was because after drinking straight gin for a couple hours a pile of hay would have tasted good.

Another of the doctors I met at that party and sat next to at dinner was a tall, dark-haired surgeon by the name of Captain Sam Gilfand. He was from New York City and was indeed, a personality. His alias at the MASH was "Hawkeye." Someone told me they called him that because he had an uncanny ability to identify critical elements in a surgical procedure that others would miss. He was considered one of the best, if not the best surgeon at the MASH. But there was another side to his personality: he had an unusually quick wit, a great sense of humor and loved to play tricks on his colleagues. The Hollywood folks exaggerated his behavior in the TV series "MASH," but some episodes I saw were like watching Sam Gilfand and the past come to life.

I'll always remember Hawkeye's greeting when we first met: "Welcome, Richard, to the 8055 FASH. That means Frozen Army Surgical Hospital," he said with an ear-to-ear smile. "That's a change from this past spring when it was MASH: Muddy Army Surgical Hospital. You should have been here before the mud froze. We had gooey mud, slimy mud, and just plain mud, didn't we, Charles?"

Enderton grinned. "That we did, Hawk."

"Welcome anyway. And don't fret, Richard, it'll be muddy time again before you know it."

Enderton told me the preceding spring had been particularly wet with the roads and camp sites a sea of mud.

After dinner, Hawkeye insisted we go over to his tent and have a nightcap. Drake and Pouhlin were in conversations with a couple of the nurses, so Enderton and I joined him and it turned out to be quite an enlightening experience for me. Hawkeye's tent had all kinds of stuff piled here and there and more hanging on nails along the 2-by-4 railing, and even more on the tent poles. In the TV series they called Hawkeye's tent "the Swamp." I don't remember what he actually called it, but it was something like that. We sat in folding canvas chairs around the stove and he pulled out a bottle of genuine French cognac.

"I want you to know I only serve this to celebrities, so I hope you are one, Richard."

"Oh, he is," announced Enderton, eyeing the cognac. "He's a WWII fighter ace."

"I knew it. I knew you were an ace of some kind," exclaimed Hawkeye.

"Hold," I said. "As much as I'd enjoy a shot of that cognac, I gotta set the record straight. I did shoot down some Zeros, but I wasn't an ace."

Enderton looked genuinely disappointed. "Well, how come Lovelady called you ace?"

"Sorry fellows, that's a little joke Al and I have between us."

"Well, you look like an ace anyway, so we're gonna have some cognac," insisted Hawkeye. He then pulled three glass snifters off a wooden shelf beside his cot, dumped nails and various other knick-knacks out of them, and poured a shot in each.

"You see, celebrities get first-class treatment in this joint—crystal snifters, no less."

"How come I didn't get the crystal treatment when I first got here?" complained Enderton.

"Sorry, Charles, you arrived on a Thursday and I only serve in crystal on Fridays." We pulled the chairs up close to the stove, touched glasses and sipped the Cognac.

"Richard, tell me why you decided to fly helicopters in Korea in-stead of jet fighters," said Hawkeye, in a seemingly serious voice. I sort of chuckled. He raised his eyebrows and smiled. "Do I detect a hint of intrigue in that chuckle?"

"It's intriguing, all right," I kind of muttered.

Hawkeye smiled. "Probably the same as why I decided to come to Korea instead of staying at warm and cozy Bellevue General Hospital, where I was surrounded by gillions of beautiful nurses."

"I suspect you're right, except for the beautiful nurses."

"Come now. I know the beautiful girls flock after you fly guys, while us ground-pounders have to settle for leftovers." (Ground-pounder was a vintage term for a non-flying officer.)

"I thought you said you were surrounded by beautiful nurses at Bellevue General?" challenged Enderton.

"That's true. And I gotta tell you about this one dreamboat surgical nurse at Belvue. She was something. She reminds me a lot of Alexis." Pause. "Richard, have you met Alexis yet?"

"I don't think so."

"No. You haven't, or you would remember it," said Enderton with a sigh.

"Great warrior Enderton speak with straight tongue. She is ichi-bon number-one girl at the 8055. Of course it depends on your taste. Others think Roxanne is number one." (Ichi-bon is a Korean term meaning the best.)

"Roxanne is a pretty girl, all right, but Alexis is beautiful, and she's a class act," pronounced Enderton.

"Yeah, she is," agreed Hawkeye. "Both Alexis and Roxanne are like beautiful roses surrounded by bramble bushes. Everybody knows they are the two best-looking nurses in Korea. But let me hasten to add, all our nurses are beautiful girls for what they do," admitted Hawkeye.

"That is the gospel," agreed Enderton.

"How many nurses are there?" I asked.

"We generally have about a dozen and they are great gals. They are dedicated and hard working under conditions that are pretty rough on them. I harass 'em a lot, but I have the greatest respect for them," said Hawkeye, turning on a sincere tone of voice.

"Well, tell me about the MASH...I mean how many—" I was interrupted when the tent door banged open and one of Hawkeye's tentmates who had been on duty came barging in.

"Meet Michael, Richard. He can smell cognac from a great distance."

Captain Michael Johnson was slender and a little on the short side. He had a full head of hair, big brown eyes and a youthful face. We shook hands and he quickly snatched his canteen cup hanging from a nail on the 2-by-4, poured himself a generous portion of the cognac and joined us at the stove.

"You must be somebody, Richard, to get Hawk to dig into his precious hoard of cognac."

"Oh he is. He's an almost ace," exclaimed Hawkeye.

Johnson looked at me suspiciously. "You have to crash five helicopters to be a full ace," I said with a straight face. Johnson just nodded and took a slug of the cognac.

"Michael, Richard wants to know all about the MASH. Tell him. Beside his talents as a super surgeon, Michael is an historian, ya know."

Johnson looked at me suspiciously again. I grinned and said, "I never even heard of a MASH until a couple weeks ago, so I really do need a history lesson."

"You never heard of the MASH?"

"Sorry. I've sort of been in hibernation, I guess you could say."

"Hibernation?"

"I was on an island in the middle of nowhere."

"Worse nowhere than this?"

"On a par," I agreed.

Johnson shrugged, took a sip of his cognac and fired a cigarette. "Well, after WWII, the Army Medical Corps decided it needed a battlefield hospital that could better support guys like General George Go-go Patton. So they created one that could keep up with Go-go and called it MASH."

"You see, didn't I tell you? Michael knows all kinds of stuff," said Hawkeye.

Johnson smiled. "Don't be distressed, Richard. Life at the MASH will grow on you. Are you really interested in the MASH history?"

"Yeah. I really am."

"All right," he said. He walked over to his corner of the tent, retrieved a canvas-backed camp chair, and sat down across from me. "This will take a while if you want the whole story."

Hawkeye was correct, Johnson did know a lot of stuff and for the next hour or so, he told the story I wanted to hear. After awhile Hawkeye crashed and went to sleep and Enderton went back to our tent and hit the sack too. But Johnson was on a roll, so I listened. From what he told me that night and from subsequent research, I developed this synopsis of developments in the Korean War that relate to the MASH and the helicopter before my arrival:

The Japanese took control of Korea in 1910 after the Chinese-Japanese War and held it until their defeat in World War II. When the spoils were divided, the communists took North Korea and the allies got South Korea. The south was given its independence and the Republic of Korea was formed. With the encouragement and assistance of the USSR and China, North Korea attacked South Korea in June 1950 for the purpose of "uniting" Korea. The United Nations declared it an act of aggression and called for its members to join in a police action to stop the aggressors. The United States, Great Britain, France, Australia, Canada, New Zealand and a bunch of others responded. Of course, the U.S. was the dominant force.

However, before the UN forces could respond in force, the North Korean Army rolled over the South Korean Army, captured Seoul, the capital, and moved right on down the Korean Peninsula to the southern tip. There, units of General Douglas MacArthur's Eighth Army finally stopped them, but only after heavy losses in a vicious running battle, with a last-ditch stand at the Port of Pusan. It was called the Battle of the Pusan Perimeter.

Out of that came horror stories about North Korean atrocities involving UN prisoners, U.S. medics and South Korean civilians. There were also great stories of initiative and heroism on our side. One of those stories involves the world's first use of helicopters on the battlefield.

MacArthur's Eighth Army fought a valiant, defensive battle against waves of communist attacks. It was bloody, with terrible casualties, so there were frantic calls for medical help. The U.S. Air Force 3rd Air Rescue Squadron, based in Japan, was one of the units to respond with rescue aircraft and that included a couple of helicopters, which at that time were pretty much a novelty and considered of limited military value. The mission of the helicopters was to try to rescue UN airmen shot down behind enemy lines, or to fish them out of the Yellow Sea, which as it surprisingly turned out, they did. Then, in answer to frantic calls for help on the bloody battlefield, the helicopter pilots began to fly wounded troops from combat areas to medical facilities. This was the world's first use of helicopters for battlefield medical evacuation.

Shortly after that, the first MASH units arrived in Korea and so did Army choppers, which also took up the challenge and began to fly critically wounded soldiers from front-line battalion aid stations directly to the newly arrived MASH units—and the first MASH-helicopter team was born. Since the new MASH units were positioned right on the battlefield, or very close to it, the wounded could now be brought under a surgeon's care within minutes. As a result, the Korean MASH-helicopter team dramatically cut the mortality rate of WWII. He was a huge boost in morale for troops who now knew that if they were critically wounded they would be evacuated by helicopter for quick medical treatment.

The MASH-helicopter team is a story about brave young men and women, and their tenacity, perseverance and good ole Yankee ingenuity. The "windmill," as the helicopter was initially called, became the legendary "chopper" that was an angel to the critically wounded soldier, or the flier shot down behind enemy lines or in the Yellow Sea. The MASH-helicopter team saved the lives of thousands who would otherwise not have survived.

When the Korean War broke out, the MASH existed only on paper. Although it had been authorized, there were no trained personnel to man it. So the medical division in MacArthur's Far East Command scrambled to find doctors, nurses and corpsmen to man the MASH units and get them into the field. It was a makeshift crew—some qualified some not—but they quickly formed three MASH units: the 8055, 8063 and the 8076. They were understaffed and ill-equipped, but the urgency rendered that acceptable and they were shipped across the channel to Korea to support the battle-scarred Eighth Army.

The first MASH units were each organized as a 60-bed hospital with 14 doctors, which included three surgeons, two anesthesiologists, one radiologist, three assistant surgeons and three general-duty medical officers, 12 nurses, two medical-service officers, one warrant officer, 93 enlisted personnel, and all the medical and other support equipment and vehicles required to be self-contained and able to move rapidly on its own. The entire hospital was housed in tents that could go up or down in a hurry. If buildings were available, they were utilized in conjunction with tents.

The Pusan Perimeter was a brutal, bloody campaign, with the UN troops barely able to turn back wave after wave of North Korean attacks. And the three inexperienced MASH units were thrown right into the thick of it, earning their stripes, so to speak, the hard way, with a round-the-clock stream of mutilated GIs to care for under makeshift conditions and often under fire.

During this period it became evident we were fighting a new kind of war with foes who did not recognize the Geneva Conventions, or the Western codes of neutrality for medical units. These combatants knew only killing and torture and a red cross was no more than a bull's eye to shoot at.

After breaking out of the Pusan Perimeter it was discovered that U.S. medical personnel captured by the North Koreans had had their hands wired behind their backs and were executed with bayonets. South Korean civilians, women and children, were found viciously assaulted and their bodies mutilated. It was also quickly discovered that enemy gunners used the red crosses on the ambulances as targets. MASH ambulance drivers and medics began carrying M-1 carbines.

General MacArthur finally got reinforcements to Korea and on September 16, 1950, launched an offensive. The Eighth Army broke out of the Pusan Perimeter and, over the next three months, fought its way right on up through the length of South and North Korea to the Chinese border.

The three MASH units and the 1st MASH—supported by a handful of Air Force and Army choppers—were with the Eighth Army all the way, evacuating and treating thousands of UN combat wounded. In three months they had become seasoned veterans. Starting with zero battlefield experience, they adjusted, improvised and learned through trial and error. They lived and worked under adverse conditions, often with enemy guns drowning out the cries of wounded who lay in rows waiting for their turn on the operating table. Add to that, they were constantly on the move, sometimes only staying in one place a few days, then striking their tent camp and moving on to the next battleground.

Another MASH, the 1st MASH, was formed to support MacArthur's X Corps, which made a surprise amphibious landing at Inchon, near Seoul, trapping the North Koreans between the X Corps and the advancing Eighth Army. Seoul was recaptured and the offensive continued into North Korea and on to the Yalu River.

By this time, the MASH and the helicopter pilots had developed medical and flying procedures through hard knocks and experience and were working together as an effective lifesaving team. From the surgeons, nurses and pilots to the GIs who put the tents up and down, they got the job done. They had started off as neophytes, but they learned to cope and to improvise under battlefield conditions. The helicopter pilots developed flying skills to cope with the type of flying they were required to do, like getting on and off the battlefield with their unarmed, primitive helicopters while flying in rugged terrain and freezing weather.

By the time the UN forces reached the Yalu River, the aggressors of North Korea had been defeated. The war was considered all but over, and the troops talked of getting home for Christmas.

Then came the Chinese.

General MacArthur and his staff at Far East Command misjudged. They didn't think the Chinese would intervene, but they did. They came swarming across the Manchurian border in hordes with blaring bugles and shrieking whistles. The U.S. Eighth Army, including the 7th Marines, slaughtered them by the thousands at the Choisin Reservoir. But they kept coming in human waves. It was mayhem, and a winter cold wave plunged temperatures to twenty below zero.

At the MASH the intravenous solutions froze and the fuel oil for the heating stoves turned to thick goo that wouldn't flow. Then the generators failed and they had to use flashlights in surgery, but the surgeons' hands were so cold they couldn't hold their instruments.

The order to evacuate came and the MASH and helicopter units fled south, stopping here and there to stake out a camp in the frozen ground and treat wounded, while the helicopters evacuated as many as possible. When the Chinese juggernaut got close, they would strike camp quickly and run south again. It was a humiliating and deadly defeat, and even though the Chinese took heavy losses, they pushed the Eighth Army and the 7th Marines back down the peninsula, out of Seoul, and on south about 40 miles, where a defense line was finally established.

General Walton H. Walker, the field commander, was killed and General Matthew B. Ridgeway assumed command on December 23, 1950. It took awhile to reorganize, but General Ridgeway got his forces on the offense again and by mid-March of 1951, they had pushed the Chinese back out of Seoul and across the 38th parallel. So the once-beautiful old city of Seoul was again devastated by street-to-street fighting—the fourth time in seven months.

With their helicopters, the MASH units followed the offense and moved numerous times during the period from New Year's Day of 1951 to the end of that May, treating literally thousands of wounded. The 8055 MASH moved nine times in that period.

Initial peace talks began in July 1951, but the brutal fighting continued for two years until the final cease-fire on July 27, 1953. This period has been called by historians the Battle of the Hills and involved savage fighting at Punchbowl, Bloody Ridge, and Heartbreak Ridge, where thousands were slaughtered.

It was this period of the Korean War in which I served. At the time of my arrival on November 17, 1952, the new Eighth Army commander,

General James Van Fleet, had built a solid defense along the MLR. But so had the Communist forces, resulting in a constant seesaw of offensive and defensive battles in the rugged mountains along the 38th parallel.

Positioned at strategic intervals in this area, the MASH units and their helicopters were now relatively static, having to move only occasionally when the MLR shifted with the loss or gain of a hill battle. Although the peace talks at Panmunjom continued, there was little progress as the North Korean delegates continued to demand outrageous concessions, while threatening a massive Chinese assault that could overwhelm the UN forces.

Chapter 4

First Mission at the MASH

I could hear the field phone. It didn't ring, it sort of clinked urgently. But the sound penetrated my sleeping bag enough to pull me out of a troubled dream where I had a Zero on my tail and couldn't shake him. It was one of those kind of dreams you hate because it keeps coming back and never seems to get settled. This time it faded to black when I opened my eyes. Out of that blackness came a growl: "You're up first, Kirkland." It was the voice of Enderton. He was a sweetheart of a guy, but a grouch before he had his first cup of coffee.

It took a minute for comprehension since my head felt like a base drum someone was beating on. "Yeah...I know," I muttered, searching for the zipper on my mummy sleeping bag and wishing I'd drunk a little less of Enderton's gin and Hawkeye's cognac the night before.

When I crawled out of the sleeping bag it was like stepping into a cold-storage freezer. "Turn up the heat," grumbled Pouhlin from inside his mummy bag.

"It's on full now," I grumbled back. The potbelly put out a lot of heat, but in a tent at subzero temperature, it didn't do very well. The field phone kept clinking until I finally got into my winter clothes and pulled the receiver out of its canvas bag hanging on the tent pole. "8055 MASH," I croaked.

"We got a patient for pickup at spot 19 in the Zebra sector," came the static-peppered voice.

"Okay...19 Zebra?" I replied, fumbling with my map, trying to open it with one hand. "Hold on," I said. I laid the phone down and opened the map with both hands. But it wasn't quite daylight so it was too dark to read.

"Turn on the light so you can read the damn map," came Enderton's growl again out of the black. A few mumbled superlatives came from Pouhlin and Drake when I snapped on the overhead light.

After a minute of searching the map, I said, "Okay, I got it."

"Make it as soon as you can, chopper, this poor guy was hit on night patrol and he's in bad shape."

There were roads to most of the battalion aid stations in the combat zone, if you could call them roads. But they were extremely rough and, at night, risky to drive on because of enemy patrols. And for a critically wounded patient, the rough ride in that vintage of field ambulance was not only agony but often fatal. So, the medics at the battlefield aid stations would try to stabilize a badly wounded patient at night and call us first thing in the morning.

"I'm on my way," I said, and put the receiver back in its case.

"You got the spot located?" asked Enderton.

"Yeah, I got it."

"What spot?"

"19 Zebra."

"Watch yourself when you turn north from the river. Those canyons up there all look alike and some are full of guys with the wrong insignia on their caps," he instructed.

"Okay."

"You want me to fly with you one more time?"

"No, I'm fine."

I wasn't. I had an awful hangover and it was so cold my hands were already numb. But I wasn't going to admit that. Enderton had already given me my orientation ride into the front lines the day before. And if I'd survived 103 combat missions in WWII, I sure as hell could manage to fly the helicopter a few miles up the damn road and back.

"Okay. Did you check the MLR?"

"No, I forgot."

"You better call I Corps intelligence," he growled impatiently and lit a cigarette.

It was critical for us to know if the main line of resistance had changed during the night because the only way to the battlefield pickup points, without getting shot at by Chinese or North Korean gunners, was to fly up the bottom of a canyon that was in friendly territory. Although the MLR generally only varied a few hundred yards during a 24-hour period, it could be enough to put you into enemy territory and in serious trouble. Intelligence was supposed to keep us posted on any overnight changes, but like everything else in war, you couldn't count on it.

I pulled the field phone back out of its case and turned the little crank. After awhile I got an operator and then several more until I finally reached intelligence and a sleepy voice told me that as far as he knew nothing had changed.

"No change in the past twenty-four hours," I reported to Enderton.

"All right, get goin' then and don't forget your medic."

I nodded, zipped up my parka with gloved hands and stepped out of the tent. It was colder than inside the tent, but not by much. I walked the short distance to the medic's tent and banged on the wooden door. "Let's go!" I shouted and a voice inside muttered, "Okay."

Daylight was just beginning to seep over the ridge adjacent to the MASH and as I walked toward the helipad I could see another bundled figure coming across the compound. It was Hawkeye. "How come you're out this early, Hawkeye?" I asked.

He pushed his parka hood back and looked at me. "Oh, I just love strolling on these crisp mornings in beautiful, breathtaking Korea," he chirped, his breath coming out like little balls of white cotton. It was classic Hawkeye. No matter what was going on, he never seemed to lose his sense of humor, and he had to be hurting because he'd drunk more gin the night before than any of us. "Just look at that beautifully sculptured Korean landscape," he said, pointing a gloved finger at the bombed-out railroad bridge. "See how those broken slabs of concrete glisten in the dawn's early light? And look at the lovely geometric design of the river ice. Not to mention that enchanting piece of broken railroad track—isn't that delightful?"

"Yeah, it's an interesting composition all right," I had to agree.

"I knew you were a man of culture. I suppose you're on your way to bring us some business this fine morning, right?"

"That's what I'm fixing to do, Hawkeye."

"By all means! Heavens to Betsy and four hands around, we wouldn't want this fine establishment to be without customers. So be on your way and I'll go sharpen my trusty scalpel," he said, pulled his parka hood up and walked off toward the main hospital tent where he was probably on the early shift.

By the time I got out to the helipad the crew chief was already there and had managed to pry open the pilot's door, which had frozen shut. But when I climbed into the pilot's seat, that chopper was so cold it creaked and groaned in protest.

"The battery won't last long this morning, capt'n," muttered the crew chief, his breath coming out like steam as he hooked up a booster battery to the Sikorsky H-5.

I nodded, knowing that even with a booster, I'd only get a brief try at starting the engine at that temperature. But I must have had the magic touch that morning because after a couple of coughs, that Pratt and Whitney R-985 engine spit out a puff of black smoke and roared to life. The chief gave me a thumbs-up as my medic came running down the trail with his medical kit slung over his shoulder. He had on so much clothing he couldn't climb into the back seat, so the chief came over and pushed him in.

Although first-generation technology with wood and fabric rotor blades, the H-5 was a significant improvement over Sikorsky's first WWII model, the R-4. The H-5 had more horsepower, was faster and could carry more weight. It was also large enough to accommodate two or three passengers in the cabin behind the pilot. It had two sliding doors, one for the pilot and one for the rear cabin where the medic rode. The patients were carried in two external aluminum pods attached to the sides of the helicopter.

As I huddled in the pilot's seat waiting for takeoff temperatures and pressures, my thoughts flashed back to my days in the South Pacific where I flew combat missions in shirtsleeves. Strange how your perspective changes. Back then I had wished for cold weather. Finally, oil and temperature gauges had climbed into the takeoff range. I pulled the cabin heater lever but the air that came out was even colder, so I shut it off. Glancing over my shoulder, all I could see of my medic was a bundle, crouched in the back seat.

"You got your headset on?" I asked over the intercom.

After a moment: "Yes, sir."

"Okay, we're off." I gave the crew chief a nod through the canopy, revved up to check the mags, then cranked on full power and pulled pitch. (Pulling pitch is an upward movement of the cyclic control stick that lifts the helicopter vertically.) As the bird became airborne I nosed it toward North Korea and medevac pick-up spot 19 Zebra.

After takeoff, I noticed the controls were stiff and sluggish from the cold, but responsive enough to continue the mission. I climbed up to just above the ridges and set the friction on the collective to hold power. The sun was just peeking over a craggy ridge off my starboard and I could see that it was going to be a bright, clear day on the battlefields of Korea.

My orientation flight with Enderton the day before had relieved some of my concern about the MASH front-line medevac mission. The chopper pilots had worked out a system of avoiding enemy fire by flying up the bottom of a canyon to the aid station, picking up the patient and flying him back down the canyon to the MASH. It was an effective procedure since that section of Korea along the 38th parallel was a maze of ridges and canyons. The trick was finding the canyon that meandered through friendly territory. When it branched, you had to know which branch led to the aid station you wanted.

There were dozens of aid stations scattered all across the hills and valleys along the MLR. And of course they also changed with the tide of battle. But I figured that for someone like me who had flown over vast stretches of jungle and water in the South Pacific for hours on end, navigation wouldn't be a problem.

I had studied the map briefly before takeoff and decided that 19 Zebra would be easy to find since all I had to do was follow the Imjin Gang River until it intersected the branch canyon that led to the aid station. After about ten minutes of flying along the tops of the ridges watching for the branch canyon, I realized I'd passed it. I grabbed the map and checked. Okay, so I would just take a shortcut across and intersect it. No sweat.

Enderton had warned me to get down in the canyon before I got near the MLR to keep from drawing enemy fire. But as I scanned the terrain below I couldn't see any sign of enemy activity or much of anything else but an endless patchwork of rocky, stark ridges and canyons, twisting and turning in all directions. A few minutes later, I rechecked the map and for some reason it didn't match the topography below. The stupid map must be wrong.

"Captain! Captain! We're taking fire!" screeched a voice in my headset. I'll always remember how that medic in the back seat suddenly came alive. His warning was a bit of a shock, as I'd about convinced myself that this was going to be a piece of cake. The shock was amplified when I saw fireballs zipping past the Sikorsky's nose. I'd seen that sight in WWII many times and it's one you don't forget and never get used to.

Glancing into the canyon below, I could see the muzzle flashes and I instinctively wanted to bank the chopper into a strafing run on the gun position. And that's what I would have done if I were flying my P-38. But I wasn't. I was flying an unarmed taxicab. Military helicopters of today have armor protection for the pilot as well as deadly fire power with which to attack a ground target. They are a formidable tactical weapon. But this was long before attack helicopters were even thought of.

It occurred to me at that point that my original assessment of the Korean helicopter was correct: it was a sitting duck for enemy gunners. And my frustration over not being able to shoot back was acutely frustrating. However, when the next batch of fireballs flashed across my canopy a couple seconds later, I knew what I had to do, frustrating or not, and that was get the hell out of there! I banked the chopper over, zipped across the nearest ridge, then dove into the bottom of the adjacent canyon—like Enderton had told me to do.

"You okay?" I shouted to the medic over the intercom as I leveled the chopper off in the bottom of the canyon.

"I'm okay, capt'n. But we may have taken some hits."

I hadn't felt or heard hits but I was so flustered over the whole thing that I might not have noticed, so I quickly went down on the collective and back on the cyclic, executing what is called a "quick stop," in chopper lingo. That brought us to a hover over a frozen creek bed.

"Keep an eye on that ridge above us and yell if you see anything," I instructed the medic as I scanned the instruments for an indication of a problem. Everything seemed to be in order, although the controls felt strange and I was considering landing and doing an outside check, when the medic's voice interrupted.

"There's guys with rifles coming over the ridge, capt'n!" he shouted.

I didn't even look. I just revved up quickly and pulled pitch—hard. I climbed the H-5 over the opposite side of the ridge and kept right on going until we were out of range.

I leveled off about a thousand feet above the ridge. The chopper seemed to be flying okay and the controls were responsive.

"You sure we took hit?" I asked the medic.

"I think so, capt'n."

So now what? My no-problem navigation had gotten me lost and I'd obviously wandered into North Korea and got the chopper shot up. I wasn't sure how bad the controls were damaged and I didn't have a clue where I was. The only thing I could do now was get out of North Korea where everybody was shooting at me and fly back to the MASH before the H-5 shot craps.

Looking down, all I could see in every direction were ridges and canyons and like Enderton said, they all looked alike. Okay. Just head south. The MASH was south of my position...wasn't it? Where else could it be? I took up a southern heading. I was flying now at a higher altitude, which I hoped was out of small arms range but made the slow-flying helicopter an even better target for anti-aircraft gunners. It did make navigation simpler, however, and after awhile I was able to get a match between the topography below and my map. The stupid map was right after all. Surprisingly, once I'd reoriented myself I realized I wasn't all that far from the canyon that led to 19 Zebra.

"Are we going back to the MASH, capt'n?" asked the medic about that time.

Was I going back to the MASH? What other choice did I have? The chopper was damaged and that's what you did when you got battle damage: go home. But then I wasn't sure that I really had battle damage. The chopper seemed to be flying okay...and what about the patient? He was badly wounded and had been waiting to be taken to the MASH...and he was still waiting. Getting lost was my fault...if you make a mistake in a dogfight with a Zero, only you pay the penalty...here, some poor GI pays. Thoughts like those were churning through my head when I suddenly knew that I had to go back. I had to pick up that wounded GI. I would have to take my chances that the helicopter was airworthy. But what about my medic? I had no right to risk his life.

"Our pickup spot, 19 Zebra, isn't all that far away and the chopper seems to be flying okay. I think we have to give it a shot," I said to him.

"I'm with you, capt'n," was the unhesitating, simple reply. I admired those medics who flew with us during the Korean War. They were brave young men who had to sit back there and hope that the pilot knew what the hell he was doing.

"Okay, keep an eye out for ground fire," I said, banking the H-5 around and heading back north. I was reasonably sure now that I had our general location spotted on the map. But I still had to identify the right canyon that would lead to 19 Zebra. And it's not easy to hold a map with gloved, frozen hands and read it while flying a machine that requires both hands and feet to maneuver. Since this was my first mission, I hadn't yet developed those little tricks that MASH chopper pilots used, like clamping the cyclic stick with both knees to free a hand for map reading. But I managed and with some degree of confidence headed for the canyon I'd identified as the correct one. It sure would have been easier if we'd had GPS in those days. (The Global Positioning System pinpoints you anywhere in the world within a few yards.)

This time I followed Enderton's instructions to the letter. I nosed the chopper down into the canyon and skimmed along a few feet above the clumps of frozen earth and rocks, banking and turning to follow its course while keeping below the top of the ridge. There was no holding the cyclic with your knees in this kind of flying since it was a constant application of controls.

All went well for awhile until I came around a bend and found myself facing a fork in the canyon and no idea which way to go. Damn! I snatched up the map for a quick check, but when I took my hand off the cyclic, the chopper lurched and I had to drop the map and grab the controls. By the time I recovered, I was already into the left fork and the decision of which way to go was made.

Well, I had a fifty-fifty chance of being in the right canyon and 19 Zebra should be near. Sure enough, a few minutes later the canyon narrowed and sloped up to a small plateau. I pulled the nose up slightly and skimmed over the rise to a leveled area directly ahead. I eased down on the collective and back on the cyclic to bring the chopper to a hover for landing.

As I came to a hover, something told me it wasn't 19 Zebra. The something was no activity and some strange-looking emplacements, which I later found out were North Korean bunkers. I kicked rudder pedal, spun the bird around and dove back down the canyon.

The good news was that the commies there were apparently still asleep or huddled in their bunkers to keep warm. So now all I had to do was go back down the canyon and take the other fork. By my calculation, that should give me a hundred percent chance of being in the right canyon. However, based on the way things had gone so far on this mission, I wouldn't have bet on it. "I don't think that was 19 Zebra, capt'n," said the medic. I didn't answer.

I flew back down to the fork in the canyon and took the other branch. About ten minutes later, I came to a cleared place on the side of the ridge with a parked weapons carrier that had a big white star painted on the hood. It seemed a pretty good bet that I'd found 19 Zebra. After I landed, shut the chopper down and crawled out, a sergeant dressed in winter combat gear walked up to me. "I sure hope you don't have a problem, sir," he said in an anxious, weary voice.

"I hope not too," I said and climbed up on the landing gear strut so I could inspect the rotor head. Normally, the chopper pilots remained in their seat with the rotor turning while the medic loaded the patient into the exterior litter pod. I would have preferred to do that since it was even colder outside the helicopter, but I wanted to give the bird a quick check to see if, indeed, it had taken some critical hits.

Two litter bearers in winter combat clothing and a corpsman holding a plasma bottle carried the patient out of a sandbagged bunker. They had him in a sleeping bag with the IV line taped in place. Under the direction of my medic, they began to load him into the aluminum carrying pod.

"I was getting worried," said the sergeant, watching me inspect the rotor head.

"We got delayed a bit," I muttered.

"Harry's in bad shape. He got it early this morning and has bled a lot. He needs a surgeon as soon as possible. He's a good man, captain. You...you'll get him to the MASH quick, won't you, sir?"

I turned and looked at the sergeant. He was carrying a carbine in gloved hands. A couple hand grenades hung on the outside of his parka. What I could see of his face behind the parka hood was haggard and dirty with a set of pleading, bloodshot eyes. "I'll get him there, sergeant," I said.

He nodded and after a pause said, "Ya know, if it weren't for you chopper pilots and the MASH, I don't think we could do this shit."

I just stood there at a loss for words. It was like when you're smug in a position on something and suddenly someone blows you away with a few simple words. That's what happened to me that day on a frozen

Korean battlefield. It didn't change my resentment about being there, but it gave me a different slant on the role of a battlefield taxi driver— and I suspect caused the first crack in my armor, so as to speak.

"The patient is loaded, capt'n. Are we okay to go?" asked my medic.

"Yeah, let's go." I said. Surprisingly, I hadn't found a single bullet hole in the helicopter, but it didn't matter. I'd already decided I was going even if there were holes.

I crawled into the pilot's seat while the medic climbed into the cabin. The litter bearers hurried back into the bunker to get out of the cold. But the sergeant stood off to one side of the landing pad and watched as I started the engine and engaged the rotor system. Even though the blast of air from the blades had to be bitter, he stood and watched. I revved up to full RPM and everything checked out okay. "You ready back there?" I asked over the intercom. "I'm all set, capt'n," was the reply.

I glanced out at the sergeant. He was still standing there with the rotor wash of freezing air buffeting his clothes and making the hand grenades jump and dance across his parka. He raised a hand and gave me a little salute. I returned it, reached down for the collective and pulled pitch. I skimmed down the canyon, banking and turning, past the fork and on to the river, keeping well below the tops of the ridges. There would be no shortcuts this time. But when I was certain I was in friendly territory, I climbed up and headed straight for the MASH with the Sikorsky running like a champ.

A few minutes later, I saw the bombed-out railroad bridge and the MASH tent tops. I eased off on the collective and nosed down toward the helipad. As I approached, I could see the stretcher bearers run out of the receiving tent and head for the pad as they always did when they heard the chopper coming. By the time I shut down after landing, my medic and the litter bearers had removed the patient from the pod and quickly carried him off to receiving, where a MASH team waited. Although much of the MASH facilities were makeshift and some down-right primitive, the care and dedication was first rate.

"Everything on the bird okay, capt'n?" asked the crew chief when I climbed out of the helicopter.

"I think so. But just to be sure, you probably should check her over, sarge," I said, stomping my frozen feet on the frozen ground.

He looked at me through the small opening in his parka. "Uh...what am I looking for, capt'n?"

"Bullet holes."

"Bullet holes?"

"Yeah. Sorry about that, but you know how it is with the new kid on the block."

"Yeah, I know how it is, sir."

When I walked into the tent, Pouhlin and Drake were still buried in their sleeping bags. Enderton was sitting on a wooden box next to the stove smoking a cigarette and drinking his morning coffee, which he always made himself on top of the potbelly. "How'd it go?" he asked, glancing at me.

I zipped open my parka, pulled out my cigarettes, fired one and took a deep pull. "It went," I said, blowing out a column of smoke.

He nodded. "You were gone longer than it usually takes to Zebra 19, so I was a little concerned. Sometimes that first mission on your own can get a little hairy."

"Yeah, I guess it can," I agreed.

The look in Enderton's eyes told me that he knew I'd gotten into trouble. "What say we go grab some breakfast at the 8055 Imjin Gang River Cafe?"

"Sounds enchanting," I replied.

It was so cold in the mess tent all you could see was hooded figures in winter parkas, huddled over the tables trying to eat before the food froze in their metal trays. The mess sergeant even wore a hooded parka with just his eyes showing so he could see to scoop out gobs of powdered eggs from the cooking kettle, which, because of the frigid air, billowed clouds of vapor like a steam locomotive. There was a potbellied stove in one corner but it might as well have been a refrigerator for all the good it did.

Enderton and I got our gob of eggs and a cup of coffee that also steamed—for a couple minutes. We sat down at one of the wooden, picnic style tables just as someone complained, "The catsup's frozen! What am I gonna do?"

"Eat it without catsup," growled someone else.

"How can I eat powdered eggs without catsup?"

"Use your imagination. Pretend this Eskimo baby shit is actually Russian caviar," said another voice, which I recognized as Hawkeye's.

"I ain't got that much imagination. And how do you know it's Eskimo baby shit?"

"It's got icicles on it."

"Oh, yeah. It does, doesn't it?"

It got quiet then with billowing clouds of cooking kettle steam drifting across huddled shapes at the tables. The only sound being the dull clank of eating utensils on metal trays and the shuffling of boots.

"Richard, is that you down there eating Russian caviar?" said Hawkeye, breaking the silence.

"It's me, Hawkeye. But mine looks more like Tejon cow dung."

"Tejon? Is that a special brand of dung?"

"Yeah. From the Tejon Ranch."

"Ah so. And just how do you distinguish the difference?"

"It's a little more lumpy."

"I knew you were a discriminating connoisseur."

"How do you know about the Tejon Ranch?" asked one of the other hooded figures.

I was taken aback. Not only because the question surprised me, but the voice was feminine. I hadn't realized there was a nurse in the group. "I grew up on the Tejon Ranch," I answered, glancing down the table to identify my female questioner. "How do you know about it?"

"I don't, but I've heard of it." replied the female voice. "I was raised on the XIT."

"You mean that miniature ranch out in Texas?" I replied, knowing that the XIT was one of the largest cattle ranches in the world.

"That's the one," she said with a laugh and it was like a touch of bright spring in that dismal setting.

"Ya know, Alexis, I been thinking of giving up all this and going into the ranching business so you and I could ranch together. Doesn't that sound exciting?" Hawkeye said.

"It does, Hawkeye. But I wouldn't want you to give up all this just for li'l ole me," said the feminine voice, which I assumed was that of the MASH's best-looking nurse, whom Hawkeye and Enderton had talked about the night before.

"I don't know how you people can be so damn glib when you're sitting here eatin' slop and freezing to death!" blurted someone who suddenly leaped up from the table next to ours, hurled his tray across the tent and stormed out.

No one in the mess tent seemed to be disturbed over the outburst. Then Hawkeye said, "Don't mind Freddie, Richard. He's that way when he doesn't get his Wheaties for breakfast."

"That does it," growled another voice. "My damn coffee has frozen!"

"So? What's the matter with iced coffee?" asked someone. I glanced down at my coffee cup. It wasn't frozen yet but it wasn't steaming any more either.

A corpsman suddenly appeared at the table and said excitedly, "Hawkeye, we're losing him!" There was a clanking of metal as several of the hooded figures at our table dropped their silverware, leaped up and rushed out of the mess tent.

"It's your boy," said Hawkeye to me as he hurried past.

"He means the guy I brought in?" I asked.

"Yeah. We're trying to stabilize him with whole blood before surgery, but he's losing it faster than we can put it in," explained the person sitting across from me as he too got up and left the table.

I thought of the sergeant at the battalion aid station. I'd promised to get his buddy to the MASH in time to save his life. "What does that mean?" I asked Enderton.

"Bad," said Enderton, leaving me with some kind of godawful feeling that if the guy died it was my fault.

"Jesus, I hope he makes it," I muttered.

"Well, he's in good hands. The conditions here may be primitive, but these folks go all out for the patients. Was he critical when you picked him up?"

"I guess so. The sergeant at the pickup point told me he'd been hit pretty bad."

We ate the awful powdered eggs and drank the cold coffee in silence for awhile.

"If you want, you can go over there after breakfast and see how he's doing," said Enderton, firing a cigarette.

"They let you go in there?"

"Sure. You have to put on a mask and gown if you go into OR, but they don't mind as long as you stay out of their way. When they get a rush of patients it gets pretty wild in there. Sometimes they got four operating tables going at the same time with rows of patients on litters laying on the ground in pre-op waiting their turn."

We both drank cold coffee and smoked silently for a moment. "Christ! Do you feel guilty every damn time you bring in a guy that doesn't make it?" I suddenly blurted.

"In a way. But you'll discover that's offset by the ones you save. And we save far more than we lose."

I shook my head and took a drink of the freezing coffee.

"You get a little action up there this morning?"

"Yeah."

"Take any hits?"

"None that I could see. But the chief's checking over the bird."

"What happened?"

"I screwed up."

Silence.

"Ya know, this isn't like flying a fighter at altitude where you can see where you're goin'."

"It sure as hell isn't. And it's sure not like having some guns to shoot back at the sons of bitches who are trying to kill you."

"Guess not. But you'll get used to it."

"I don't think so, Charles."

"I don't know that you have any choice."

"Yes I do. I can put in a request for transfer to a fighter squadron."

"Which has about the same chance as a snowball in hell."

"Maybe so. But I'm gonna have to try."

"I wish you luck, but meantime—"

"Don't worry. You got my word that I'll give this thing my best shot regardless of any personal feelings."

"I can't ask for any more than that, Richard."

We sipped more cold coffee and smoked. Finally, I said, "I assume that nurse I spoke to was the one you guys were talking about?"

"Ah yes, that was she. Alexis is a lovely, lovely lady...but untouchable."

"Well, that's okay since I'm not interested in touching her. But she sure has an intriguing voice."

"Wait till you see her out of winter garb. She's got more than an intriguing voice. Besides being a knockout, she is a neat person and an excellent nurse."

"A triple-threat gal, huh?"

"A-men!"

"You single, Charles?"

"I sure am. But so far I haven't got to first base with that girl. Every hot dog in Korea has tried to make it with her and flunked out. She's engaged to a Marine and she is playin' it straight."

"Good for her."

"Yeah, well you can afford to say that, bein' an old married man. But it's tough on guys like me."

"Well, you get to Tokyo every eight weeks, don't you?"

Enderton smiled. "Yeah, and those little jo-sans down there are indeed lovely."

"So I've heard."

Two new hooded figures walked into the mess tent. "Don't tell me, let me guess. I got my choice of eggs any way I want 'em as long as they are powdered and scrambled, right?" grumbled Pouhlin.

"What uncanny perception you have, Lieutenant Pouhlin," said Drake as he fanned the steam with his gloved hand so he could peek into the cooking kettle. "Christ, Sarge, when are we gonna get some real eggs?"

"Whenever the quartermaster give me some, that's when!" replied the mess sergeant.

"You spose the quartermaster is open to a bribe?"

"Probably," said the sergeant.

"What would it take?"

"Got any Jack Daniel's?"

Jeff shook his head. "If I had some I'd drink it," he replied, picked up a mess tray and held it out.

The sergeant scooped up a gob of the powdered eggs and dumped it into the tray. "So would I," he muttered.

"Well, it's better than C-rations, and who's covering the field phone?" asked Enderton.

"Not much better," mumbled Drake.

"Jon's up there," said Pouhlin, as the sergeant dumped a gob on his tray.

"What's he doin' here this early?"

"He stayed in the village last night and nearly froze to death. So he came early to thaw out," explained Pouhlin.

Jon was our houseboy at the MASH and lived in nearby Uijongbu. He was a handsome 15-year-old who looked a lot like Kim, my houseboy at K-16. He had black eyes and hair and a big smile, which he used often, despite the fact that most of his family had been killed during the first North Korean attack. Jon could speak pretty good English so he would answer the field phone if no one was there, then run and get whoever was on alert. The rule was, however, that the alert pilot stay close. When a pickup call came, the alert pilot would then respond and, after flying the mission, would drop to the bottom of the schedule and the next pilot in line would assume the alert. We normally had two choppers at the MASH in case we needed them or if one went AOG (aircraft grounded for maintenance or whatever).

"How did your first mission go, Richard?" asked Pouhlin as he and Drake sat down across from Enderton and me.

"It went," I replied.

Both pilots looked at me. "Get lost?" asked Pouhlin.

"Yeah."

"Don't feel like the Lone Ranger. I still get lost once in a while and I've got thirty-three missions," said Pouhlin, trying to shake frozen catsup out of the bottle.

"Timing is the key to not getting lost," proclaimed Drake. "I got the flying time to each pickup spot marked on my map. That way I know exactly when I should get there."

"And what if you're not there when the time is up?"

"Don't get picky, Charles."

"The damn catsup is frozen," groaned Pouhlin.

Enderton ground out his cigarette in an ashtray made from a shell casing and said, "One of the birds is due for a hundred-hour inspection so I'm gonna fly it down to K-16 this morning. Major Lovelady says he should have another bird ready for me to bring back by the time I get there. Fortunately the MLR is quiet. Probably because the chinks are holed up trying to keep from freezing to death. Any questions?"

"Yeah. Could you stop off at the supermarket and get a pound of bacon and a dozen fresh eggs?" said Pouhlin.

"Hey, good idea," agreed Drake.

"How many missions a day do you normally fly?" I asked.

"If there is no major attack going on, there is usually only a handful of casualties from patrol action. And that can be covered with one bird," replied Enderton as he got up from the table. "See ya later."

After finishing my cold coffee, I started back to our tent and I met one of the surgeons that had attended our party the night before. "Do you know how that guy I brought in is doing?" I asked.

"No, I've been in post-op. I think Hawkeye is working on him now. You can go on over there and check it out." He pulled his parka hood back up and walked off.

I stood there a moment watching the steam from my breath make white clouds. I knew I was hesitating because I was afraid of the answer I'd get. But I had to know. Finally, I walked over to the pre-op tent. When I entered, I came face to face with Hawkeye dressed in a blood-spattered surgical gown and cap with a surgical mask hanging down around his neck. When I saw the look on his face, it was like someone suddenly ripped through my insides with a chain saw. "Sorry, Richard. I did my best," he said in a voice I would not have recognized as his. I just nodded.

"We didn't lose him because of anything you did or didn't do, Richard," he said quietly. "His wounds were so severe there just wasn't a chance. We do everything possible to save lives, but sometimes it's out of our hands. Believe me when I tell you it's tough when you lose, because you can't help but wonder if there was something more you could have done. We may appear to be a bit callous and I suppose in a way we are. But I can tell you I've never failed to feel like I've been kicked in the stomach when I lose. So I do everything in my power to avoid losing a patient. And that is the way you gotta see it too. All you can do is your best."

I nodded again, turned and walked out of the tent and over to the MASH orderly room where I asked the clerk if he would give me an application for transfer. He looked at me strangely then shrugged and after a search through his beat-up desk, handed me a form. "Here it is, captain, but I'm not sure it will work because it's an Army form and you're Air Force."

"It doesn't make a rat's ass anyway, corporal. But it might make me feel better," I growled, snatched the form from his hand and stomped out. I filled out the form, scratched out Army and wrote in Air Force, addressed it to Far East Air Force Commander, walked over to the mail tent and dropped it in the slot.

Chapter 5

Action on the MLR

Submitting an application for transfer didn't improve my depressed state of mind. I lay on my sack in my winter parka most of that day sulking. Fortunately, things remained quiet on the MLR so there were no more calls for our services and Pouhlin and Drake joined a poker game in one of the other tents. Enderton called on the field phone and said that the replacement helicopter wasn't ready yet so he would be spending the night at K-16 and would return to the MASH sometime tomorrow. I skipped dinner, dug out an old candy bar from my B-4 bag and crawled in the mummy sleeping bag with all my clothes on except my boots and parka.

The next morning I was still in a depressed mood, but had to get some breakfast because I was hungry. The fare hadn't changed—it was still scrambled, powdered eggs. But they had installed a couple more potbellied stoves, which at least kept the coffee from freezing and the mess sergeant had his parka hood pushed back so you could see his face. I saw Hawkeye and he assured me again there was nothing I did or didn't do that would have made a difference in the loss of my patient. And I guess I actually knew that but I just couldn't seem to come to grips with the whole thing.

After breakfast I walked down the trail to the riverbank. While I stood there in the freezing cold looking at the frozen river, I heard the helicopter rev up and take off. I glanced up and saw it bank around and head north. Pouhlin, who was up next on the schedule, was on his way to pick up a MASH customer.

After awhile it occurred to me that I was standing out there probably getting frostbite and proving nothing, so I started back up the trail and saw the helicopter returning. It came down the valley, landed, and had taken off again before I arrived back at the tent.

"You're up next," said Pouhlin, who was standing over the potbelly warming his hands when I walked in.

"We got business?"

"We got business big time. The gooks are on a rampage along the MLR in the Echo sector. I just brought in two patients and there's more waiting. Jeff is on a run now."

I was in no mood to fly but I knew I had to, regardless of my personal feelings. I nodded, dug out my map and joined him at the potbelly.

"The pickup spot is Echo 31. It's on the side of the ridge at the fork of those two canyons," he said, pointing his finger. "You can follow the canyon all the way up from the river. It's a piece of cake to find. But stay low because there's a hell of a firefight going on just over the ridge."

"I can't imagine those guys starting an attack in this weather," I grumbled. I took off my parka, strapped on my service .45 and pulled the parka back on.

"Well, the gook general who ordered the attack ain't gonna be out there freezing, you can bet your ass on that. Intelligence says this looks like a major offensive, so I called K-16 on the land line and left a message for Capt'n Enderton to get his tail back here with the other chopper as soon as possible," said Pouhlin as the sound of the returning helicopter filled the tent.

I zipped up my parka, slammed out through the tent door and headed for the helipad. The medics were already unloading patients from the litter pods when I got to the helicopter. Drake had kept the rotor turning to save time, so I reached in and held the cyclic stick while he scooted out of the pilot's seat.

"Stay low in the canyon! There's groundfire all over the place!" he shouted above the noise of the engine and rotors.

I nodded, crawled into the seat and quickly closed the door to shut out the blast of subzero air. After fastening my crash straps, I checked the instruments and glanced out to see if the unloading was finished. The patients had been lifted out of the pods and were being carried to receiving with litter bearers at each end of the litter and one holding the plasma bottle. They looked like walking mummies in their heavy clothing and hooded parkas.

The medic who would fly with me was putting replacement litters back in the pods, then securing the pod covers in place. (The MASH personnel had learned early in the game that it was faster and much easier on the patient to leave him in the same litter from battlefield pickup through surgery and post-op.) I recognized him as the one I'd had on my first mission. After he had climbed into the helicopter and closed the door, I pulled pitch and headed up the valley. "I'll try not to get us lost and shot at this time," I said over the intercom.

"I'm sure you'll do fine, captain," he replied. The tone of his voice suggested that the medics were aware of my problem. It was a cold but clear day and all I had to do was follow the Imjin Gang River north until it intersected the canyon that led to Echo 31. But then that was all I had to do the day before and still managed to screw it up.

I climbed up to 500 feet, leveled off and set the friction on the collective to maintain power. Holding the cyclic with my right hand, I picked up the map with my left hand and checked the terrain below to make damn sure I turned into the right canyon this time. I could see smoke rising over the ridges at my ten o'clock position. It was probably artillery fire and probably where I was headed.

A few minutes later I spotted what looked like a bombed-out building with a few brokendown huts along the riverbank. It matched my map, so I reduced collective and headed down into the canyon, leveling off just a few feet above the rocks and frozen turf. "You watch the ridge on the left and I'll keep an eye on the other one," I said to the medic. He gave me two clicks on the mike, which meant he understood.

I flew the chopper along the bottom of a frozen creek bed, banking and turning with the contour of the canyon as it meandered toward the north and the rising smoke. I kept my peripheral vision on the ridge off my starboard, but saw only rocky, treeless earth. When I reached the point where I could see the ridgeline where the smoke was billowing, I spotted pickup point number 31, right where it was supposed to be. Great going, Kirkland, you did it!

The chopper landing spots all along the Korean battle line were about the same: a level, or fairly level, area near a medical aid station or bunker. They would generally be at the head of a canyon on the side of a ridge opposite the enemy positions, or in a saddle below the ridgeline so that we could approach and land without being exposed to the enemy gun positions. That worked well as long as you went to the right spot and they weren't under fire.

The instant I touched down, my medic was out of the chopper directing the battalion litter bearers in the patient loading: one into each pod, strapped down securely, the IV bottle and lines taped into position, and the pod covers back in place. The battalion bearers quickly backed away and my medic climbed into the helicopter, shut the door and gave me a thumbs-up. I revved up takeoff RPM, pulled pitch, and scooted back down the canyon as fast as the bird would go.

"They've got a bunch more of real bad wounded, capt'n," said my medic over the intercom.

"All we can do is bring them out as fast as we can," I replied.

The return flight to the MASH went as uneventful as the trip up and a few minutes later I was on the helipad at the MASH where the litter bearers quickly unloaded the patients from the pods and carried them to receiving while my medic put new litters into the pods and secured the lids. "Everything go okay?" shouted Pouhlin, crawling into the pilot's seat as I scooted out. I nodded and hurried out of the bitter cold rotor wash.

As I walked up to our tent from the helipad, it dawned on me that I felt pretty good. I suppose it was because I'd been able to fly the mission without screwing it up, so at least that had soothed my conscience some. When I entered the tent Drake was sitting on his sack smoking. "Went okay, huh?" he asked.

"I got up there and back." I pulled off my gloves and held my numb hands over the potbelly.

"This kind of flying takes a little getting used to."

"Yeah."

"You'll get the hang of it before this run is over. I got the feeling this slaughter is gonna last for awhile."

Suddenly the tent door swung open and one of the MASH administrative officers burst in. "We just got word the road to Echo 31 has been cut so we can't get in there with ambulances. You're gonna have to bring all the wounded out. Can you get some more choppers?"

"I don't know, but I'll call K-16," said Drake, snatching the field phone from its case and spinning the crank.

Normally, the helicopter was only called to ferry out the critically wounded from the battlefield. Minor wounds and walking wounded were brought to the MASH by ambulance. With the road cut, all wounded would have to be evacuated by chopper. "You were just at Echo 31— did you take any fire coming down the canyon?" the administrative officer asked me.

"Not that I was aware of."

"The gooks must have cut the road right after you left. Echo 31 isn't under fire, just the road going in there."

When Drake got through to K-16 they told him that Enderton would be on his way shortly, but there were no more choppers available. The administrative officer grimaced. "Well, I guess we're gonna have to do with what we got. We called the 8063 and the 8076 to see if we could send some of their choppers down to help out, but they also got action. I guess the gooks are attacking all along the MLR. And by the way, we're on alert for a bug-out," he said, and hurried out of the tent.

"Does bug-out mean what I think it does?" I asked Drake.

"It means pack up and get the hell out, the gooks are on their way."

"Super."

"Well, a bug-out alert is just a precaution, it doesn't mean it's gonna happen. We get those ever once in a while. But I guess it could happen if the gooks make a breakthrough. They don't seem to care how many of their troops they sacrifice. I guess that's because they got a bunch of 'em."

At the sound of Pouhlin returning, Drake grabbed his gloves and headed out the door. It only took about 15 to 20 minutes to make the round trip, so by the time I got my feet and hands warmed enough to smoke a cigarette, I heard Drake coming back and it was my turn again. When Drake got out of the helicopter, he left the engine running but disengaged the rotor because he wanted to talk to me. "The gooks are in the canyon, so you gotta go up the next canyon to the west then cross back over about here," he said, showing me on the map.

"Okay, I got it, but what about the pickup spot. Is it under fire?"

"No. There's fighting all around, but it's clear. Just don't over-shoot the spot or you'll get a hot reception." He waved and hurried off.

The patients had been carried off and my medic was already aboard so I climbed in, engaged the rotor, cranked in takeoff RPM, and pulled pitch. "This time we gotta make a detour and the bad guys are all over the place, so keep a sharp watch," I told my medic as we flew up the river.

I found the alternate canyon without a hitch and followed it to where it made a sharp bend. I had just started to cross back over into the main canyon, as Drake had instructed, when I saw an ambulance dead ahead in the bottom of the canyon. There were two guys standing beside it waving frantically.

"Captain! That's one of our ambulances!" the medic shouted at about the same time I saw it.

I quickly went down on the collective and back on the cyclic for a quick stop, then set the H-5 down in the rocks a short distance from the ambulance. I pulled open the door as they ran out to the chopper. They were dressed in winter clothes and carried carbines. One was a corporal, the other was a private first class. "Hey! I think those guys are from the 8055!" said the medic as the two men pulled their parka hoods back.

"Boy are we glad to see you, capt'n!" shouted the corporal. "We tried to detour around the roadblock and broke an axle on the ambulance. There's gooks all over the place!"

"Okay, hop in and let's get out of here!" I shouted.

"We can't, we got two patients in the ambulance," said the corporal.

Two patients, one medic and a pilot were all the H-5 helicopter could carry. Even if I could cram in two additional passengers, the bird would be so over weight it would never get off the ground. So now what?

"Okay. Load the patients into the pods. I'll take them back to the MASH, then come back and pick you up," I instructed.

The medics looked at each other then at me. "Any way you can take us all?" asked the corporal.

I shook my head. "No. The bird can't do it. Hurry up and get the patients loaded in the pods."

"Okay, capt'n," said the corporal and there was no more hesitation. They scurried across to the ambulance while my medic jumped out and got the pods ready.

I hated to go off and leave them, but I had no choice. I scanned the ridges on both sides of the canyon while they loaded the patients. I couldn't see any sign of enemy activity. "I'll be back in about fifteen minutes!" I shouted as my medic climbed into the bird and the other two backed away from the chopper with an awful expression on their faces—as though they were watching the last lifeboat pull away from the Titanic.

I twisted the throttle, revved the rotor and took off. About six or seven minutes later, I landed back at the MASH and yelled impatiently at the litter bearers to hurry up and get the patients unloaded. I shouldn't have. In their rush, they tilted an empty litter upward and the rotor struck it. In those days our rotor blades were made of wood and fabric. If they hit something, pieces flew in all directions. Fortunately, in this case no one was hurt. But after I got the helicopter shut down, I just sat there in the cockpit telling myself again that I should heed all the signals the Big Guy was sending me: this just wasn't my line of work.

I tried to get on the field phone to K-16 to tell them we needed a new rotor blade desperately, but the line was tied up with priority traffic because of the big battle going on up at the MLR. Until Enderton got there with the other bird, we were dead in the water…and there was no way of knowing the fate of the two medics I had left in the canyon.

The land line operator at big switch, the key connection, promised to patch me through to K-16 as soon as possible. Meanwhile, Pouhlin and Drake sat around the stove smoking and I lay on my sack smoking and in a worse mood than ever.

"It wasn't your fault, Richard," sympathized Pouhlin.

"And you were right. There is no way you could carry six people in the H-5," added Drake.

I was in such a foul state of mind, I didn't even answer. A few minutes later, the field phone rang and I was off my cot in a flash and grabbed it out of the canvas holder. "Yeah?"

It was a medical lieutenant at I Corps headquarters and he was shouting, "Where are the choppers? We got wounded all over the place that need urgent medical attention! What are you guys doin'?"

"We're sitting on our ass, what'a ya think we're doin', you asshole!" I snarled and slammed the phone back into the holder. Pouhlin and Drake looked at each other then at me as I flopped back down on my sack. When I heard the chopper coming, I was out the tent door and down to the helipad by the time Enderton landed. As soon as he touched down, I pulled the pilot's door open and yelled, "Don't shut it down!"

"What's goin' on?" he asked as I more or less pushed him out of the pilot's seat.

"Jerry and Jeff will fill you in—I gotta go!" I replied, slammed the door in his face, cranked on full throttle and pulled pitch.

I flew back up the canyon and was at the stalled ambulance within six or seven minutes. But no one was there. I hovered around but couldn't see any signs of anyone, friend or foe. I didn't want to, but I had to land. I had to know if the gooks had killed the medics and left them in the ambulance. I set the bird down, disengaged the rotor but left the engine running. With cocked .45 in hand, I got out of the H-5, ran over to the ambulance and peeked in. It was empty. I breathed a conditional sigh of relief for eliminating one possibility. I quickly ran back to the chopper, engaged the rotors and revved up. They had either been captured or, when I didn't show up, had decided to walk out. But if they had walked, I would have seen them as I had just flown up the canyon. They wouldn't have walked back to Echo 31, with the gooks all around...or would they? The only thing left to do was go up there and find out.

I took off and climbed over the ridge and into the canyon that led to Echo 31. I had flown off without a medic so I was on my own to watch for ground fire. The first thing I saw when I cleared the ridge was smoke and fire all along the opposite ridge. It looked too big for artillery fire, and that was confirmed when I caught a glimpse of a diving aircraft. For a second or two, my old WWII senses kicked in and I thought, Bogie! (enemy aircraft). Then I could see that it was one of our jets making a bombing run on the North Korean positions across the canyon. It might even be a jet from my old fighter squadron with one of my buddies flying it. I could imagine what he'd say if he knew I was down there in the helicopter. The jet swooped down and laid his bombs along the ridgeline, sending up a huge ball of fire, smoke and debris. Good run. That should put some of those sons of bitches out of action, I said to myself, watching the fighter pull up in a steep bank to clear the target for his wingman, who followed and was already on his bombing run.

About that time, Echo 31 landing spot appeared ahead and I had to switch my attention. The instant I landed, litter bearers appeared carrying two patients. A lieutenant dressed in winter battle gear ducked down and ran out to the helicopter. I opened the door and he shouted, "We got a lot of wounded and the damn road is cut. Can you get some more choppers?"

I shook my head. "This is it for now. Have you seen a couple of ambulance drivers?" The way he looked at me told me he hadn't, even before he shook his head. I had to accept the fact there was nothing more I could do for the 8055 ambulance drivers, and GIs were in desperate need of medical attention. That had to be the priority now.

"We'll take out your wounded as fast as we can, lieutenant," I assured the haggard-looking officer watching me. He nodded. I climbed back into the chopper, engaged the rotors and pulled off Echo 31 just as another jet swooped down and laid another string of bombs on the ridge across the canyon. I saw the fire and smoke in my peripheral vision, but I was concentrating now on the job I had to do, which was to get these wounded GIs to the MASH.

When I landed back at the helipad a few minutes later, the litter bearers and Enderton were there waiting for me. "Did you find the ambulance drivers?" Enderton asked, climbing up into the pilot's seat as I slid out. I shook my head.

"What happened to them?"

"I don't know."

"The gooks get them?"

"I don't know. Do we have another rotor blade coming?"

"Yeah. I finally got Lovelady on the land line and they are trucking up a rotor blade. It should be here later today."

"They got a lot of wounded up there, Charles."

"I know. Is the spot under fire?"

"No. But there's plenty of fire all around so stay low in the canyon and don't overshoot the spot," I advised. He looked at me in surprise as I jumped down off the helicopter and walked off.

When I got back to the tent and assured Pouhlin and Drake I had no idea what happened to the ambulance drivers, Pouhlin told me the colonel wanted to see me as soon as I got back.

"He wants to see me?"

"Yeah. Probably about the ambulance drivers."

"He'll have to wait till I get thawed out," I said holding my hands over the potbelly. The truth was I didn't want to talk about it. What the hell was there to talk about?

"I think you're burning your hands, they're smoking," warned Drake. Sure enough, they were smoking, but they were so cold I couldn't feel it.

"You hear any more about when the truck will get here with the rotor blade?" I asked.

"Yeah, Major Lovelady is coming with it and they should be here in a couple hours," said Drake.

"That's good. We need that other bird. There's a bunch of wounded GIs laying out in this miserable cold waiting to be brought in," I muttered.

"Yeah and they're stacking up over in pre-op and all the operating tables are in use. By the way, when there's a run like this, the MASH crews work around the clock so they keep the mess tent open for at least hot coffee and some kind of snack if you're interested," said Pouhlin.

"With four of us flying the missions and only one chopper, you'll have about forty-five minutes before your turn again," added Jeff. I could surely use some hot coffee, so I went to the mess tent. No one was inside, but there was a big kettle of hot coffee and a tray of some kind of baked stuff, so I helped myself and sat down at one of the tables. I had just taken a sip of the coffee when someone sat down across the table from me. I glanced up and was surprised to see that it was the nurse from the XIT Ranch. She was wearing a parka over OR clothes with her hair in one of those white stocking caps and a surgical mask hanging around her neck. But I could see, as Enderton had claimed, she was an attractive girl.

"Hello Tejon Ranch," Lieutenant Alexis Markey said in that same distinctive voice I'd heard the day before, although the weariness from long hours in OR was evident.

I managed a smile and said, "Hello, Alexis."

"Any news on our ambulance drivers?" she asked. I shook my head and sipped the coffee. She nodded and sipped her coffee. I guess she could see I didn't want to talk about that.

"You pretty busy in OR?"

She nodded. "It's always the same when there's a battle on one of those stupid hills. A lot of GIs get all shot up and we have to try and put the pieces back together."

"That has to be a tough job."

"It would be difficult in any event, but considering the conditions it's remarkable the surgeons do as well as they do."

"I imagine it's difficult for you nurses too...I mean considering the conditions."

"Yes. It's not easy...not easy at all," she said, her voice trailing off. It was quiet for a moment except for the distant rumble of artillery fire.

"But the satisfaction of saving lives is very compensating," she suddenly said.

I nodded. "How long have you been here?"

"Not quite six months, but it seems much longer."

"Yeah. I don't doubt that."

She stared into her cup of coffee then looked at me and said, "I must admit there are times when I find it difficult to keep my perspective. Then I remind myself that it's a matter of attitude. You have to keep a positive outlook, otherwise you're in big trouble."

"Yeah, I guess so."

She held her coffee cup in both hands and looked across the top of it. "You know, you can make any job difficult with the wrong attitude. But if you accept your situation and do the best you can, no matter how much you dislike it, you can function. Otherwise, you just don't do a very good job, you're miserable, and the time drags."

Jesus! She was giving me a lecture on my attitude! No doubt the word had gotten around. Enderton said she was a nice person and an excellent OR nurse. Maybe so, but I didn't give her the right to counsel me. It wasn't any of her damn business, and because of my lousy state of mind, it pissed me off.

"Attitude affects behavior under any condition, lieutenant, particularly when you've been thrust into a situation that is totally incompatible with your training and experience. In which case it's pretty damn difficult not to have an attitude problem," I pronounced sharply.

She gave me a surprised look and said, "I'm not sure I understand what you mean."

"You know what I mean."

She continued to stare at me, then said, "I'm sorry if I've offended you. I...I had the feeling that..." She paused and got up from the table. "I think you misunderstood, captain. I was talking about myself and my own terrible struggle to keep a positive attitude," she said quietly, and walked out of the mess tent.

I sat there feeling like an idiot. This whole thing was really getting to me. I'd always had a positive, optimistic outlook on life before I went to Korea. I had rolled with some pretty bad stuff in WWII, including being shot at day after day and spending weeks on end in a New Guinea jungle hospital with dengue fever and malaria. But I'd still maintained a pretty good attitude. At this point in Korea, however, I wasn't doing well at all. I walked back to the tent and flopped down on my sack.

"You see the colonel?" asked Pouhlin, who was pulling on his parka at the sound of the chopper off in the distance.

"No. I didn't see the damn colonel."

Pouhlin rolled his eyes, and walked out of the tent. Drake shrugged and went back to the letter he was writing. Okay, so I acted like a jerk with the nurse. But it was an honest mistake.

A couple minutes later Enderton came into the tent and made a beeline for the potbelly. "Any word from Lovelady?"

"Only that he'll be here later today," answered Drake. "How are things at Echo 31?"

"Not good. The gooks still have the road cut and the casualties are piling up."

"Anything on the ambulance drivers?"

Enderton shook his head and asked me, "What did the colonel want?"

"I don't know."

"You see him?"

"No."

"Well, get your ass over there and do it." I swung my feet off the bed, and stomped out through the door without a word.

When I entered the receiving and pre-op tent, it was a sea of activity. There were patients lying on litters everywhere with IV and whole-blood bottles attached to makeshift racks. They had a couple potbellies that were on full-fuel flow and glowing red, but it was still brutally cold. Most of the medical personnel were wearing so much heavy underclothing they looked like overstuffed teddy bears. X-rays hung on a clothesline between two tent poles. Hawkeye was there in a blood-splattered OR smock reading an x-ray and pointing at it with a scalpel. I saw Alice Smith off to one side changing Johnson's badly stained OR smock while he scrubbed his hands at a wooden stand that held several five-gallon cans with the tops cut off and filled with scrub water and soap. When Hawkeye saw me he waved and went back to what he was doing.

I walked over to Alice and asked her if she knew where the colonel was and she said he was assisting in OR. I put on one of those white stocking hats and a surgical mask and gown and went into the operating room. What was being used as an OR had been an old wooden shed of some kind with no windows and open rafters. But it had a solid wooden floor that was crammed with medical instruments, trays, IV stands and four portable operating tables. All four had patients with surgeons, nurses, anesthesiologists and medics crowded around. Piles of bloody sheets and towels were overflowing from canvas bags on the floor. The overhead floodlights were attached to crude wooden beams and held in place by surgical tape. A potbelly in one corner of the room glowed red, but it was still bitterly cold.

It was my first experience in an operating room and I stood there in the corner with a sick feeling in my stomach. But as I watched them work, I realized that despite the primitive surroundings and the splattered blood, they were like a well-oiled machine. All movements were calculated and at each surgeon's command, the response was precise. The instruments changed hands quickly and accurately, despite the cold and the bulky clothing.

One of the surgeons dropped his instrument into a pan and held up his hands. Two helpers appeared, picked the litter off the table and carried the patient out into the post-op tent. Two other helpers carried in another patient on a litter and placed him on the operating table. The anesthesiologist immediately began his part of the procedure as the surgeon scanned an x-ray that was attached to the patient with a clothespin, while a nurse exchanged the surgeon's rubber gloves.

About that time someone tapped me on the shoulder and I recognized the MASH commander. He motioned for me to follow him and we went out into the pre-op tent. After we pulled off our surgical masks he said, "Would you give me your best guess as to the disposition of my two ambulance drivers, Captain Kirkland?"

I was so uptight about everything, I'd resolved not to take any bullshit from the colonel, even if it meant a court-martial. But the tone of his voice told me that his concern was about his drivers. "Colonel, I don't know. They were gone when I got back to the ambulance and I simply don't know what happened to them."

"Is it most likely they were taken prisoner?"

"Probably."

He nodded. "I appreciate your effort to rescue them, captain. I know you did all you could."

"Thank you, sir."

"Thank you, captain." He turned to leave, then stopped. "By the way, that asshole at I Corps *is* an asshole," he said with the hint of a smile, then walked back into the OR. (I found out later that the lieutenant at I Corps had phoned the colonel complaining that I had called him an asshole.)

My first experience in the MASH OR was upsetting. But the colonel's attitude had a kind of settling effect on me and I returned to the tent in a somewhat better frame of mind. That was enhanced when I walked in and found Ace Lovelady warming his hands over the potbelly.

"Hey there, Ace, how are you doing?" he asked.

"A little better now," I admitted.

"That's good to hear. You sure picked the right time to get your feet wet on the MASH mission."

"Yeah, I guess so. Did you bring a rotor blade?"

"I did, and my troops are putting it on the bird as we speak."

"That's good, Ace. We can sure use another chopper."

"That's what I hear."

"You stayin' over, Ace?"

"You bet. As soon as they get the blade on I'm gonna join you and fly some missions."

"All right. I'll see ya later," I said as I left to fly the next mission.

The Third Air Rescue Group's policy for going home was one year in the unit and for every 30 combat missions you could subtract one month off your tour. The maximum missions allowed was 90, so a combat tour could be completed in nine months and you could go home. Pilots like Al Lovelady and Bill Ryan, who had administrative jobs, would come out to the elements once in a while and fly missions with us so they could cut time off their tour.

We got the other chopper back in commission and the five of us flew nonstop as fast as we could go until darkness shut us down. Fortunately, our troops, with some deadly air support, stopped the North Koreans and Chinese drive and got the road back open. That enabled the ambulances to get through to the battalion aid stations and bring in the backlog of walking wounded. The bad news was that the MASH was inundated with critically wounded and worked around the clock for the next several days.

We were beat that evening, but Pouhlin broke out a bottle of gin and a precious bottle of olives he'd been saving and we had martinis with real olives, which made for a very happy happy hour. Then later, while we were in the mess tent having dinner, the colonel came in and told us that the ambulance drivers had been picked up by some GIs in a weapons carrier and were okay and would be back at the MASH later that night. It was the news that everyone was happy to hear, particularly me.

The battle on the ridge in Echo sector was fierce and bloody, but didn't pan out to be the big offensive that was initially feared. Maybe one of the gook generals did come out and decide it was too cold. In any event, it only lasted three or four days, so the press didn't give it the attention that other hill battles got, like Heartbreak Ridge and Pork Chop Hill. But it kept us flying out wounded from first light to dark for several days and the MASH on 24-hour duty.

By the time things settled down again, I had learned what it was like to fly battlefield medevac with a helicopter. I had also learned that, indeed, there was a satisfaction in saving lives that was a world apart from blowing away an enemy ship or aircraft with machine guns. I still believed, however, that if I had to be in Korea, it should be in my old fighter squadron doing what I'd been trained to do in war. I did make a conscious effort to improve my attitude, despite my conviction, and a few days later when I saw Alexis sitting alone at a table in the mess tent one morning, I sat down next to her with the intention of apologizing for my previous behavior.

She nodded coolly at my greeting and took a drink of her coffee. She was dressed in her bulky winter clothes, but the parka hood was back which exposed her huge blue eyes and glistening auburn hair. "You folks have had a rough time of it these last few days, haven't you?" I probed. Another nod.

I took a drink of my coffee and a bite of whatever it was we had for breakfast that morning. It looked like some kind of hash that had already been eaten once. "I...uh, want to apologize, Alexis, for my behavior the other day."

She turned and looked at me as though she wasn't sure what I had said. Her eyes were a shade of blue that was unmatched in my paint box. At first they appeared cerulean, then I decided they were more a shade of cobalt. Whatever the color, they were intoxicating—but not all that friendly.

"I was really in a bad mood that day over a bunch of things and I...well, I misunderstood what you were saying."

"Yes, that was obvious."

"I'm...uh, having a little problem adjusting."

"You have more than a *little* problem, captain, and unlike most of us, you don't try to hide it."

I was determined to mend the fence, so I laughed and said, "It's that obvious, huh?"

She gave me the hint of a smile and said, "Yes, I'd say so. But I have the feeling that your way of dealing with an attitude problem is probably healthier than mine."

"Why do you say that?"

"I keep mine to myself."

"Not always."

She dropped her eyes and studied the top of the wooden table for a moment then looked at me. "Frankly, captain, I don't know why I said what I did to you. I'm not one to discuss my personal problems with anyone. But for whatever reason it just came out."

"Sometimes that happens."

"My problem is that contrary to outward appearances, I hate being here," she suddenly admitted. Her admission surprised me. I suppose because Enderton had told me she was a trooper and a dedicated nurse. "Oh, I do my job and keep my feelings to myself...or at least I try to."

"Maybe the time has come to let your feelings be known, Alexis."

"It must be, because here I am again confiding in you, whom I don't really know and don't particularly like."

That hurt my feelings some, but I was determined to see this thing through. I smiled and said, "Maybe it's a sort of kinship because we have a similar problem?"

"No. I don't feel any kinship to you because I don't even know what your problem is."

"Well, it's similar to yours."

"I don't think so. My problem is pretty simple. Being a nurse in a nice, warm, well-lighted, well-equipped hospital in the States is so far removed from a Korean MASH, it's like being on another planet. Oh, I volunteered, so I have no one to blame but myself. But I just had no idea of the...the conditions...the savagery. I've worked emergency OR and I know about gunshot wounds and automobile accidents, but it's nothing like this...nothing," she said, her voice trailing off.

I wanted to say something sympathetic, but I could tell she had more to say so I held my tongue. After a pause she added, "Back home I concentrated on being efficient in the OR and that way I helped the surgeon save lives. When I arrived here and found myself thrust into conditions I couldn't have imagined in a million years, it took all the stamina I possessed to keep my perspective. So far I've done it because I'm part of a team that depends on each other and who work to save lives under terrible conditions."

The emotion in her voice and the way she was expressing herself left no doubt of her sincerity. "I believe I understand, Alexis. In a sense I'm in that same boat."

"No, I don't think so," she said quietly.

"What I mean is that, like you, I understand the importance of the job, particularly after these last few days. But I don't belong here and because of that resentment I'm having a difficult time adjusting."

"You're not alone. We all understand that what we're doing is important. But that doesn't mean we like being here any more than you do."

"You can always request a transfer."

"Yes. That is an option. Are you going to request a transfer?"

"I already did."

"Well, you were right about one thing. Talking about my problem with you sort of put things back in perspective. So I guess I owe you one and here it is. You chopper pilots are doing wonderful work. You're saving lives that otherwise wouldn't be saved. It may be dangerous, but you couldn't do anything in Korea any more important or worthy. So quitting just because you resent being here is chicken shit, if you'll excuse the expression."

And what do you say to that?

About that time some others sat down next to us, which ended the conversation. The next morning our element left the MASH for our next assignment so I didn't see Alexis again for awhile. But her stinging accusation that my request for transfer was chicken shit hung on my conscience for some time.

Chapter 6

Ch'O Do Island

We were happy campers when our replacements arrived at the MASH in a Sikorsky H-19 helicopter. That meant we would fly it back to home base at K-16 with our crew and not have to make the trip in the back of a GI truck. The H-19 was the latest Sikorsky model, which could carry eight to ten passengers and had more range than the H-5s that we used at the MASH. It also had a heater and although not very efficient in subzero temperatures, it was heavenly compared to the back of a GI truck.

When we arrived at K-16, the other four pilots and medics of our element joined us. They had been on aircrew rescue duty at K-2 in the south and K-18 on the east coast. These were rescue locations where Air Force, Marine and ROK (Republic of Korea) fighter and bomber squadrons were based. When rotating elements through home base at K-16, we generally would spend the night to get some clean clothes, pick up mail, and get a briefing from either Bill Ryan or Major John Woods, the detachment commander. This time it was Woods. He filled us in on the latest war information and new directives from rescue headquarters in Japan.

The major was a mild-mannered fellow with a teddy bear appearance and a pleasant smile. Before the briefing he introduced himself to me, as I hadn't met him. He welcomed me to the unit and asked how I'd gotten along on my first tour at the MASH. I had planned to tell him exactly how I felt and that I had submitted a request for transfer. But it didn't seem like the time or place...or was I still smarting from the nurse's accusation? Whatever it was, I just replied "Okay," and let it go at that.

It was as cold at K-16 as it was at the MASH so we sat around the potbelly on some beat-up folding chairs and listened to the major.

"Congratulations, guys, on a job well done during that last gook attack. Bill Ryan tells me he believes you set a record for combat missions flown without a serious incident other than the loss of one rotor blade. Intelligence advises that things have settled down now and the peace talks at Kaesong are continuing. However, progress remains slow, with no estimate as to when there might be a cease-fire. Frankly, I think the North Koreans are still playing games and probably planning another all-out attack with massive Chinese support. But who knows? Not much official news from headquarters. However, the scuttlebutt has it that we may be upgraded to squadron status so we can get a higher priority on logistical support."

"That'll be the day," grumbled Enderton.

"Now Charles, think positive," counseled the commander.

"Sure, major."

"I want you to know we finally got a new generator and you'll notice we built an enclosed shower room too. And it's got a potbelly in there."

"Hey, that is progress!" admitted Enderton.

"Thank you, Charles. By the way, I'm sorry the Tiger element has to pull another island tour before you get R and R, but the weather has fouled up the schedule. Good luck, fellows, and keep up the good work. Bill will fill you in on operational matters," said Woods as he made a tactical retreat, turning the briefing over to Captain Ryan.

Normally, an element only pulled one island tour between R and R. This time Enderton and crew were going to have to do two tours, which they weren't all that happy about. There were a number of small islands off the west coast of North Korea. The UN forces had captured two of them, from which we flew rescue missions to pick up aircrew shot down over North Korea or the Yellow Sea. One was named Paengnyong Do, which we called the South Island. It was about 100 miles northwest of

Lt. Richard C. Kirkland, U.S. Army Air Corps, climbing into a P-47 fighter at Gusap, New Guinea, December 1943.

A P-38 fighter, with pilots of the 49th Fighter Group, 5th Air Force, nicknamed the "Terrors of Tachloban." Major Richard Bong, America's all time leading ace, stands directly beneath the nose of the aircraft. The author, Lt. Richard Kirkland, is on the wing second from left. Picture taken on Biak Island, Dutch East Indies, September 1944. (Courtesy 49th Fighter Group Association)

Home base tent camp of Helicopter Detachment 1, 3rd Air Rescue Group, USAF, at Seoul, Korea, designated K-16. Photo taken shortly after author's arrival in November 1952.

Maj. Albert P. Lovelady, on left, and Capt. Kirkland, standing in front of a Sikorsky H-5 helicopter, at K-16, December 1952. The H-5 was the primary helicopter utilized by the USAF Air Rescue Service for battlefield pickup of wounded and rescue of downed aircrew from behind enemy lines during the Korean War.

Capt. Kirkland, taking off in an H-5 at the 8055 MASH near Imjin Gang River.
Mission was to pick up critically wounded from the battlefield and bring them to the MASH.
Aluminum pods on the H-5 are for carrying patients.

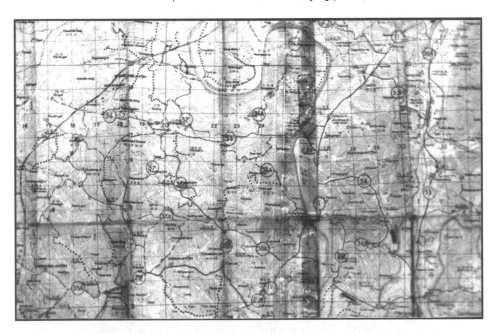

Map of the Korean battlefield I used when flying missions from the 8055 MASH. It is the area
along the MLR, north and east of Seoul, with the locations of helicopter pickup spots marked. This
map was Korean helicopter pilot's only navigational aid, which made finding the locations difficult,
as ground-fire abatement necessitated that we fly in the bottom of canyons that all looked alike.

Capt. Sam Gilfand, alias "Hawkeye," at 8055 MASH.

A young, brave 8055 MASH nurse after her turn in the shower.

Photo taken shortly after their escape from North Korea on Oct 26, 1951.
From left to right: Lt. Col. John Dean, 1st Lt. Charles DuPont, Cpl. Gerald Fryer,
Capt. Robert Barnhill, 1st Lt. Vernon Wright. Photo courtesy Charles DuPont.

Area in North Korea where Lt. DuPont's H-5 helicopter was shot down
after picking up downed jet pilot Lt. Vernon Wright.

This sketch I did in late afternoon after the H-5 returned with a wounded patient from the battlefield.

My houseboy, Kim, at K-16 in front of our tent. He had just been riding through camp blowing his new two-tone horn I got for him while on R and R in Japan.

Operating room at the 8055 MASH was a makeshift structure connected to the main tent of the hospital. During a major battle, four operating tables would be utilized.

The wreckage of Capt. Charles Enderton's H-5 chopper on the battlefield along the MLR. Fortunately his patient was in the carrying pod on the left side, which was undamaged.

Capt. Kirkland and Korean children beside the H-5 helicopter the author flew
into North Korea with life-saving serum in the winter of 1953.
Photo taken by the Korean doctor who did the inoculations.

Author, Capt. Michael Johnson and Hawkeye in front of officer's quarters tents at the 8055 MASH,
spring of 1953. Note the sleeping bags hung on tent to air out.

Seoul. The other was Ch'O Do, which was another 50 miles or so northeast of Paengnyong Do. We called it the North Island.

Both islands were just off the coast, so the inhabitants were North Korean although they were more or less nonpartisan—and kept that way by a garrison of ROK soldiers on each island. The commies didn't like our being there, but as we had naval superiority there wasn't much they could do about it. Oh, they shelled the islands from the mainland once in a while, and made an occasional bombing raid, but to no major consequence other than make our duty there a bit more uncomfortable.

"Greetings, gentlemen," began Ryan. "And welcome back to your home away from home on the shores of the beautiful Haun River, which is frozen over, as is the Yellow Sea all along the beautiful shores of North Korea."

"Oh shit!" groaned Enderton.

"Well spoken, Charles," said Ryan.

"Is the sea frozen out to Ch'O Do?"

"Not yet, but we're concerned that it might be."

"So what are we gonna do?"

"We're gonna keep an eye on it."

"Keep an eye on it?" said Enderton with a frown.

I spoke up, "I'm not sure I understand."

Ryan shifted in his chair, took a puff of his cigarette and said to me, "There are a number of warships in the area, including a British cruiser we call Big Daddy. It keeps an eye on the North Korean coast up there, which includes the two islands we use. So, if the mainland gooks try to come out to the islands, Big Daddy blows them out of the water. That is normally a powerful deterrent. But the concern now is that if the ice reaches the island, they can walk across at night in small groups for guerrilla raids that Big Daddy's radar might not be able to detect."

"So they sneak into our camp in the middle of the night and slit our throats whilst we're dreaming of Varga girls," said one of the pilots. (Varga was an artist of that day who painted pictures of beautiful, shapely girls.)

"Well, the experts say it's unlikely the sea will freeze out to the island, but just in case, we're beefing up the garrison of ROK guards there on the island and giving them some artillery pieces."

"And if all else fails, Charles will takes care of them with his hog leg," added Pouhlin. Enderton wore a pearl-handled Colt .38 instead of the regulation .45. The guys accused him of imitating General George Patton of WWII pearl-handled fame.

"Anyway, you're scheduled to swap out tomorrow with Captain Kerr's element. No change in procedure for now, but Major Woods ask me to remind you there will be no single-ship missions this time of year from the North Island. You fly in pairs, so if one goes down the other can pick 'em up. And everyone wears an exposure suit, no exceptions. Any questions?"

"What if one ship is AOG and we get a MAYDAY call?" asked Enderton.

"The policy is two ships only, Charles. But as the on-scene commander, you have the authority to override that if you deem it necessary. But bear in mind that if you go down in the Yellow Sea this time of year, that water is so cold you're unconscious in a few minutes, even in an exposure suit."

The next morning, six pilots and four medics of Enderton's Tiger element put on rubber exposure suits and climbed into a couple of H-19s, lifted off the helipad at K-16, and headed for the islands. I was with Enderton in one chopper with our medics and Pouhlin and Drake. The other two pilots and their medics flew the other chopper. We flew west out of Seoul in loose formation and over the Inchon tidelands where MacArthur made his famous amphibious landing in the early days of the war. It happened to be low tide so I got a grand view of that unique marine marvel which was a vast expanse of mud flats, shoals, small islands and marine life of every description.

"How in the world did MacArthur get his X Corps over that?" I asked Enderton from where I sat opposite him in the cockpit. The H-19 was configured for two pilots in an upper cockpit above the passenger cabin. It could hold up to six litter patients or ten passengers.

"It wasn't easy," he replied over the intercom. "The trick was in the timing. MacArthur's troops had to disembark from the big transport ships out in deep water and cross the tideland in landing craft at exactly high tide. And I can tell you there was little room for error. They have enormous tides here where the Yellow Sea rushes in and out like a tidal wave. There could be none of the usual SNAFUs that plagued most amphibious landings in WWII. But the landing was a remarkable success with little loss of life. And it was a tactical coup that routed the commies and recaptured Seoul. Ole Dugout Doug may have been an egomaniac, but he was a brilliant military tactician."

After about a half-hour of flying, we made a course correction and turned northwest, flying just off the shore line of a group of North Korean islands. If we had been on a mission to pick up downed aircrew, a fighter CAP (Combat Air Patrol) would be covering us. But for our rescue crew change, we just stayed out over the Yellow Sea far enough from the coast to be out of small-arms fire, so the risk was minimal.

After about an hour, we arrived at Paengnyong Do Island, which was the first of the two islands where we operated. It was small, about six or seven miles long and about the same distance from the mainland. There was a short dirt landing strip on the island. Normally we would have been flown up on a Gooney bird for element change, but in this case we were swapping out choppers because the birds there were due for inspection.

"Is that what I think it is along the shoreline?" I asked Enderton as we approached the island.

"That is indeed ice. Too bad salt-water ice doesn't work well in martinis."

Paengnyong Do island was mountainous with some coves along the shoreline and a couple of small fishing villages. On the east side there was a stretch of sandy beach with aircraft wreckage scattered here and there, the evident result of some unsuccessful crash landings.

The chopper site at Paengnyong Do consisted of a couple of tents and a helipad in a small valley. The Air Force operated a radar site on the nearby hilltop. Their call sign was "Rankin" and they were responsible for radar identification of aircraft and relay of information on enemy aircraft coming down from the north. They also scrambled our chopper crew for MAYDAY calls. One crew and one H-19 were positioned there to cover emergencies in that area.

Our backup for the South Island was a Grumman SA-16 air-rescue amphibian aircraft stationed in South Korea or Japan. They would fly up to be on station for MAYDAY calls, or to respond if the South Island chopper got in trouble. Their call sign was "Dumbo." The helicopters had the primary responsibility to make the water pickup of downed air crew. But if for some reason they couldn't, or got in trouble, the Dumbo could land in the open sea as long as the water wasn't too rough or frozen.

We landed and the new crew replaced the one there who then flew their chopper back to K-16. Enderton, Pouhlin, Drake, our medics and I, flew on to the North Island. Ch'O Do looked about like the South Island except it was smaller but the mountains were higher. We landed at a similar site on the slope of a barren ridge that also led to a radar site on the adjacent mountaintop, call sign "Kodak." This radar site had the primary responsibility for aircraft identification and tracking of both our aircraft and enemy aircraft in that area. Those were Russian and Chinese MiG fighters that came down from across the Yalu River in China to engage in aerial combat with our fighters in what became known as "MiG Alley" where the world's first jet air battles were fought.

Ch'O Do Island was about five or six miles long but it was only four miles off the plainly visible mainland, which created a problem: it was well within enemy artillery range. The island was covered with barren mountains that surrounded a small, narrow valley. There were some rice paddies in the valley and a couple of small, pitiful-looking villages that looked deserted and frozen.

On one end of the island was a larger coastal village where the majority of the Koreans lived. Its name was Sosa Ri. We called it "so sorry." And it did look pretty sorry although it was picturesque in a primitive sort of way. It was primarily a fishing village with boats of various sizes and descriptions dotting the shoreline. Most of the houses were straw-roofed but there were a few wooden structures, including one that looked like either a temple or a community center of some kind. It was painted a bright orange color that made it look out of place.

Our camp consisted of two tents on the side of the ridge with a couple pieces of perforated steel for a helicopter landing pad. Next to the pad was a stack of 55-gallon fuel drums for the choppers. The fuel drums were brought in at intervals by landing craft and lugged up the hill by native workers. Out from the camp was an outdoor privy we called the deep freeze. Our bomb shelter consisted of a shallow cave dug into the rocky ridge and sandbagged at the entrance. Down the slope about 50 yards was a typical North Korean well where we got our water. The circular top was made of adobe bricks over which was an ancient wooden frame and crank. An old iron bucket on a rope provided the means of retrieving the water. It worked fine except the water was polluted and couldn't be drunk unless you boiled it for 30 minutes.

The tent did have a wooden floor and door, which had a sign over it that read: "You ditch and call, we bitch and haul, behind the lines, anytime, rain or shine." Hundreds of pilots and crews had to ditch or bail out in the Yellow Sea during the Korean War. They called for help and our choppers hauled them out. Our tent on Ch'O Do was a standard GI pyramidal with a cot in each of the four corners and a wooden box used for a chair, or whatever else. There were two homemade wooden tables. One was for general use and the other held the grid map of the area and a field phone that was connected to Kodak, the radar site on the hill behind us. That is how we got our MAYDAY calls. On the other side was a footlocker with a couple pots and pans and some staples such as salt and pepper, flour, sugar, coffee and such. Each of us had been issued three weeks' worth of C-rations at K-16. Any sustenance beyond that was up to our individual resourcefulness.

The temperature was subzero, so everything was frozen solid. The only heat was a "Korean stove," a 55-gallon fuel drum with about eight inches of sand in the bottom. From a hole in the lid, a piece of pipe was vented out through the tent top. A steel line from an outside fuel drum fed 100-octane aviation gas into the sand and acted like a blowtorch.

That steel drum would get cherry red. I don't know why it didn't blow up and cremate us, but it didn't, and it kept us from freezing to death.

After landing and securing the chopper, we gathered in the tent and I met Captain John Kerr and his crew. We all stood around the Korean stove in our cumbersome exposure suits for a few minutes and visited before they left in their H-19 to fly back to K-16.

"Anything new, John?" asked Enderton as they prepared to leave.

"It's colder than a witch's tit and everything is frozen, even the damn C-rations," grumbled Kerr. "And I guess you noticed the icepack is almost out to the island and the guys at Kodak are concerned that the gooks might come across at night."

"So we've been advised," said Enderton.

Captain Kerr was tall and thin with an easygoing personality and when he smiled it went clear around to his ears. He turned on one of those smiles and said, "Hey Chuck, you might get to try out that pearl-handled shooter of yours."

"It would almost be worth it to pop a couple of those bastards," replied Enderton.

"Well, Big Daddy will be watchin' over ya," said one of the pilots in Kerr's element.

"Maybe not. Ryan told us the ice distorts the radar and they aren't sure they could detect them coming," advised Drake.

"Nobody mentioned that to us," said Kerr.

"They sure as shit didn't. Let's get the hell out of here, boss," said another of Kerr's pilots.

"Yeah sure, go ahead and desert us like rats leaving the sinking ship," said Pouhlin.

"Don't fret, Jerry, the ROKs will protect you," said another of the pilots.

"Uh, huh. I know exactly where those guys are: holed up some-where trying to keep from freezing to death," replied Drake.

"Do you blame them?" said someone.

"No. Not really."

"You had many calls?" asked Enderton.

"Yeah. We've had some. We picked up a couple last week. But we...lost one yesterday up in the Chinampo Estuary."

"You went clear up to the Chinampo?" The Chinampo estuary was on the mainland and the good part of another hundred miles further north.

"Yeah. It was a long haul. And the bastards were firing at us from shore batteries. A marine pilot was down in the estuary. We found him, but he was in bad shape. Water was so cold...full of chunks of ice... He couldn't get into the sling, so the medic went in the water after him, but...but he was just too far gone..." Kerr's voice trailed off.

We all puffed on our cigarettes in silence for a moment, each of us with our own private thoughts. Mine went to that first patient I'd picked up at 19 Zebra...the one that didn't make it.

"All you can do is give it your best shot," said Enderton.

"Yeah," muttered Kerr, and ground out his cigarette. "Hey, you guys watch out for knife-wielding gooks and have a nice stay on lovely Ch'O Do isle. We gotta hit the road."

After they lifted off in their chopper and headed south, Enderton checked in on the field phone with Kodak. They advised there were no ongoing air strikes. That meant the probability of our getting a call was remote, so we peeled off our uncomfortable, rubberized exposure suits and put on winter parkas over wool fatigues and longjohn underwear. With that, and the Korean stove a cherry red, it was survivable in our canvas igloo.

"Did Kodak say anything more about the gooks coming across the ice?" asked Pouhlin as we huddled around the stove.

"There is still almost a mile of open water and if the gooks try to get across that in boats, Big Daddy will spot them on radar and blow 'em away. Besides, it's too cold out there for man or beast," declared our element commander.

"I hope the gooks know that. I have a thing about not wanting to get my throat slit in the middle of the night," said Drake. "A buddy of mine was on an Island in the South Pacific in WWII and he said the Japs would sneak into their camp at night and slit throats."

"You were in the South Pacific, Richard. That ever happen in your outfit?"

"No. But when I was on Biak Island in the Dutch East Indies, the Japs were holed up in caves above the camp and would sneak out at night and watch our movies."

"How'd you know they did that?"

"Well, the movies were all outdoors and you sat on the ground on the side of a hill and the movie started after it got dark. One night I was sitting there watching Errol Flynn in 'Objective Burma,' and every time Flynn would shoot a Jap, this guy sitting next to me would say: 'Sclew you Ellol Frynn; sclew you Ellol Frynn!'"

That got a laugh and seemed to ease the tension we all felt. "On that note, I'm going to fix my filet mignon," said Enderton, which prompted all of us to survey our C-rations and choose one for dinner. Since it was below freezing in the tent the cans of C-rations were frozen and had to be thawed out on top of the stove. There were several choices like beans and franks, stew, spaghetti and meatballs, etc. The ration actually wasn't too bad, but my problem was that my stomach rebelled at the formaldehyde, or whatever it was they used in those days as a preservative. So I could only eat a limited amount which I mixed with a crumbled hardtack (a hard cracker) and a piece of the fruit bar. I survived on that concoction during my first island tour. On subsequent tours I came better prepared with peanut butter, jelly and boxes of crackers I bought in Japan. It wasn't like the great peanut butter sandwiches I used to have back home on the ranch, but it kept me alive.

When we went to bed, Drake spent some time rigging an alarm with pots and pans that would fall and wake us if someone forced the door open. After he had it all done, Enderton said, "The gooks won't come through the door, Jeff. They simply slit the tent open with their sharp knives." We crawled into our mummy bags wearing all our clothes except our boots. It was rather precarious considering the Korean stove was going full blast on 100-octane aviation gas, and the four of us were crouched in our sleeping bags with loaded .45s in hand waiting to start shooting at the slightest sound.

Although my concern over survival in WWII was generally relegated to aerial dogfighting with Zeros, there were times when things got a little tense during night bombing raids. Like on my first night on Leyte, in the Philippines, when we were bombed 52 times. But even that wasn't as nerve-wracking as that first night on Ch'O Do Island with the concern that some knife-wielding North Korean or Chinese might be coming through the tent after me. But Enderton was right, they didn't come and after a miserable, fitful night we were awakened by the field phone the next morning. It was Kodak warning us they had an early morning strike going on in MiG Alley. So we reluctantly crawled out of our sleeping bags and into those godawful exposure suits.

They were like a pair of kids' pajamas, where your feet and all go in, then you pull it up around your neck and tie it with a drawstring. They were made of heavy rubber so that when you were in the drink no water could get in. It was probably akin to how the old knights in armor felt when they were all buttoned up.

"Be careful not to tear your suit, Richard. If you have to go into the water and there's a tear, the damn thing will fill with water and then you're really in trouble," advised Enderton.

"I'm not sure the prevention isn't worse than the bite," I replied.

Our first chore of the day was to preflight-check the choppers, including running the engine and engaging the rotors. Those poor birds were so cold the metal would actually groan in protest when you crawled in. Once we got them going and warmed up, we would go out every couple hours and run them up a few minutes so that if we got a MAY-DAY call we could get airborne quickly.

After we preflighted the choppers, Enderton made coffee on the Korean stove. He filled a gallon tin can with water and after it boiled, dumped in several cups of coffee and boiled it some more. That made black java that would curl your hair when you drank it. But it got the ole blood circulating and popped your eyes open.

The Korean War-vintage fruit bar tasted more like flavored sawdust than fruit, but it helped neutralize whatever that preservative was in the C-rations. I was washing a bite of it down with the java when the field phone rang frantically. Enderton grabbed it, listened for a few seconds and snapped: "MAYDAY! I'll lead this one, you fly backup," he said to me as we hurriedly strapped on our .45s and Mae West life preservers. "Satan Red Two, an F-86 Saber jet took some hits in a dogfight and is coming down out of MiG Alley with a sick engine. Kodak will vector us to an intercept."

"Roger," I said as we banged out through the tent door.

"Medics, let's go!" shouted Enderton. Within seconds, two medics and our mechanic scrambled out of their tent, which was a few yards down the hill from ours. The medics, carrying their medical kits and wearing the same survival gear, crawled into the cabin of the choppers while the mechanic readied the portable fire extinguisher. Drake, my copilot, and I climbed up the side of the helicopter and into the cockpit via the access slots on the side of the Sikorsky.

As soon as I got the engine going, Drake punched dog channel on the VHF radio. That put us on the emergency frequency where we conducted all MAYDAY voice communications. By the time I got myself strapped into the pilot's seat and engaged the rotor system, my headset cracked with Enderton's voice: "You ready, Pedro Two?" Pedro was our call sign during the Korean War and remained the call sign for all US Air Force Rescue Helicopters around the world for nearly a half-century after the Korean War.

"Roger. Pedro Two is ready to go." Enderton lifted off, flew out over So Sorry and headed north. I followed close behind.

"Kodak, Pedro One and Two are airborne," reported Enderton. "Roger Pedro, this is Kodak. We got you on a 360-degree track." came the quick reply from the radar site. "Now turn right to zero one five. What angels, Pedro?" ("Angels" meant altitude.)

"We'll climb to fifteen hundred, Kodak."

"Roger. The MAYDAY aircraft, Satan Red Two, is at angels twenty-five about fifty north."

"What's his status, Kodak?"

"He's still got partial power and is headed home with three friends. As soon as you get a little further out I'm gonna put you in an orbit and we'll see how he does."

"Roger, Kodak."

"Criminee! Look at that ice!" groaned Drake over the intercom. "It's damn near out to the island." I glanced down and could see that he was right. The whole shoreline of North Korea was frozen over with ice that went out several miles into the Yellow Sea.

"Kodak, this is Satan Red Leader, over," came a transmission in my headset. "Satan Red Two still has partial power and is able to hold angels so we're gonna head straight for K-16."

"Roger. Are you canceling your MAYDAY?"

Hesitation.

"Is Pedro airborne, Kodak?"

"Affirmative."

"Okay. As long as you got 'em up, let's stay on the safe side and see how our boy does for awhile. Why don't you orbit where you are for a bit and we'll see how it goes."

"Roger Wilco. Pedro orbiting." Enderton went into a gentle right bank and I followed a couple hundred yards behind. The pilot of an airplane sits on the left side of the cockpit with the co-pilot on the right. In most helicopters the pilot sits on the right. Therefore, our turns would normally be to the right for better visibility.

"Sure would hate to go down in that stuff," Drake said to me on the intercom as he looked at the Yellow Sea below. Beyond the ice pack the water was covered with floating chunks of ice. It was a chilling sight that for some strange reason reminded me of watching a shot-up B-24 bomber ditch in the Banda Sea during WWII. The concern then wasn't ice cubes, it was sharks. A flight of four of us P-38s, orbited the downed Liberator and saw that some of the crew escaped the sharks and got into life rafts. I don't know what ever happened to them.

"Satan lead, I just lost it, Frank," came the clear, calm transmission on dog channel.

"She's stone dead?"

"Yeah."

"Kodak, this is Satan Red Leader. We need Pedro!"

"Roger, Satan Red Leader. I have Pedro orbiting about thirty south of your position. What are your intentions?"

"Bill, what'a ya think?"

"I'm gonna try to make it to Rankin and belly it on the beach."

"I don't know, Bill. You're sinking fast. I don't think you can make Rankin from here." The F-86 was an excellent airplane, but like all fighters it did not glide all that well without power.

"I got to try to make it, Frank. I ain't gonna eject into that frozen shit."

"Hey man, Pedro's down there."

"Where?"

"Pedro, this is Satan Red Leader. You read me?"

"Satan Red Leader, this is Pedro One. I read you," responded Enderton.

"Ya see? He's down there. He'll pick you up."

"Pedro, this is Satan Red Two. Where are you? Can you see me?"

"Satan Red this is Pedro. I don't have you visual yet, but I'll spot you when you get closer."

"Satan Red Two, this is Kodak. You're still too far out for Pedro to get a visual. Turn right to a heading of two zero zero degrees for an intercept. What's your angels?"

"I'm down to fifteen, Kodak. But I'm going for Rankin. Give me a heading please."

"Satan Two from Leader. It's your decision, Bill, but you're not gonna make Rankin."

"I gotta try Frank...gotta try."

"Satan Red Two, this is Kodak. If you're going for Rankin, turn right to one eight five degrees."

"Roger."

"Kodak from Pedro One. If Satan Two is going for Rankin, would you ask them to scramble Pedro South."

"Roger. You gonna track Satan Red?"

"Yeah Kodak, give me a steer."

"Okay Pedro. Take a heading of one seven zero and I'll keep you posted."

"Roger Wilco."

The Satan Red flight of jets was now headed for Paengnyong Do Island, where the pilot of the MAYDAY aircraft planned to crash-land on the east shore that had a stretch of sandy beach. A number of other MAYDAY aircraft had bellied in there, but the wreckage strewn along the beach was evidence that it was a high-risk gamble.

We discontinued our orbit and headed south at full power knowing that if Satan Red Two didn't make it to Rankin, we would have to pick him up. It was understandable why he was reluctant to bail out into that paralyzing water. But even with a dead engine, he was gliding at twice our speed and if he didn't make it and had to eject, his survival would depended on how long it took us to get to him.

"He'll never make it," said Drake on the intercom. Radio silence followed for several minutes.

"Bill, you're not gonna make it."

"I gotta make it."

"You're not, Bill. You're not! Pedro! Where are you? You see us?"

"Satan leader, I don't have you spotted. Pedro is just south of Kodak."

"Satan Red Leader, this is Kodak. You're about seven south of Pedro. What's your angels?"

"We're down to ten. Bill, you got no choice now. You gotta turn back and have Pedro pick you up."

Silence.

"Pedro, this is Satan Two. You see me?"

"I don't have you in sight yet, Satan."

"Satan Red Two, this is Kodak. Recommend you turn back to three five zero degrees for an intercept with Pedro."

"Aw shit...all right. Satan Two turning to three five zero degrees."

"Good show, Bill. We're heading back, Pedro. What's your angels?"

"We're at fifteen-hundred, Satan."

"Okay, we're down to six. Satan Red Flight keep your eyes peeled for the chopper."

"Pedro from Kodak, correct right ten degrees."

"Roger."

Satan Red, correct left ten degrees."

"Roger."

"Satan and Pedro from Kodak, you're closing to about three miles. You should be visual shortly."

"Bill, get ready to punch out."

"Not till I see the chopper."

"Can't go much lower...we're down to three."

"I got you Satan! I got you visual!" came Enderton's transmission.

"He's got you, Bill! Punch out! Punch out!"

"You see me, chopper? You see me?"

"I see you, Satan Red Two!"

A second or two later I spotted the jet as the canopy flashed in the sunlight and tumbled away. Then came a puff of gray smoke when the pilot fired the ejection system that shot him from the cockpit and out into the blue sky, his parachute popping open a couple seconds later. Then my peripheral vision picked up the abandoned Saber jet on its death plunge. I glanced over and saw that it was headed directly toward me and again I experienced one of those crazy flashbacks to WWII where I thought for an instant that I was going to crash head on into a Zero.

"Look out!" shrieked Drake.

Before I could react, the fighter dipped down and I watched, fascinated, as it struck the sea directly in front of us, sending up a huge geyser of water with pieces of wreckage spewing along a hurtling path over the surface of the water. One wing came off and flew wildly into the air while the fuselage bounced along the icy surface like a skipped rock, finally coming to a stop in a cloud of vapor, and disappearing into the Yellow Sea.

"A whole damn ocean to crash in and the damn thing heads right for us!" groaned Drake. "I thought we were goners."

"Yeah, so did I," I muttered, watching the pilot of Satan Red Two float down in his red-and-white parachute a couple hundred yards off our nose.

"Pedro Two from One, you got him spotted?" transmitted Enderton.

"Roger, I got him in sight."

"Okay. As soon as he touches down I'm going in for the pickup. You be ready if anything goes wrong."

"Roger."

We had descended and were now flying about a hundred feet above the ice-clogged water with the descending parachute a couple hundred yards ahead. The instant the pilot hit the water, Enderton moved quickly forward, with the "horsecollar" rescue sling lowering on the cable so that by the time the chopper was over him, all the pilot had to do was reach up and grab it. The horsecollar was a semi-round, buoyant device on the end of a cable, used to hoist a survivor into the helicopter. And that was exactly how it went. The pilot had inflated his Mae West, hit the release button on his parachute, put his arms and head through the horsecollar, and was winched into the hovering helicopter within seconds.

"Pedro One from Satan Red Lead. You got him, chopper?"

"We got him, Satan Red," said Enderton.

Several cheers from the other members of Satan Red Flight could be heard over the emergency radio frequency. "All right Pedro! Is he okay?"

"He's turned a bit blue, but we got him wrapped in blankets."

"Thanks Pedro. We owe you chopper guys and that's no shit."

"We aim to please, Satan Red."

"You sure do, Pedro. Big time."

"Pedro One from Kodak. Understand the pickup has been made?"

"That's a roger, Kodak. We're headed for Rankin with the survivor."

The formation of the remaining three Satan Red Sabers swooped low over us, the roar of their jet engines audible, trails of black smoke visible against the morning sky. I was momentarily struck with a surge of nostalgia from my fighter pilot days, but at the same time I was experiencing a new sense of satisfaction at having been a part of saving the fighter pilot's life.

"Thanks again, Pedro. Come see us and the drinks are on the house."

"We'll take you up on that, Satan Red," replied Enderton.

"Kodak from Pedro One, would you tell Rankin that we'll be down there in about twenty minutes and advise JOC [Joint Operations Control at K-16] to arrange a ride home for our guest?"

"Roger Wilco, Pedro."

JOC would then call rescue operations and they would either divert an on-station SA-16, or send up our Gooney bird to the South Island to pick up the survivor and fly him back to his home base. That was a service never dreamed of in WWII.

"Pedro, from Kodak. Well done guys. If we had anything to drink, we'd invite you up." (Sometimes when we had a bottle, or the guys that ran the radar site got one, we'd climb the hill after sundown and have a little party. They couldn't leave their post but we could after dark. It was a bit risky to be out hiking at night in North Korea. But what the hell, you needed some diversion now and then.)

We dropped off the Satan Red pilot at the South Island, flew back to Ch'O Do and went back on alert again. Fortunately, there were no more calls for our services that day. The successful mission did give us all a little boost in morale and that evening after dark, Enderton broke out his last bottle of gin and Pouhlin still had some olives left, so we had a happy hour.

"I'd share it with the guys on the hill but it's just too damn cold to hike up there," he said pouring shots into our canteen cups.

Each of us pulled our box chairs up around the Korean stove and I said, "Here's to Pedro One. Good job, guys." We touched cups and drank.

"It sort of makes up for all the bullshit, doesn't it?" said Enderton, firing a cigarette.

"It's a good feeling when you get it done. And those fighter jocks really appreciate us. Jeff and I went over to their club at K-2 one night and they treated us like visiting royalty," said Pouhlin.

"It wasn't always that way. Some of the guys that were here in the early days of the war said that the fighter pilots used to ridicule 'wind-mill' drivers...until choppers snatched a few of them from behind the lines or fished them out of the Yellow Sea. After that, their tune changed," said Enderton looking at me.

I nodded and said, "Yeah. If we'd had a Pedro back in WWII several of my squadron-mates would still be around."

For whatever reason—the satisfaction of the successful mission, or maybe the British gin—the second night on Ch'O Do Island went much better than the first night. The North Koreans didn't come to slit our throats and although it was just as cold, I slept pretty well.

The next day a weather front moved over North Korea and all air operations ceased for the next several days. It was good not to have to wear the rubber survival suits all day and the temperature did go up a little. But it was still bitter cold and we continued to worry about the North Koreans walking across the ice. That didn't happen, but one morning our crew chief reported some of our gas drums had disappeared during the night.

"I got a feeling I know what happened to them," said Enderton. "Those poor bastards up in So Sorry stole them for fuel to keep from freezing to death."

"Yes sir. I can see where they rolled the barrels up the hill toward So Sorry," said the sergeant.

"Are we short of fuel now?"

"No. We got enough till the next resupply. But I think we should report it, capt'n."

Enderton was reluctant, but he called Kodak and asked them to contact the ROK commander to tell the villagers not to take any more of our gas. Later that day it started to snow, and Pouhlin was watching it through the Plexiglas door window when he suddenly said, "Holy moly, come look at this!"

A couple of us grabbed our .45s and rushed to the door. We could see several villagers rolling 55-gallon fuel drums up the road from So Sorry, with ROK soldiers in winter uniforms prodding them with their rifles.

"Ah shit!" groaned Enderton. "That's what I was afraid of."

"Well, there's nothing you can do about it now, Charles. The ROK are gonna do it their way," said Pouhlin.

We watched the poorly dressed Korean villagers, some with their feet wrapped in rags, roll the fuel barrels back to the fuel storage area. Then at a command from the ROK commander, they lined up facing our tent. They were a pitiful sight, with the snow coming down on them. I couldn't imagine how they survived the bitter cold. Enderton stepped forward and said "Okay, that's fine. Thank you."

The ROK commander nodded and gave a command. A big, burly ROK soldier with a wooden stick the size of a baseball bat then started down the line of villagers clubbing them with the bat so viciously they staggered with each blow. But none uttered a cry and no one fell. We watched helplessly until the first clubbing was over, but when he started the second round I got in the act. "Hey! That's enough!" I yelled. The big guy stopped and looked at me, then at his commander as if uncertain of what to do. "I said that's enough!" I repeated. The commander gave me a dirty look and snapped a command. The ROK sergeant repeated the command and they prodded the villagers back down the road toward So Sorry.

"That's a no-no, Richard," said Enderton when they were out of earshot. "The rules here are you can't interfere with the ROK com-mander."

"Yeah. Well, I'm ignorant of the rules."

"So you are," said Enderton, grinning.

The next day dawned clear and Kodak called and advised us that an SA-16 Dumbo was going to make a mail drop. That was great news as we hadn't had mail for a couple weeks. Sometimes we would jokingly refer to the SA-16 amphibians as "Slobber Albert sixteens," but that wasn't meant to be derogatory. They were not only our backup, sometimes they brought our mail when we were on the island and that made them welcome visitors. But there was another reason we were glad to see them fly over our camp: they often brought us goodies such as fresh fruit and real bread, which they dropped to us by parachute.

We all ran outside and Enderton contacted them by walkie-talkie radio on a special frequency. After he contacted them, they flew down over us at low altitude and dropped our mail and a couple loaves of fresh bread on a small cargo chute. We immediately cut the bread into equal parts and greedily ate it as we read our welcome mail. I've never forgotten how good that chunk of crusty bread tasted. I have also never forgotten how much getting mail meant. Having been through two wars and isolated duty on Eniwetok, I can attest that mail plays a key role in a military man's morale. I know it did for me, and for the vast majority of my fellow servicemen.

Later that afternoon, I was answering some of the letters I'd received and counting the hours till I could take off the exposure suit, when the field phone screeched. It was Kodak and he had a MAYDAY call for us.

"You ready to make the pickup on this one?" asked Enderton as we hurriedly waddled out to the choppers in all our gear. "Yeah, I'm ready as I'll ever be," I said.

"We got some pretty gusting winds today, so you're gonna have rough sea conditions for the pickup."

The temperature had plunged again and it was godawful cold, but we had just completed a warmup on the choppers, so it didn't take long after engine start to get takeoff temperatures and pressures. I called Kodak on dog channel and pulled pitch. I knew as soon as I was airborne that Enderton was correct. The winds were whipping the Sikorsky around and I could see the whitecaps on the Yellow Sea.

"Okay Pedro, I got you on the scope. Our MAYDAY is still about seventy-five north, so take up a heading of three six zero degrees," instructed Kodak.

"Roger, Kodak, three six zero degrees and I'm climbing to fifteen-hundred," I replied. Enderton was a short distance behind me in the other chopper. Kodak had told us on the field phone before take off that the MAYDAY aircraft was a F-84 thunder jet, Demon Three, on a dive-bombing mission. He'd taken some flak hits over the target and was nursing the aircraft homeward but with only marginal control.

"Demon Lead, this is Kodak. We got Pedro en route. What's the status of your MAYDAY?" I wasn't receiving Demon's answers because I was still at low altitude and too far away.

"Roger, Demon Lead, this is Kodak. Understand he's down at angels five on a 180 heading?"

"Roger, Demon. Pedro One, the MAYDAY has engine power, but is having trouble controlling his aircraft and may have to eject any moment. Hold your heading and expect intercept in about ten."

The next ten minutes seemed to take forever. Another flashback reminded me of my own experience of flying back a disabled P-38 that had taken a flack hit that nearly severed one of the tail booms. I'd slowed down to lessen the chance of structural failure and it seemed like it took a year to get home. I could well imagine what the pilot of Demon Three was going through.

"Correct ten degrees right, Pedro, and you should have visual in a couple minutes," transmitted Kodak.

"I got you in sight, chopper," came the sudden transmission in my headset.

"Who has me in sight?" I asked.

"Demon Lead has you visual, Pedro."

"Okay, Demon Lead. I don't have you yet. Are you with Demon Three?"

"Yeah. I'm off his right wing. We're at your two o'clock position at angels five."

"I got him!" shouted Drake, pointing.

"Okay, Demon. We have you in sight. What are your intentions?" I asked.

"Demon Three, how you doin', Fred?"

"I can't hold this thing much longer. She's about to come apart...you got Pedro in sight?"

"Yeah. See him down there at nine o'clock low?"

"I...I can't see him...too much vibration."

"He's there, Fred. He'll pick you up. You better punch out before you lose it."

"Pedro, this is Demon Three, you got me? You can see me?"

"You're in sight, Demon Three."

"If I punch out, you'll get me all right, won't you, chopper?"

"We'll pick you up, Demon Three," I assured him.

"My wife and kids will owe you."

"We'll get you."

"Okay. I'm outta here."

I could see the F-84 plainly now at our two o'clock high position. The canopy jettisoned and tumbled away, followed by the ejected pilot. The aircraft immediately snapped into a series of wild gyrations before it slammed into the Yellow Sea in a geyser of foaming water and pieces of flashing aluminum. It was evident the pilot had been struggling with an aircraft that was critically unstable from battle damage. The red-and-white parachute blossomed in the late afternoon sun and began its gentle descent. I swung the H-19 around and flew adjacent to his track to make sure I didn't get too close until he hit the water.

Gusting surface winds chopped the rolling swells into whitecaps that were studded with bobbing chunks of ice. I slowed to hover flight and waited until the pilot splashed down, then I eased the helicopter up over him and turned hoist control over to the medic in the cabin below. Now my job was to concentrate on maintaining my hover position both horizontally and vertically over the downed pilot. It was the medic's job to operate the hoist with an electric hand control.

I glanced down and saw the pilot bobbing in the icy water below. My memory suddenly flashed back and I was looking at my WWII squadron-mate George Haniotis bobbing in the Bismarck Sea. It was intensely distressing recalling that terrible feeling of helplessness I experienced in that long-ago tragedy. There had been no one to save Haniotis. But I could save this fighter pilot with the helicopter, and I would!

I could see that he had popped his Mae West and gotten out of the chute but his face, framed in a white crash helmet, had already turned a shade of cobalt blue from the powerful shock of the icy water. He was struggling desperately to grasp the horsecollar that was whipping about him in the foaming windswept waves and downwash from the rotors.

The medic was on the intercom giving me instructions as he worked the hoist to place the horsecollar where the downed pilot could grasp it: "Right! Right!...Hold!...Forward! Easy...Back! Back, captain! Back!" he barked, reeling cable to compensate for the vertical movement of the waves. One second the horsecollar would be on the water surface then the wave would drop away and it would be suspended in space.

The surface wind was buffeting the Sikorsky, causing the tail to swing one way then another and the rotor RPM to vacillate from dangerously high to critically low, which required constant throttle twisting to maintain RPM while manipulating the controls to hold a steady position over the churning water.

"Demon to Pedro. You got him yet, chopper?"

"Left, capt'n, left!...Hold!...Back, back!"

"Pedro One, from Pedro Two, you got trouble?"

"Pedro! Answer me! You got Fred?"

"He's on! He's on. He's got the horsecollar!...aw shit, he lost it."

"Pedro One, you need assistance?"

"Forward! Forward!...Hold!...Back a little!...Hold!" I glanced down at the pilot in the swirling spray and churning sea and saw that he was desperately struggling to grasp the swinging horsecollar, but it was evident the frigid cold was draining his energy quickly and he was only seconds from unconsciousness.

A terrible fear gripped me. Fear that I wouldn't be able to save him any more than I had been able to save George Haniotis! Then my earphones cracked with, "I got him! I got him, capt'n! He's in the collar and coming up!" At that moment those were the most beautiful words I'd ever heard.

"Pedro, from Demon, have you got Fred?... Answer me, goddamnit!"

"Demon Lead, this is Pedro Two. Affirmative. We have picked up Demon Three," I transmitted as calmly as I could.

The cheer of approval on the emergency radio frequency was like that I'd heard when Enderton picked up Satan Red Two. But it had significantly more impact on me now: it was a personalized feeling of relief and satisfaction. In a sense it seemed to wipe out that horrible sense of failure from long ago over the Bismarck Sea.

The cheer also reminded me of the one my squadron-mates gave me one day in New Guinea when I shot down my first Zero. It hadn't been easy and when I finally did it, I experienced a unique sense of accomplishment. And when we landed back at our home base, I painted a miniature Japanese flag on the side of my P-38. In those days that's what a fighter pilot did when he got a confirmed victory. In Korea the fighter pilots painted little red stars on their jets. The chopper pilots in Korea didn't paint miniature fighter pilots on the side of their helicopters when they saved one's life, but they felt just as good about it. I had experienced similar satisfaction at the MASH, although perhaps not as intensely. Not that a jet pilot's life was any more precious than a battlefield GI's, but it struck closer to home for me.

"Thanks a lot, Pedro, the drinks are on us!"

"Glad to be of service, Demon."

"Is Fred okay?"

"His teeth are chattering, but we got him wrapped in blankets and we'll have him home in time for beer call." Another cheer came over the radio and a couple minutes later, as I watched the flight of jets swoop over us and streak for home, I felt another of those nostalgia twinges...but it was fleeting.

"Good job, Pedro One," came Enderton's transmission.

"Thank you, sir."

"We'll have to hustle, but we should be able to get him to Rankin and make it back to Kodak before dark."

"Let's hit the afterburner."

As it turned out there was a Gooney bird en route to the South Island on a cargo haul, so when I landed they were waiting for the survivor, but I doubt he made beer call that night. I only got a glimpse as the medics carried him off the helicopter, but I could see that he was still suffering from hypothermia. He did manage a smile and a little salute and that said it all.

We were scrambled several times during the next few days at Ch'O Do. Enderton made another MAYDAY water pickup of a Navy pilot, and two days later I picked up another Air Force pilot. There were a number of other MAYDAY calls, but they all made it home except one: a British jet that crashed on approach to his carrier. We flew out to the carrier and looked around but there was no trace of the pilot. He had apparently gone to Davey Jones' locker with his aircraft. Since we never contacted him by voice or saw him crash, it wasn't quite as emotionally distressing as when we were directly involved with a MAYDAY and lost the pilot.

The day after that mission another winter storm moved in and dropped a layer of soft snow, followed by a freezing rain. Then the temperature took a nosedive and we had a six-inch layer of ice on everything. That shut us down for awhile, since there was no way to get the ice off the helicopters. In fact, it was a life-risking chore just to get to our deep-freeze privy and back. The good news was that it was so bad it shut down the whole war for a few days.

To pass the time we played cards, wrote letters and read. I worked on a drawing of my wife, which I later turned into a painting when my footlocker finally arrived. I only had a portrait of her but I wanted to make it full length, so I did a sketch of a Varga girl from a picture and substituted my wife's face. I worked on it for some time during my gypsy travels around Korea and it got a lot of attention. I also got a lot of technical advice, particularly from Hawkeye and the doctors at the MASH who claimed, of course, to be the masters of anatomy.

Kodak advised that the alert was back on again for North Koreans to come across the ice and slit our throats. That had become kind of a Chicken Little thing that we tried to ignore, but it was still on our minds. By the time the weather finally cleared, we were climbing the canvas tent walls. Our two-week tour on Ch'O had stretched to nearly a month. That's rough when there's no way to take a shower and we'd been eating hardtack and drinking melted, dirty ice because the well had frozen over.

The day the weather finally broke we rotated and another element took over at Ch'O Do. When we got back to K-16, I took back all the bad things I'd ever said about it, I was so happy to be there.

Chapter 7

Turning the Corner

When I walked into my tent at K-16 the day we returned from the island, I had a pleasant surprise. Kim, our houseboy, was all smiles and said, "Hava big surprise faw you, capt'n. Lookee what come," he said excitedly waving his arms for me to come see.

I looked where he was pointing and there on the floor beside the bed was my footlocker. "Hey, all right, Kim! This is a surprise," I exclaimed. And it did please me as I hadn't really expected it for another month or so. "Now I can do some painting."

He looked puzzled. "What you paint?"

"Maybe your house," I said, smiling.

He grinned. "Ah so. My house a need painting awright. You hava lots of laundy faw washee?"

"I sure do," I said, then unzipped my B-4 bag and dumped it all on the floor. There had been no washing of clothes on Ch'O Do, and I hadn't had a shower for the good part of a month, so both my clothes and I were pretty rank.

"Okay, me get clothes washee. You go shower. Water is a hot." That was what I wanted to hear, and Kim had the potbelly going full blast so it was tolerable in the tent.

Getting from the tent to the shower was the challenge, but it was worth the dash as it was warm inside once you got there. They had done a good job building the shower house. It was made of heavy wood, sort of like a sauna, and it had a large tank of water that was heated with a homemade blowtorch heater that one of the mechanics had designed and built with good ole Yankee ingenuity. It worked like a charm. Shower time was scheduled and limited since it was shared by the whole outfit, but it was like a slice of heaven to stand under that hot water after not having a shower for so long. Afterward I put on clean clothes from longjohns out and felt like a new person.

That evening a bunch of us had a little get-together in Ace Lovelady's tent to catch up on the latest scuttlebutt. As usual, we sat on boxes and homemade stools around the potbelly in a fog of cigarette smoke, drinking some kind of brandy called "Dragon Fire." Pouhlin had bought it from a sergeant who smuggled it back on a courier flight from Hong Kong.

"It tastes more like dragon piss to me," said Drake when he took a drink.

"How do you know what dragon piss tastes like?" challenged Pouhlin.

"I don't, but I have a great imagination."

"Beggars shouldn't be choosers."

"What's the latest scuttlebutt, Al?" asked Enderton.

"The scuttlebutt has it we're gonna become the 2157th Air Rescue Squadron next month," announced Lovelady.

"And what does that mean?" asked Pouhlin.

"I can tell you what it means," said Drake. "It means diddly squat."

"Well, I hope it means a higher priority on getting stuff," said Lovelady. "And I sure hope it's soon because we need some more dadgum helicopters." Dadgum was another of Al Lovelady's limited vocabulary of swear words. "We lost another H-5 last week and there's no replacement available."

"What happened?" I asked.

"Walt McCoy got shot down on a behind-the-line pickup. Bill McKinney went in and picked up Walt and his medic all right, but we lost McCoy's chopper and Bill got his all shot up in the process. So now his bird is AOG for a new engine and we don't have any spare engines and they don't know when we're gonna get one."

"Did they get the downed pilot?"

"No. The gooks killed him before Walt could get to him."

Everyone took a slug of Dragon Fire and it was quiet in the tent for a moment. Although the chopper pilot had done all he could to save the downed fighter pilot, it was a psychological blow. Almost like you had failed in your duty when you didn't make a pickup.

"Kirk made a couple water pickups at Ch'O Do," announced Enderton.

"Hey, congratulations, Ace," said Lovelady. "Did everything go okay?"

"Yeah, it all went well."

"Satisfying isn't it?" I could tell the way Lovelady was looking at me that he was probing to see if my attitude had changed any since our last conversation. He was the kind of commander who was genuinely concerned about his men. And even though he was no longer my commander, that instinct was still there.

"Yeah, it was satisfying," I admitted.

He nodded and took a pull on his perennial cigar.

"What's this about John Molloy?" asked Pouhlin.

Lovelady shifted on his wooden box. "Uh, he's kinda under house arrest...but we're tryin' not to let that get out, so when you all go on R and R next week, don't say anything to the guys at headquarters, okay?"

"What did John do?"

"Well, I guess you could say he went AWOL. He kind of flipped out. You remember he went down in the Yellow Sea off Inchon here a couple months ago, and just couldn't get over it."

"That was before I got here. What happened?" I asked.

"He was on a MAYDAY call and had some kind of mechanical failure and had to autorotate into the water. He got out okay, but the medic didn't and went down with the bird. That really got to him and he just couldn't shake it. He disappeared here a couple weeks ago and the MPs found him holed up with some little Korean gal in a brokendown hovel in Seoul."

The first time you go to war it's usually when you're very young so you don't have to put up with all these flashbacks you get the second time around. This one took me back to the day I got out of the hospital in Port Moresby, New Guinea, in early 1944. I'd been there for weeks with malaria and dengue fever. The guy in the bed next to me, Richard Strommen, was also a fighter pilot who had bailed out over the jungle and spent months with stone-age savages. He eventually escaped, but he had caught all the same fevers and stuff I had. When we finally got out of the hospital they gave us a couple weeks' rest and recuperation. We went to Sydney, Australia, rented a two-bedroom flat overlooking beautiful Bondi Beach where there were great seafood restaurants and lots of pretty Aussie girls. We ran out of money after about six weeks and had to hitchhike our way back to New Guinea. When I reported in to my squadron commander, he wanted to know where the hell I'd been. I told him I was recuperating from the fever. He mumbled something about taking my damn sweet time about it. But that was the last I heard about it. He knew I'd had a rough time with the fever and needed the time to recover, so nothing was ever said about my being AWOL.

"What's the major gonna do?" I asked, looking at Lovelady.

He shook his head. "I don't know. And I don't think he does either. It's really a bummer because Molloy is an excellent pilot and a good officer. He just flipped out, that's all."

When the Dragon Fire was all gone, we went to the mess hall. After sawdust-flavored fruit bars and hardtack sandwiches for nearly a month, dinner tasted great, whatever it was.

The next morning Bill Ryan told me that Major Woods would like to see me. After breakfast I went over to the Quonset hut that served as his office. It was an austere room with just a table he used for a desk, a rusted filing cabinet, a couple folding chairs and a large map of the area nailed into a two-by-four that ran along the corrugated metal wall. A potbelly was going full blast so it was tolerable, although we both had on winter fatigues and heavy parkas.

"I hear that you made a couple water pickups during your island tour," he said after I sat down in a folding chair in front of the homemade table desk.

"Yes, sir."

"Good. I know it's difficult duty up there this time of year, but we save pilots' and crewmen's lives that otherwise would not survive."

"Yes, sir."

He hesitated a moment, reached over and pulled a paper from the wire basket on his desk. "If you're going to request a transfer you will have to resubmit it in proper form and through the proper Air Force channels," he said, handing me the Army form that I had mailed at the MASH.

I looked at the form that had several endorsements all the way from Far East Command down through the subcommands. Each said my request was a no-no. "Okay. Do we have the forms?"

"Lieutenant James, our adjutant, will give you the proper procedure. But I have to tell you, captain, I'm not going to approve it. Major Lovelady has briefed me on your status and I understand your problem. I also don't believe in keeping a man where he doesn't want to be. But we simply can't afford to lose a pilot right now."

"I understand, major. But as a matter of principle, I will be submitting a request for transfer...in accordance with the proper procedure."

"That's your prerogative, but I will not approve it."

"It's nothing personal, major. And I can assure you I will do the best job I can while I'm with this unit, regardless of my feelings."

"I believe that, Richard, or I would transfer you right now."

"That's a catch twenty-two, isn't it?"

"Sure is," he said, smiling, "Incidentally, if there is anything I can do to make your stay in this unit more tolerable, let me know."

"Thank you. Uh...could I ask you about Lieutenant John Molloy?"

"Do you know John?"

"No. I just heard about his...problem."

"What's your question?"

"This may be a bit presumptuous, major, but...uh, are you considering a court-martial?"

Woods' eyes narrowed. "It is presumptuous, captain, considering you don't even know him."

"Well, I had a similar experience in World War II and—"

"You personally?" The commander looked at me curiously.

I'm not sure just what prompted me that day, but I recall feeling it necessary to tell Woods my story. I guess my objective was to let him know that extenuating circumstances should be considered in these types of situations in the business of war. When I had finished, he nodded and picked up his cigarettes that lay beside the framed picture of a pretty woman, his wife. He flipped his Zippo, fired the cigarette and took a deep pull. "Thanks for the candid input. It always helps to get another slant on these kinds of decisions."

"Yes, sir."

A couple days later, I was pleased to hear that Molloy rejoined his element and went back on the flight schedule.

Our extended stay on Ch'O Do Island had screwed up the schedule again, so our element was held over at K-16 for a couple weeks of alert duty at home base. Duty at K-16 was primarily to provide rescue coverage for the fighter bombers based at Kimpo Airfield and others in that area who were flying ground support missions along the MLR and bombing missions into North Korea.

The weather had turned bad again, however, and there wasn't much flying going on so I got out my painting gear and started work on converting the drawing of my Varga-wife into a painting. When Kim came in and saw it, his eyes got big and I could tell he was embarrassed. I put it away and talked him into posing beside his bicycle inside the tent while I painted his picture. It wasn't very good, but he thought it was great so I gave it to him.

The next morning the weather flip-flopped and turned clear and mild enough to paint outdoors, so I went over to operations to make sure I wasn't the alert pilot. When I walked in, Bill Ryan was talking to an Army major and a ROK officer from UN Headquarters. The major was speaking: "ROK intelligence reports there is a serious outbreak of fever on Poing Do Island. We have the serum and we need to get a doctor up there as soon as possible to vaccinate the villagers. Because of the ice the only way we can get there is with a helicopter. Can you dispatch one?"

Ryan looked at the major. "I don't understand. Why didn't they just call and assign the mission?"

The major hesitated. "Well, uh, Poing Do is a North Korean island."

"Where in North Korea?"

"It's up in the Zebra section."

Ryan hesitated. "Come and show me," he said and walked over to his operations wall map. The major studied the map a moment then pointed to a small Island. It was in the red-shaded area designating enemy territory. Ryan shook his head. "That's a no-fly zone for us, major, unless it's to rescue downed UN aircrew. And I don't think the commies are gonna stop the war long enough for us to go up there and treat one of their villages for the fever?"

"Well, Poing Do is off the beaten path, as you can see. It has no military installations, so we're hoping we can slip in there, do the inoculations and get out before anyone on the mainland knows about it," said the major. Glancing at the ROK officer he added, "Captain Sung is a Korean doctor who used to live on the island and has family there. He has volunteered to go."

"You say this is unofficial?" said Ryan.

"Well, it's an official request for a volunteer to fly an unofficial humanitarian mission."

"All our missions are humanitarian."

"I know, and this mission truly falls in that category. Intelligence reports this thing is bordering on epidemic, particularly for the children. The commies apparently have little concern, or the means, to deal with it since the island is of little strategic value to them. A boat going up there would be spotted for sure, even if we could get through the ice, which we couldn't. So the helicopter is the only way."

Ryan glanced across to where I stood next to the potbelly smoking a cigarette. "You want to come look at this?" he asked. I opened the door of the potbelly, got rid of my cigarette and walked over to the operations plotting map. The major identified the island's location. It was inside the red zone, but I could see that it could be reached without flying over the mainland.

"You say there are no troops there?"

"Not that intelligence is aware of."

"How long will it take for the inoculations?"

The major turned to the Korean officer. "Me think it take maybe two hour," he replied in broken English.

"Okay. I'll fly it," I said to Ryan. There's an old soldier's warning against ever volunteering for anything. But someone always does. This time it was me. It had to do with the children. Mine were five and seven years old.

The ROK doctor had the serum and the inoculation equipment with him, so all we had to do was find a helicopter. Ryan couldn't let the alert ship go, but Lovelady managed to come up with an H-5, and we scrounged an extra exposure suit for the doctor to wear.

I cross-checked our intelligence reports, which were supposed to be updated daily with enemy troop locations. Of course, there was no way of knowing if the information was accurate. But it agreed with the major's claim that there were no reports of North Korean troops on the island.

"You're not gonna have any backup since Dumbo can't land in the ice cubes, so I'd advise you to minimize your time over water by flying along the coast as long as you can," Ryan suggested. We loaded the Korean doctor and his gear in the back seat of the Sikorsky and I pulled pitch a short time later and headed out toward the Yellow Sea. I climbed up to 5,000 feet so I could stay out of small-arms fire yet be within autorotation distance of the mainland. If something went wrong with the chopper, I could autorotate to the shore and take my chances as a prisoner of war. As bad as that prospect was, the alternative of having to ditch in that ice water without backup was worse.

At 5,000 feet helicopter pilots get nosebleeds, as the saying goes. You don't wear a parachute in the chopper because most helicopter flying is at altitudes too low to use a parachute, but at 5,000 feet, you feel naked without one. Low altitude is more efficient for a chopper, unless someone is shooting at you. I was also flying high in this case so Rankin could keep me on radar and I would have someone to talk to if I got in trouble.

Since I wasn't involved in a MAYDAY, I was on a tactical radio frequency and about the time I was well into North Korea, Rankin called me on that frequency and gave me some disturbing information: "Pedro, this is Rankin. Be advised we just picked up unidentified aircraft headed your way."

"Rankin from Pedro. Roger, unidentified aircraft. How close is he?"

"Pedro, it looks like a flight of three or four of them and they're about thirty northwest of you with no squawk." (That meant no identification.)

"They're headed my way?"

"That's affirmative. Their speed indicates jet fighters, probably MiGs. I've alerted a flight of Satan Sabers [F-86 jet fighters] for an intercept, but the bogies will be in your area before they can get there, so be prepared for defensive action."

Yeah sure, I mumbled. I'll prepare to shoot them down with my index finger. Or maybe I could do like the first fighter pilots in WWI: haul out my .45 and take potshots at them through the side window.

"Rankin, this is Satan, where are the bogies now?" came a new transmission in my headset a few minutes later.

"Satan, from Rankin. The bogies are about forty southeast of your position. I don't know how they got down that far without us or Kodak painting them...unless they came overland on the deck. But we got 'em now and they're headed this way. Be advised we have a Pedro in the area."

"Okay Rankin. Give me a vector."

"Steer one six zero degrees, Satan."

"Roger, one six zero. We're on our way. Satan flight from Satan Lead, let's go max...now!"

I realized that if enemy aircraft were after me, I'd be better off on the deck where I could take advantage of the terrain for evasive action.

But then I would be out of radio contact with Rankin and also subject to ground fire. I elected to hold my altitude and keep a sharp eye out. Hopefully I would spot the MiGs before they saw me, then dive for cover.

A few minutes later: "Pedro, this is Rankin. The unidentified aircraft is still headed in your direction."

"Roger, Rankin. Let me know when they are close enough for a visual."

"They are balling the jack so it won't be long, Pedro."

It was coming up on decision time. If those MiGs caught me at angels five, they could blast the chopper right out of the sky. But they had to find me first and they were easier to spot than I, so I held my altitude and course, and kept a sharp eye northward.

"Rankin, this is Satan, are the bogies still headed south?"

"Affirmative, Satan."

"How close are we?"

"You're still about thirty northwest."

"They gotta turn back north soon. Advise me the minute they do. That's when we'll nail 'em." The MiGs were almost always at high altitude when they flew into North Korea from their bases across the Yalu River in China. They were usually identified quickly by our radar at Kodak. But this flight had apparently flown down at low altitude to evade radar detection and were much farther south than usual.

"Pedro, from Rankin, you should get a visual on the bogies shortly."

"Okay, Rankin. Pedro is looking."

I was now flying over the rocky shoreline of the mainland with several offshore islands visible ahead. If my calculations were correct, I was within a few miles of the one I wanted, so it was time to drop down to lower altitude. I advised Captain Sung on the intercom that we were going to descend. I had just released the friction on the collective in preparation for a descent when Rankin transmitted: "Satan, this is Rankin. The bogies have made a one eighty and are headed back north."

"Good show, Rankin. Keep us on an intercept. Satan flight from Lead, prepare to engage."

I breathed a sigh of relief at hearing that exchange. At least the threat of being attacked by MiGs was history and I could concentrate on identifying the island. But hearing Satan Leader say "prepare to engage" did stir another of those old WWII memories as I could imagine the activity in the jet cockpits: snapping on the gunsight, flipping the gun-arming switches, tightening the seat straps, watching the sky ahead intently, because he who sights his opponent first has the advantage.

"Pedro, this is Rankin. The bogies are leaving your area, you copy?"

"Roger, Rankin. I copy."

"Rankin, from Satan, we got contrails west, heading north."

"That should be your bogies, Satan."

"Okay. They are hightailing it for home, but we're goin after 'em...Satan flight, let's go!"

That meant Satan had spotted the MiGs and would engage them in aerial combat if they could intercept them. At that point in the Korean War the American F-86 Sabre jet was as good as or better than the Russian jets and the communist pilots knew that. So unless they had superior numbers or altitude advantage, they would run for safety across the Chinese border (the Yalu River), which was off limits to UN aircraft.

After the debacle at the Choisin Reservoir when the Chinese entered the war, it was decreed that UN aircraft would not pursue enemy aircraft into China. That frustrated our fighter pilots, particularly when the MiGs came across the Yalu and attacked our jets, sometimes shooting them down, then they would run for safety back in China. It reminded me of when I was a kid this mama's boy would hit me in the alley, then run to the safety of his yard and stick his tongue out at me. Well, I'll let you in on a known secret in Korea: sometimes our pilots would ignore the rules and go after the MiGs anyway. They would zip across the Yalu at low altitude so radar couldn't spot them, shoot down the fleeing MiGs and zip back across. The gun-camera film would show an enemy aircraft being destroyed. Who was to say where it occurred?

About that time the doctor was jabbering and pointing down to tell me we were over the island. As much as I wanted to remain at altitude so I could listen to the radio chatter of a good ole aerial dogfight, I reluctantly nodded and began a descent to Poing Do Island. (I found out later that our guys did engage them and scored three victories.) I descended to 500 feet over the island and rechecked my map. It matched, so now I had one remaining concern: Were there enemy troops down there who would pounce on me the minute I landed?

Poing Do was a small island, so I did a low-altitude surveillance flight and could only see typical, austere village with some frozen rice paddies and a few fishing boats. I saw no sign of soldiers, so I landed on the rocky beach near the village and within a few minutes the helicopter was surrounded by the islanders. They were poorly clothed and looked half starved to death. Since it was probably their first close-up look at a helicopter they were curious, but thankfully kept their distance from the rotors as they spun down after I cut the engine. One of the spectators, wearing some kind of official hat, seemed to be the leader and knew we were coming. He and Dr. Sung began an immediate conversation with a lot of jabbering and arm waving.

"No soldier in village. But maybe come. I hurry," Sung said to me.

"Dr. Sung, remember, I must go if soldiers come, you understand?" I replied. We had agreed beforehand, at Ryan's insistence, that I would stand by at the helicopter while he did the inoculations. But if the commie soldiers showed up, I would have to depart without him. That was assuming, of course, that I saw them in time to make my getaway. He nodded and after some more chatter they took the inoculation equipment and a couple crates of C-rations we had brought and hurried off to the village, leaving me sitting in the cockpit of the Sikorsky. Fortunately the tide was out so I had parked the bird far enough from the shore that if I spotted soldiers the minute they came over the bank, I should have time to crank up and get away before they reached me...if the engine started on the first try.

Although the rocky shore was covered with chunks of ice and everything was frozen, it was a relatively warm day and a bright sun shone through the canopy, warming the cockpit. I was comfortable enough, sitting there waiting for the doctor's return, but I was nervous. Every once in a while a couple of villagers would appear and give me a momentary scare. But they were just curious and after a while would disappear. I was reminded of the anxiety of flying a combat mission in enemy territory when you expect at any moment to have a batch of enemy aircraft come screaming down from out of the sun, except in this case it would be screaming commies with bayonets.

I kept a sharp eye on the bank the enemy soldiers would probably come charging over while I smoked one cigarette after another. After a couple of hours passed, I was squirming and began to suspect that something had gone wrong. No curious villagers had appeared for some time and I had the feeling that I was being stealthily stalked. Had the North Korean troops arrived in the village and were they getting ready to come storming over the bank? And could I get the engine started and the rotor up to takeoff speed before they swarmed over me? I had thought so before, but now I began to have doubts. I had one cigarette left in the pack. I would smoke it and if Dr. Sung hadn't come back by the time I finished, I would crank up and do a reconnaissance flight over the island.

Just as I flipped open my Zippo lighter, the commies came swarming over the bank. I spit out the cigarette, dropped my Zippo and hit the engine starter button. The Pratt and Whitney roared to life and I had flipped the rotor engagement lever before I realized that the swarm of commies was just a group of young village boys with Dr. Sung.

I've always wondered if I would have made it if they had been North Korean soldiers. It would have been a close call. As it turned out Dr. Sung had promised to let the boys see the helicopter up close if they would submit to inoculation. So I shut the bird down and even though I was anxious to depart, I let them come close and Dr. Sung insisted on taking a picture of me with the boys beside the chopper. I'm glad I did because even though I couldn't talk to them since they spoke no English, I could tell just by being with them for a few minutes, that they were just curious young boys. But that didn't change anything. They were North Korean. The enemy.

After lifting off, I flew low over them and they all waved. Then I climbed up to angels five and called Rankin. "Pedro is airborne, Rankin. Do you read?"

Happily I got an immediate answer. "Roger, Pedro, I read you five square. Where you headed?"

"I'm going to K-16. You got any more unidentified visitors?"

"Not at the moment. That last group didn't like our hospitality."

The trip back to K-16 went smoothly and from what Dr. Sung told me, the serum was badly needed and probably saved some children's lives on Poing Do Island. There were moments when I was sitting there in the helicopter waiting for Dr. Sung that I wondered what madness had possessed me. But afterward, I was pleased with myself and have always considered that the key mission that I flew during the Korean War. The reason I say that is because on the flight back to K-16 my Korean experience suddenly became into clear focus in my mind. I suspect it was a combination of things: the satisfaction of saving GIs lives at the MASH, the fellow pilots I'd pulled out of the Yellow Sea while on Ch'o Do Island, and now the children at Poing Do Island. It all seemed to form a clear picture of what I was doing in Korea and it was good...very good.

It was tough duty and not as glamorous as being a fighter pilot. The news reporters all talked to the jet aces, not the helicopter pilots. But that's okay, they deserved it. As the old Army Air Corps song went: "They live in fame or go down in flame." And those Satan pilots who shot down the MiGs would celebrate happy hour that night. But so would I. Because I knew, as they say in football, that I had "turned the corner." I wouldn't be submitting any more requests for transfer.

Chapter 8

Pedro Down

Pulling alert at K-16 was good duty except when you got a MAYDAY call and had to fly into North Korea to rescue a downed pilot. Those were rough missions. The fighter-bomber pilots flew air support for the infantry or went on bombing missions into North Korea, both of which were high risk. When shot down, they would either crashland or have to bail out in enemy territory. In either case we had to go and try to pick them up and that's when we earned our big pay.

We always had fighter protection on those missions and they would keep the enemy ground fire suppressed pretty well, until we went in for the pickup. Then the enemy gunners knew the fighters would have to back off and they would come pouring out of their holes and open fire on the chopper with everything they had. On one such mission I took enough enemy fire to be shot down but I managed to stay airborne long enough to get back across the MLR before I actually went down. I was flying an H-19 and fortunately none of us were wounded.

I had planned to include that mission in the MASH Angels story. However, I convinced a chopper pilot friend of mine, Lieutenant Charles J. DuPont, to let me tell his story instead. It is about a mission he flew in the Korean War that gives the reader a more compelling example of what a chopper pilot faced flying into North Korea to rescue a downed pilot, and the consequences of being shot down behind enemy lines. DuPont's mission occurred in the fall of 1951, which was before I got to Korea, but he told me the story. I've added the dialogue, but it's just as he related it to me.

• • •

The tall, lanky pilot sitting on his cot in the GI tent fished a ciga-rette out of his shirt pocket and stuck it between his lips. As he fired it with a Zippo lighter, a field phone hanging on one end of his cot screeched. He reached across his bed and pulled the phone from its canvas case. "Pan Mun Jom; Lieutenant DuPont," he said with puffs of smoke tumbling out.

"This is Captain Durbin at JOC. We got a pilot down and we're trying to locate a chopper to go get him. You got one available?"

DuPont frowned. "This is special operations at Pan Mun Jom, cap-tain. You need to call rescue control at K-16."

"I've already called them and they don't have a chopper available that could get up there in time."

"Well, we got one. But as you know, it's here at Pan Mun Jom on special duty to ferry the VIPs to the peace talks at Kaesong."

"This is an operational emergency, lieutenant. We got a pilot down in enemy territory and that chopper is the only one that can possibly get to him before dark."

DuPont stood mute for a moment, holding the phone in one hand and a burning cigarette in the other, while his thoughts raced.

"Lieutenant?"

"Yeah...Where is he, capt'n?"

"He's down in sector 14 Zebra."

Bad place. He knew where 14 Zebra was: not all that far in a fighter plane, but a long way into enemy territory for a slow-moving chopper. "Okay, capt'n. We'll go get him."

"Great. Have the pilot call us on the emergency frequency as soon as he's airborne and we'll give him details and CAP info." DuPont dropped the phone back into its case, took a last puff of his cigarette and ground it out. He lifted his survival vest and .45 pistol belt from where it hung on a two-by-four tent railing and started out through the door when the field phone screeched again. He turned and picked it up. "DuPont here."

"Charlie, this is Bob Barnhill. What's going on?" Barnhill was the operations officer of the helicopter rescue unit at that time.

"I just told JOC that we'd send our VIP chopper to pick up the downed pilot," replied DuPont.

"Have you cleared it with the general?" asked Barnhill.

"No. He's not here." Hesitation. "Bob, this chopper has to go now if we're gonna pick up that pilot before dark."

"Yeah, you're right. Who's flying the mission?"

"Yours truly, and I gotta get goin'."

"What? You can't do that, Charlie. You're grounded from combat flying. Get somebody else to fly the mission."

"There ain't anybody else, Bob. I'm the only one here. The other pilots are up at Kaesong at the peace conference. I either go pick up that pilot or he's in deep kimchee. As soon as it's dark his CAP [Combat Air Patrol] will have to leave and the gooks will grab him...or kill him. One is as bad as the other."

"I know but...damn, Charlie, you've flown your ninety missions and that's gonna be a rough one—14 Zebra is in a heavy concentration of North Korean troops."

"Well, I sure as hell don't like hearing that. But it doesn't change anything. I gotta go try to get him. There isn't any other option, is there?"

"No...no I guess not. We don't have another chopper available that could get up there in time...I guess you drew the short straw, ole friend."

Yeah. So it goes. He'd picked up wounded GIs off the battlefield and snatched downed aircrew from the Yellow Sea and behind enemy lines 90 times. That had been his job and he'd done it and he didn't regret it. But he knew when he finished his missions that he'd stretched his luck to the limit and it was time to go home. But about that time, the North Koreans had agreed to hold peace talks—while the war continued to rage—and the colonel had talked him into staying for awhile because they needed chopper pilots to fly the UN delegates from Pan Mun Jom, South Korea, to Kaesong, North Korea. Since 90 was the maximum missions a pilot was allowed to fly, he would no longer be flying combat missions but would be performing a great service for his country and the United Nations…so the colonel said.

DuPont walked to the tent next door and stuck his head in. "I need a volunteer for a pilot pick up in North Korea."

Medical technician Sgt. Joe Frier, sitting on a wooden box sewing up a hole in his sock, looked at DuPont, then glanced around the empty tent and grinned. "By process of elimination, I guess that means me, lieutenant."

"You'll do. And hustle it up, Joe."

"How come you're flying a combat mission, Lieutenant DuPont? I thought you were grounded from combat missions?"

"Yeah, so did I."

A few minutes later, with Frier, his medical kit and .30 caliber carbine in the rear seat of the Sikorsky H-5, DuPont pulled pitch and headed toward Inchon. "JOC, this is Pedro Zero Nine. I'm airborne," he transmitted on the emergency VHF radio.

"Roger, Pedro. We have confirmed that 14 Zebra is the grid location of the downed pilot. He is from the 51st Fighter Interceptor Wing and he's being CAP'ed by F-80s from his squadron, call sign "Hammer." The call sign of your CAP is "Grenadier Love." They're a South African flight of four F-51s and they should be up on dog channel shortly."

"Roger, JOC."

That's one bit of good news, thought Charlie. He'd been CAP'ed before by the South Africans and they were good and the F-51 fighter, of WWII fame, was an excellent CAP aircraft. It could get down where the jets couldn't.

"Pedro, for rendezvous with your CAP, what's gonna be your ingress position and altitude?"

"I'd like to rendezvous with Grenadier Love over Inchon at five-thousand feet, JOC."

"Okay, I'll so advise them."

DuPont knew that going into the interior of North Korea at 5000 feet would make him a perfect target for anti-aircraft gunners, but it would probably be even worse at low altitude because of small-arms fire. It was a crap shoot in either case. All he could do was hope to thread the needle between anti-aircraft batteries.

To minimize exposure, his plan was to fly west until he was directly south of 14 Zebra, which was near Inchon, pick up his CAP then turn north. If the pilot's location was correct, he would have to fly 35 to 40 miles inside North Korea—a long time to be exposed to enemy fire. But his South African CAP would be merciless to whomever shot at him. Each fighter packed deadly firepower.

"Pedro, this is Grenadier Love, we have you in sight," came the radio call as he approached Inchon.

"Roger, Grenadier Love, I have you in sight also and I'm making my turn north," replied DuPont as he spotted the formation of four F-51s arching across the sky above him.

"Roger, ole chap. Let us know if you take any fire."

"You'll hear me loud and clear, Grenadier Love. Request you send one of your birds on up to 14 Zebra and give me a report on conditions."

"Roger. Number four, pop on up there and take a look."

"Righto, lead. Number four breaking off."

DuPont watched one of the P-51s peel off and accelerate to the north. The remaining three circled above the slow-flying helicopter as it flew northward. Below and ahead stretched the vast Inchon tidelands, dotted with islands. To the north, a cloud cover blocked the late afternoon sun and cast a dull gray over the distant mountainous area, as though a harbinger of what lie ahead.

"Rankin, this is Grenadier Love. We're a flight of four capping a Pedro and we'll be up in your part of the woods for a while, ole chap."

"Roger, Grenadier Love, I have you on the scope."

"Good show. Let us know if you see any red stars headed our way."

"You'll be the first to know, Grenadier Love."

"Thank you, my good man."

"Grenadier Love lead, this is four; go to tach frequency," transmitted the F-51 that had been sent north to reconnaissance the area at 14 Zebra.

"Negative! Negative!" barked DuPont on the radio. "I'm the one that's gotta go in there, so I want to hear what's goin' on!"

"Roger, ole chap, we'll stay on this frequency. What's the story, Robert?"

"Not good," replied the pilot of Grenadier Love Four. "The downed pilot is hiding in a graveyard. But the place is swarming with North Korean troops. They do have a flight of eight F-80s up there and they're tearing up the countryside, but there's troops all over the place."

"He's hiding in a graveyard?"

"Yeah, he's on a hill in the graveyard and the gooks are all around it."

Damn! DuPont grumbled to himself. That meant heavy ground fire when he went in to make the pickup. It was going to be a rough mission all right.

"Pedro, did you receive that information?"

"Yeah. I'd rather not have, but I got it, Grenadier Love."

"More bad news, Pedro," transmitted number four. "There's weather moving in. You can see the storm front over the mountains to the north, and I'd guess it will be over that area within the next half hour or so."

"Super," DuPont muttered. Checking his map against the landmarks below, he estimated his position to be about 15 miles from the downed pilot. He should be there before the bad weather struck. But that was the least of his worries. The only good news was that he'd taken no anti-aircraft fire...so far.

Turning around in the seat, he shouted, "Keep an eye out for anti-aircraft fire, Joe!" Since the early-vintage choppers in Korea did not have an intercom, communications depended on good old shouting. The medic scooted forward in the back seat and shouted, "Okay lieutenant! This gonna be a hot one?"

"I'm afraid it is, Joe!"

Frier nodded and moved back into his seat. DuPont felt sympathy for the young medic who could do nothing but sit back there and hope for the best. At least he, as the pilot, had some control over his destiny...or did he?

"Pedro, this is Hammer. You read?" came a new transmission in DuPont's earphones.

"Roger, Hammer, Pedro reads you."

"We're the CAP on station. What's your ETA, Pedro?"

"About ten minutes, Hammer. How does it look?"

"Our guy is okay for now, but you're gonna be just in time. The valley is swarming with troops. We've kept them off the mountain where he is, but a few may have slipped through so we need to get him out of there—the sooner the better."

"Okay, Hammer, how is the weather?"

"Not good. It's moving in fast. But we'll be able to work the area over once more before you get here."

A few minutes later, as he approached the area of 14 Zebra, DuPont could see mushrooming clouds of black smoke caused by the attacking flight of jets that were strafing and firing rockets into the North Korean troop installations. He could also see the dark weather clouds moving down from the north.

"Hammer, this is Pedro. I'm over the south end of the valley now with my CAP, Grenadier Love. I'll be in position in a couple minutes to go in for the pickup," transmitted DuPont.

"Roger, I got you spotted. Hammer flight from lead, break off. Repeat, break off, the chopper is here and starting his run. Pedro, you got the graveyard in sight?"

After a short visual search, DuPont spotted the mountaintop graveyard. "Okay, Hammer and Grenadier Love, I got the graveyard in sight and I plan to make my approach to the north."

"Sound off if you take any fire, Pedro," responded the Grenadier Love leader.

DuPont lowered the collective, nosing the helicopter downward. "Joe, keep a sharp lookout for ground fire!" he shouted.

As he flew down over the valley, DuPont could see the mountain ahead with the graveyard on top, and suddenly he remembered that Koreans bury their dead sitting up. The graveyard was covered with grave mounds! He wouldn't be able to land and the helicopter he was flying did not have a personnel hoist! What else could go wrong?

"Joe, we're goin' in for the pickup. Don't open the cabin door till I tell you!"

"Yes sir! Are you gonna try to land?"

"Can't land because of the grave mounds! I'll come to a hover and you signal the pilot to grab onto the helicopter, then try to pull him inside!"

"Okay, but I don't see him!"

"Neither do I!"

"Maybe the gooks got him!"

It would be a hell of a note if the pilot had been captured at this point, thought DuPont as he eased in aft cyclic and lowered collective pitch to set up his approach to the mountaintop.

"You getting any ground fire, Pedro?" came the voice of Grenadier Love from the cockpit of his F-51, as the four South African fighters circled over the small valley.

"So far it's negative on ground fire, Grenadier Love. But I can't see the pilot. Where is he?"

"There he is, lieutenant!" shouted Frier suddenly, leaning forward from the back seat and pointing a finger. DuPont saw a figure run out from behind a grave mound, waving his arms frantically. "I got him," he said, banking slightly and pulling pitch to establish a hover. But as the H-5 settled toward the graveyard, DuPont realized the swirling winds from the approaching storm had shifted and the helicopter began to yaw and buck violently.

He pulled pitch, nosed off to one side and kicked rudder pedal to bring him back around for another approach. He could see the pilot chasing after him through the grave mounds, apparently afraid the helicopter was leaving without him. "Open the cabin door!" DuPont shouted. "When I come to a hover over the mounds he's gonna have to grab on!"

"Lieutenant! There's soldiers with guns right below us!" shouted the medic. DuPont saw the North Korean soldiers in his peripheral vision, but his concentration was centered on bringing the helicopter into a hover that would allow the pilot to climb in. But if he went too low, the tail rotor would strike one of the burial mounds and that would be all she wrote.

He glanced out and saw the pilot, who was racing toward the helicopter, suddenly stop, raise his arm and fire his .45 at two soldiers who were chasing him. Then he turned and ran toward the helicopter that was yawing and pitching as DuPont struggled to stabilize a hover in the shifting winds.

The pilot ran up to the helicopter and made a desperate lunge for the open door. Frier, hanging out the door, grabbed him and hung on. All DuPont could hope was that Frier had a good grip on the pilot because soldiers had suddenly appeared directly in front of the helicopter. It was either pull pitch now or take a head-on fusillade of North Korean lead. DuPont twisted the throttle full open and pulled all the pitch he could get.

"Pedro, from Hammer. Did you get him?"

DuPont heard Hammer's call but his total concentration was on flying the helicopter as fast as it would go away from the ground fire that he knew was pouring into the H-5. He glanced back. The pilot was still hanging onto the side of the helicopter with Frier struggling to pull him inside. "Answer me, chopper!" came the angry voice of Hammer.

"I don't know yet," said DuPont.

"What?"

"I got him in, lieutenant!" shouted Frier from behind.

DuPont felt that sudden, acute feeling of relief that he'd always felt when he'd snatched someone from the enemy's grasp. "We got him, Hammer," he said calmly over the radio.

"Hey! That's great! Everybody hear that? The chopper got Vern!" Cheers could be heard over the radio as the CAP pilots looked down and saw the flashing blades of the Sikorsky helicopter skimming out across the mountain ridges of North Korea.

In the helicopter, Frier leaned forward and tapped DuPont on the back and shouted, "Lieutenant, the pilot says that when he jumped onto the chopper he saw oil streaming out of the engine! He's got it all over him!"

Lady Luck giveth and she taketh away, thought DuPont as he glanced at the oil pressure gauge and saw the needle fluttering on a downward course.

"Grenadier Love, this is Pedro. I got trouble."

"What's the problem, Pedro?"

"I took ground fire and I'm losing engine oil pressure."

"What are your intentions, ole chap?" Yeah, DuPont…What are you gonna do? You can't will that Pratt and Whitney to keep running without oil. How long will it run?…not long…you're gonna have to land down there and it's too late in the day to get another chopper up here to get the three of you out. The commies will be coming when they see you go down, and the CAP can't protect you at night. They will have to go home. You should have known your luck couldn't last forever…

DuPont glanced down at the terrain below. The canyons were already turning a dark blue-gray as nightfall approached and the storm clouds moved relentlessly over the ridges. Not many places down there to make an autorotation landing…but that's what he had to do. The engine can't run without oil and, barring divine intervention, the helicopter was going down when it quit. Maybe he could make it to the coast before it quit…it wasn't too far, was it?…maybe…?

"Grenadier Love, I'm gonna try to make it to the coast. Call JOC and have them launch an SA-16. If I can make it, they can pick us up over there."

"Roger Wilco."

"Pedro, this is Hammer. We're low on fuel but we'll help cover you as long as we can."

DuPont turned his head and shouted. "Joe, buckle yourselves in tight! We got a rough landing comin' up!"

When he turned back to the instrument panel, he saw the cylinder head temperature gauge raising and the oil pressure gauge pegged on zero. It wouldn't be long now till engine failure.

"Grenadier Love, from Pedro. Can you see how far it is to the coast?"

"Yeah. I can see the coastline. It's not too far after you cross that next ridge."

Directly ahead was a heavily wooded ridge. If the engine quit while flying over it, he would have to autorotate into the trees...not good...somebody would get hurt for sure. Directly ahead, just before the ridge, was a small plateau of rice paddies. He could land there all right, but they were North Korean rice paddies. If he could just make it over that ridge...come on, baby, you can run just a little longer, can't you?

Oil pressure zero and cylinder head temperature gauge were pegged in the red and the engine beginning to make strange noises. It was decision time and DuPont knew it. He eased off on the collective and back on the cyclic for an approach to the rice paddies directly ahead. "Grenadier Love, I'm gonna have to land in the rice paddies up ahead, let me know if you see any activity."

"Pedro, you're not all that far from the ridge and JOC has an SA-16 en route to the area."

"I gotta feelin' that I can't make it over that ridge, Grenadier Love."

DuPont had discovered in his first 90 combat missions that when he got that certain feeling, he should act on it. And it was well that he did. As he brought the helicopter up over the rice paddies, the engine gave out a groan and quit dead.

His instinct was correct. But he was just a few yards short of the rice paddy and had to make his landing on the lip of the paddy, which caused the H-5 to topple over on its side. The rotor blades struck the ground and the helicopter thrashed around violently until the blades had beat themselves to death, hurling pieces in all directions.

When the thrashing subsided and all the pieces came to rest, the three men crawled out of the wreckage, fortunately uninjured. They stood for a moment with ambivalent emotion as they stared at the twisted, broken helicopter. They had lost their means of escape but somehow they knew the fallen chopper had given its all.

"She did pretty well, considering," said DuPont, pointing to all the bullet holes in the engine compartment of the H-5. "Yeah, and it got me out of that graveyard," said Lieutenant Vernon Wright, the jet pilot.

DuPont glanced around the plateau of rice paddies. "I don't see any activity, but you fellows keep a sharp watch while I get out my URC-4 radio."

"You got one of those?" asked Wright.

"Yeah, I'm lucky to have it. They're new and there's precious few of them around. I just hope it works," said DuPont, fishing the small, handheld emergency radio out of his survival jacket.

"Come on baby, work," he mumbled, pulling up the antenna and switching it on. "Grenadier Love, this is Pedro. Do you read?"

No answer. Then: "Who is calling Grenadier Love?"

"It's me! Pedro...uh, I'm on the ground with a URC-4 radio."

"I say, ole chap, what a pleasant surprise, and I can read you five square," came the response on the URC-4 receiver.

Charlie knew at that instant the playing field had been leveled again. With ground-to-air communications and a little luck, they could still get out of this alive. This is believed to have been the first emergency use of the URC-4 radio in the Korean War. The tiny radio subsequently became required survival equipment for aircrews, and it was responsible for saving many a downed airman.

"Pedro, are you okay down there? Your helicopter looks done in."

"Roger, Grenadier Love. But the good news is that no one was hurt. What's the word from JOC?"

"They just called and said that the Dumbo [SA-16 Amphibian] had to turn back because of weather and darkness. I'm afraid you chaps are gonna have to spend the night. But JOC has rustled up two choppers and will launch them at dawn, weather permitting."

Yeah…weather permitting, Charlie muttered to himself, as the cold wind of the season's first winter storm whipped his clothing. "Okay. Do you see any activity around us?"

"We can't see any in your immediate area. There is some kind of military installation a couple miles north of you, and we spotted what looked like troops moving out. You might want to get out of that area rather quickly."

"Okay. Grenadier Love, we're gonna do just that."

"Roger, Pedro. You can count on our being back up here at the crack of dawn…weather permitting."

"Thanks. Look for us south of here. When I see you overhead, I'll contact you on the URC-4. And, uh…Grenadier Love…if it doesn't work out, we want you to know we appreciate your efforts."

"Pedro, all the pilots and crews in Korea know the great work you chaps do, so you can count on us doing everything we can to get you out of there. Good luck, and we'll see you in the morning," said the Grenadier Love leader, who then winged over with his flight of F-51 fighters and swooped down over the three figures standing beside the wrecked helicopter. When the sound of the Rolls Royce engines in the F-51s had faded, it was replaced by the howl of a winter wind sweeping across the hulk of the fallen chopper.

"We're in for a rough night, fellows, no matter what we do. But I think we better get on out of here before some of our North Korean foes show up," said DuPont glancing up at the ridge. "I suggest we climb about halfway up the side of that ridge, then head south. I've got a magnetic compass with a luminous dial to keep our direction."

"Why halfway up, lieutenant?" asked Frier.

"Well, I'd bet that North Korean GIs are no different than any others, so they will do what looks to be the most obvious and easiest. And that is to search the valleys and the tops of the ridges."

Wright nodded. "Sounds reasonable to me. What's the plan if we do encounter soldiers?"

The three looked at each other. DuPont and Wright wore sidearms. Frier held a regulation .30-caliber carbine. "I suggest we let the decision to fight or surrender depend on the situation," offered DuPont. The others nodded.

The three men forged their way through the woods until they were about halfway up the side of the ridge. Then DuPont took a bearing with his magnetic compass and they headed south. Darkness had settled now, which made traversing the forest a stumbling, falling, cursing exercise, exacerbated by a howling wind and a heavy cold rain. The winter storm had struck with a fury and within a short time all three were soaked to the skin and numbed by the freezing rain. But they forged on, stopping occasionally for a short rest and to listen for sounds of possible pursuers.

"I'm so cold I got no feeling in my hands," groaned the medic as they halted for a rest after several hours of trudging doggedly through the freezing downpour.

"I'm so cold I can't feel anything anywhere," said Wright. "You suppose we're freezing to death?"

"They taught us in medical training that just before you freeze to death, you feel warm and comfortable," advised Frier.

"Well then, I'm not freezing to death," growled DuPont. "Because I'm one cold, miserable son of a bitch!"

That touch of humor spurred them on through the dark forest. They traveled as quietly as possible, but couldn't suppress an occasional outburst of cursing when someone fell or got a twig jabbed in his eye. At one point Frier stepped off a 20-foot cliff and bruised his hip badly. "Maybe we should stop and try to find some find of shelter," suggested Wright.

"The only shelter we're likely to find if we don't keep going, is a North Korean prison," voiced DuPont. "If Joe can walk, we got to keep going."

"Yeah, I'll make it, lieutenant. I'd rather freeze to death than end up in a gook prison camp."

Sometime in the early morning hours the temperature dropped below freezing, but the wind and rain slacked off and occasionally the moon would peek through the clouds. The moonlight was a morale booster, but in a way made their travel more treacherous, since at one moment they would be in bright moonlight and the next, pitch blackness.

At one point they stopped to rest and suddenly heard voices coming through the woods. They grabbed their firearms and dove for cover behind a clump of trees. They remained motionless, hardly daring to breathe for some time. Was it soldiers or villagers? They never found out, as whoever it was went past them without visual contact.

After that tense experience, they struggled on until shortly before dawn, when Frier could not continue on his injured hip. DuPont had wanted to get to an open area in the forest where the CAP could see them the next morning, but he realized they were all too exhausted to continue. He would have to rely on the URC-4 radio. If it worked like it had earlier, the CAP could find them and the rescue choppers could be directed in to pick them up. If it didn't work…sayonara.

Afraid that a fire would give their position away, all they could do was huddle in the wet brush and count the minutes till dawn. Without movement, the terrible cold was now a serious threat to their survival. DuPont had realized this would happen if they stopped walking, and he had pushed them to the limit. But now there was nothing to do but hope the rescue aircraft would arrive early, as promised.

When the first streaks of dawn broke across the North Korean ridges, DuPont checked off one of his worries. The storm had passed and the sky was going to be clear. That meant they would come. The rescue aircraft would come! He reached into his survival vest for the radio, but his hands were so cold he couldn't grasp it. Then came a terrifying thought: would the URC-4 even work in this bitter cold?

DuPont climbed to his feet and began to beat his hands together to get some feeling. His cigarettes had turned to wet mush early in the night, but the faithful Zippo flamed when he flicked the little start wheel. Then he held his hand over the flame until he smelt flesh burning…and he heard the distinct sound of a F-51.

"They're here! They're here!" he croaked. And they were. As promised, the flight of four South African F-51s streaked across the early morning sky above where DuPont was frantically trying to get the antenna up and the URC-4 radio turned on. Was it on? Was the radio on? He'd pushed the switch...hadn't he? It was difficult to tell with frozen hands. He waited. The F-51s passed over and continued on. They would go by, of course, because they couldn't see him in the trees.

"Grenadier Love! Grenadier Love! You passed us!" shouted DuPont into the mic on the URC-4 radio. The sound of the F-51s faded as they flew on north. "Son of a bitch!"

"Christ, they flew right on by us," rasped Wright, who had struggled to his feet beside DuPont. "Is the radio working?"

"I don't know."

"Grenadier Love! This is Pedro! This is Pedro! Do you read?" No answer.

DuPont repeated his frantic call several times, with no answer.

"Hey, I hear them coming back!" said Frier, who had also stumbled to his feet.

"Pedro, this is Grenadier Love. Do you read me?" came the clear voice on the URC-4 radio.

DuPont let out a shout: "Yahoo! You bet I do!"

"I say, ole chap, it's good to hear you," came the reply.

"Times that by ten and you'll know how good it is to hear you, Grenadier Love!" croaked DuPont.

"Good show. Are you okay?"

"Other than frozen stiff, we're fine now. Are the choppers coming?"

"Righto. They are en route. Where are you?"

"We're just south of your position. You're coming toward us now. We're in the trees on the ridge just to your right."

"Roger. Tell me when I'm directly over you."

Charlie could see the F-51s approaching. "Turn left a little...okay, that's good...keep coming...a little more left...hold...you're almost there...now! You just passed directly over us!"

"Okay Pedro, I got you spotted. There are two choppers coming and they should be here within the next thirty minutes. We'll set up a CAP over you until they get here."

"Grenadier Love, suggest you keep an eye on our location but orbit a bit north of us. That should mislead any of our North Korean neighbors who might be interested in what's going on over here."

"Good idea, Pedro, we'll move north a little."

"And Grenadier Love, we should destroy the chopper. I hate to do it, but I don't want the commies to get hold of it."

"Righto, we'll take care of it."

"Oh man, I think we're gonna make it," said Frier, leaning against a tree.

"Sure we're gonna make it—I never had any doubt," said DuPont with a grin.

"Me either. I knew you Pedro guys would come through," added Wright.

"I hope they got a hoist on those choppers, cause there ain't no way they can get us without one," said Frier glancing up at the overhead trees.

Christ! Wouldn't that be a bummer thought DuPont suddenly. "Grenadier Love, this is Pedro, would you check with JOC and make sure those choppers have a personnel hoist?"

"Pedro, this is Colonel John Dean in Pedro Zero Two. Are you reading me?"

DuPont was surprised to hear the voice of his commander on the URC-4 radio. "Roger, colonel, I read you."

"We got a hoist, Charlie, and we'll be up there in a few minutes to pick you up."

"That's great, colonel. We're gonna have to be hoisted out. When I hear you coming, I'll talk you into our location."

"Okay. Bob Barnhill is flying Pedro Zero One. He'll come in and get the first two. Then I'll come in and get you, ole buddy." Charlie grinned. His commander had never referred to him as his ole buddy before, but under these circumstances that was just fine.

A few minutes later, the two Sikorsky H-5 helicopters came into view and DuPont directed them to his location with the URC-4 radio, as he had Grenadier Love. While the South African CAP watched over them, the first chopper came in over DuPont's position and lowered the horse collar on the cable. Frier and Wright were winched up, one at a time, to the helicopter, which hovered above the trees. Then the colonel in Pedro Zero Two, came in and lifted DuPont up in the same way. With Grenadier Love watching over them, the two choppers then flew out of North Korea and landed safely at K-16.

Korean War records indicate that this mission, flown on October 25 and 26, 1951, was the first successful rescue of a downed Air Force chopper crew from behind enemy lines in the Korean War. Lieutenant Charles DuPont was sent home after this mission, his 91st, and was recommended for the Distinguished Service Cross.

I knew about DuPont's mission, but needed some details to write the story. We have kept in touch all these years, so he gave me the details and a couple of additional anecdotes: He said the Grenadier Love leader told him afterward that they fired rockets and thousands of rounds of .50-caliber machine-gun fire into the fallen Sikorsky helicopter before they finally got it to burn. DuPont also admitted it took two days for him to thaw out, but that didn't bother him because that's how long he stayed inebriated.

Chapter 9

Rest and Recuperation

Finally, the pilots and medics in Enderton's element got orders for R and R and we flew over to Japan from Seoul in a C-124 Globemaster. It was a huge four-engine transport that would carry a couple hundred passengers. It rattled and shook, but it had efficient heaters and it got us there. We landed at Tachikawa Air Base, which was the big terminal in the Tokyo area where all the troop carrier and MATS aircraft operated.

Most of us got quarters over at Johnson Air Force Base for our one-week R and R. I had planned to find a hotel in Tokyo, but Enderton convinced me to stay on base because he claimed the quarters were good and the officer's club dining room was excellent. It turned out he was right on both counts.

The air base, at a town called Irumagawa, had been a Japanese military installation during World War II. It had been repaired and remodeled and was headquarters for a number of Air Force units including our outfit, the 3rd Air Rescue Group. The BOQ (Bachelor Officer's Quarters) rooms were spacious and well heated and the shower had hot water anytime you wanted it, day or night. I stayed in it so long that first day I was waterlogged when I finally came out.

Three of the pilots in our element who had been there before headed for their "ranch," so I didn't see them again till it was time to leave. When I first heard that expression I was intrigued. I thought it might be fun to spend my R and R on a Japanese ranch. But then Enderton explained to me that this ranch wasn't what I thought it was. It was private Japanese quarters in the city with a built-in, multi-talented female caretaker. It was a package deal including lodging, meals and caretaker services that you paid for by the week.

The other five pilots in Enderton's element went to the officer's club for happy hour and dinner that night: Enderton and I, plus Pouhlin, Drake and Lieutenant George Hayes, whom I hadn't met because he'd been pulling duty down at K-3 in the southern part of South Korea.

The Officer's Club was decorated in an interesting mixture of Japanese and American style. The tables, chairs and silverware were all Western, while the interior decoration was Japanese for the most part with colorful murals and paintings. The club was supervised by Air Force officers but staffed by Japanese civilians who were courteous and efficient.

We started off in the lounge where they served martinis in big crystal glasses with huge green olives. Our waiter, a young Japanese fellow who was eager to please and could speak enough English to be understood, took our order with a big smile and was back in a flash with our martinis.

"Here's to seven days of food gorging, booze, and other decadent activities," toasted Drake.

"Hear hear!" we all replied and drank.

"We're off to a good start, this is an excellent mart," I declared.

"They do a good job here," said Enderton. "The O Club is well managed and so are all the other base services, including a large and well-stocked Base Exchange. Incidentally, this base is named after one of our WWII fighter pilots, Lieutenant Colonel Gerald Johnson."

"Yeah. He was my CO," I said.

"Colonel Gerald Johnson was your CO?"

"That he was, only he was a captain when I flew with him in the 9th Fighter Squadron in the Southwest Pacific."

"I've heard of him," said Pouhlin. "He was one of our top aces, wasn't he?"

I nodded. "He had twenty-two confirmed victories, and a bunch more that weren't. He was a great fighter pilot and a great commander. Gerry went all through the war without a scratch then gets killed here in Japan shortly after the war in an operational accident."

"Ain't that a bitch?" said Jeff.

"Lady Luck plays a big role in any game, particularly the game of war," said Enderton.

"True, but I'm gonna forget all that war shit for the next seven beautiful days," declared Pouhlin.

"Speaking of luck, what say we hit the Tachi Ballroom after dinner?" suggested Hayes. Maybe she'll be there."

"George, are you still thinking about that girl?" asked Jerry.

"Yeah, I am," said Hayes, taking a big gulp of his drink. He was fresh faced with big brown eyes, curly hair and a dimpled chin. He was young and single and had been sent to Korea fresh out of helicopter school.

"George thinks he's in love with a little freelancer he only saw one time and doesn't even know her name."

"She's not a freelancer, Jerry. And I do know her name. Her first name anyway," replied Hayes.

"I thought all those girls were freelancers."

"Kanuri isn't."

"What's a freelancer?" I asked.

"It's the same as a street prostitute only they don't let 'em walk the streets here, so they hang out in clubs and dance halls like the Tachi Ballroom," explained Enderton.

"She's not a prostitute, Charles. I know some of the girls there are, but a lot of them aren't. Girls like Kanuri go there to make a little money to survive on, that's all," Hayes informed us. "They give the girls a cut for every drink the guys buy them. Kanuri is an orphan. Her parents and her two brothers were killed during the war and although things are getting better in Japan, it's still tough to get a job that pays enough to live on, so she works a couple nights a week at the Tachi to make ends meet."

"You only saw her once?" I asked.

"Yeah. I met her on my last R and R. She is really a sweet girl, and she speaks English pretty good so we can talk. She just doesn't fit the mold of the girls that come there. But when I said that to her she got indignant and said that she was no different than the other girls who were only trying to survive on what little they made hustling drinks."

About that time the waiter showed up with our second round of martinis. Enderton held up his and said, "Here's to Kanuri and all lovely ladies, wherever they may be."

We drank the toast and I said, "So what happened, George?"

"We had a wonderful time dancing and talking the whole evening until they closed the place. She thanked me for buying her drinks and said she had a wonderful evening...then said goodnight."

"Aw come on, George, don't give us that," scoffed Pouhlin.

"That's the truth, Jerry. She wouldn't even let me take her home or anything. I asked her if she was gonna be at the Tachi again and she said maybe. So I went back the next night and every night for the rest of the week, but she didn't show."

"So you never saw her again?" I asked. Hayes shook his head.

"Who knows, George, maybe she'll show up tonight and you'll score," said Pouhlin.

"You probably won't believe this, but I really wasn't looking to score. I just wanted to be with her...she's like no other girl I've ever met."

"Those are danger signals, my boy," said Enderton. "Maybe you and I better go into Tokyo after dinner. I know a place that specializes in making you forget all about lost loves."

"You got lost loves, Charles?" I asked with a grin.

"Doesn't everyone?"

We all laughed, polished off our marts and headed for the dining room. It felt good to be dressed in class-A uniform and sit at a real table with white linen tablecloth and genuine silverware and china. You don't realize how much you miss such things until you're away from them for awhile. And Enderton was right about the food. It was excellent, the service outstanding and they had a live Japanese orchestra that played great American dinner music. I don't remember what I had for the main course, but I do remember that I had a huge piece of Japanese cherry pie for dessert that was almost as good as my mom made back on the ranch.

When we finished dinner, Enderton said, "They have all kinds of games and books and stuff here in the club for you old married guys, so have a nice evening. George and I are headed for the Tachi Ballroom."

"Hold the phone. Tell me some more about this Tachi Ballroom," I said.

"It's where a bunch of lovelies come to show their wares and I mean they are lovely and I don't dare go down there or I'll get in more trouble than poor George," said Drake.

"My bride says it's okay to look as long as I don't touch, so I think I'll go along with you guys and do a little lookin'," said Pouhlin.

"Yeah. Well let me tell you, once you look at those dollies, you're gonna want'a touch," counseled Drake.

"What about you, Richard, you gonna go look?"

"Absolutely. I'm an artist, ya know, and artists have to observe."

That brought some guffawing, and Enderton said, "Okay that makes four of us. Come on, Jeff, I'll keep an eye on you."

We grabbed a couple of those little skoshi cabs (very small cars) and headed over to the Tachi Ballroom. I have always been glad I went that night because it was quite an experience and on a subsequent R and R, I went back and did some sketches. You know, me and Tolouse Lautrec.

The Tachi Ballroom was a huge indoor pavilion filled with all kinds of colored, glittering decorations and a dance band that must have had 50 musicians. But the most glittering of all were the girls. They were lovely. All were dressed in floor-length gowns made of bright silk and brocade and designed for maximum effect.

The place was packed, mostly with young military guys from all branches of the service and all countries. Many were on R and R from Korea. The game for the girls was to dance with the customers who would buy them drinks. Their drink had a fancy name but was nothing but colored water. The girls got a cut of the drink price and could polish off one after another since it contained no alcohol. They were free to make their own deal with the customer, and apparently some did and some didn't. I marveled that they could even walk in those tight gowns, let alone dance. But they did. I enjoy dancing so I danced with a couple of the girls and, of course, bought them drinks of colored water. They were pretty good Western-style dancers considering their dresses were so tight they could only take about a four-inch step. Their English was limited but they spoke enough to be understood and they were quite pleasant, smiling and giggling like little schoolgirls.

I enjoyed that evening at the Tachi Ballroom, the highlight of which was meeting the Japanese girl Kanuri—and observing Hayes' reaction when he discovered that she was there. If I've ever seen a guy taken with a girl, it was Hayes that night. The girl wasn't what you would call beautiful, but she was cute with flawless skin that looked like pink velvet. Like most of the girls there, she was petite with a trim figure and coal-black hair. But I think what attracted George as much as anything was her beaming, childlike smile. It made you feel like it was special just for you. It was also evident, as Hayes had claimed, that she was a cut above her contemporaries at the Tachi Ballroom. Her dress, although stunning, was not as provocative as most of the others and her mannerisms were more conservative. But I was surprised that all the girls at the dance hall were relatively reserved, even those who were for hire.

The three of us married troops left about midnight and went back to the BOQ, where I enjoyed another treat: sleeping in a warm room in a real bed with sheets and pillows. It was mid-morning the next day before I finally crawled out, showered, dressed, and went to the officer's club for breakfast.

Enderton was the only one of our group in the officer's mess when I walked in. He was sitting alone drinking coffee and smoking a cigarette. We talked about our evening and he said he'd found a companion.

"What a lovely thing she was. We danced the night away while I bought her at least a dozen of those colored-water drinks. She must have had a hollow leg to hold it all. I have to admit I was seriously tempted to pay the price, and take the gamble for a full evening of her company. But I'm afraid I rendered myself ineligible since my drinks were something more than colored water."

"So how did it all work out for George and his little gal?" I asked.

Enderton raised his eyebrows and took a sip of coffee. "I guess it depends on your perspective. He spent the whole evening with her and I suspect also bought a dozen or so glasses of colored water. I lost track of them somewhere along the line but I have the feeling that little Kanuri acquiesced to George's boyish charm. I gotta feeling he didn't come back last night."

"Well, he's a big boy now."

"Yes, but I don't think he fully appreciates the reality of what he's getting into and it was evident to me that he is getting in pretty deep. I believe George is emotionally involved with Kanuri and that's a bridge too far."

"East is east and west is west and never the twain shall meet?"

"Something like that."

"That will change."

"Not in this generation."

After eating the biggest breakfast on the menu, which included real eggs, ham, bacon, potatoes, toast, fresh fruit, breakfast sweet rolls, milk, and fruit juice, Enderton said, "Ya know, Richard, the silver lining of having to survive on Ch'O Do Island for a month is that it makes you appreciate all the good things in life that we take for granted."

"Yeah. But I already knew that from surviving in New Guinea for a year."

Enderton laughed. "Was it really as bad as Ch'O Do?"

"Not really. Ch'O Do is in a class of its own."

"I'm gonna get my car after breakfast and if you would like, I'll give you a tour of the Japanese countryside."

"I would like that very much, Charles. How is it that you have a car here?"

"I was stationed in Japan for awhile before I went to Korea and I bought myself a little English MG convertible that I keep here at the base. It's too cold this time of year to drive with the top down but it's got a good heater."

Enderton drove his MG with the touch of an expert and he not only knew the roads and how to get around Tokyo and surrounding area, he was like a well-versed tour guide. He gave me a running commentary beginning as we drove out the air base entrance where they had a Japanese Baka plane on display. It was a WWII Kamikaze. Just looking at it triggered some hair-raising memories for me as I was on the receiving end of one during the Battle of Leyte in the Philippines.

"The Baka was a rocket-powered Kamikaze that was air-launched from a Betty bomber. It had a 2,250-pound bomb in the nose. The pilot flew a one-way mission," commented Enderton.

"Yeah, I know. The commander of a 'divine wind' squadron had a high turnover of pilots." (Kamikaze means divine wind.)

As we traveled, Enderton described the scenery with some history thrown in here and there. It was hard to believe there was almost no open space or unused land. And Tokyo was the same: every inch taken. I don't know what I had expected, but I remember what struck me when we entered Tokyo: it was a busy, bustling city with crowds of people, tall buildings, neon signs flashing everywhere, and cars going every which way. I was incredulous that this could be the same city that had been all but destroyed just seven years earlier.

"I think ya gotta give MacArthur a lot of credit for all this," said Enderton when I expressed my surprise. (General Douglas MacArthur was the occupation commander of post-WWII Japan.) "He figured out how to get these people to shift gears from centuries of subservience under warlords and that bullshit Bushido philosophy [Bushido: the warrior's way] and at the same time keep their god Hirohito. It worked and now they are beginning to roll. Give 'em another few years and Japan will become an economic giant."

The tour of city and country made a fascinating and enlightening day and I promised myself that when I came back on my next R and R in the spring, I would bring my sketchpad and paints. Enderton's exposure and good commentary painted a picture of Japan I couldn't have imagined, and I told him so when he pulled up in front of the BOQ at the air base late that afternoon.

"I figured you would enjoy it. I'm headed out of town for a couple days." He smiled. "I have a special friend I want to visit."

"Keep it in perspective," I said with a grin.

"Absolutely. Incidentally, if you go into Tokyo, the downtown Tokyo Officers Club has a Japanese concierge. He speaks good English and can tell you whatever you need to know or make reservations for you. Have fun," he said, then waved and roared off in his MG.

I met Pouhlin and Drake for dinner at the O Club and they reported that Hayes had disappeared. They speculated that he and little Kanuri were off somewhere doing what lovers do.

"He's really got it bad. I hope he doesn't do something stupid, like marrying her," said Pouhlin.

"According to the indoctrination lecture I had when I got to Japan, you can't marry Japanese girls without your commander's permission."

"Yeah, but he might do it anyway. When the ole love bug bites you..."

That night I had another great sleep in a bed with sheets, took a long hot shower the next morning and topped it off with another giant breakfast. Then I got on an electric train to Tokyo. It was fast, efficient and crowded. The passengers, nearly all Japanese, glanced at me but avoided eye contact except for an elderly man sitting across the aisle from me. He stared at me with dark eyes and a deep frown. It gave me an uncomfortable feeling.

The train stopped often and crowds of people scampered on and off and I would lose sight of him for awhile, then I would see him again and he would still be glaring at me. Finally I thought I heard the announcement of my station, but I wasn't sure. I turned and asked the guy next to me before I realized it was the glaring man. His frown instantly transformed into a wide, beaming smile as he nodded and said, "Ah so, ah so!" waving his arms to tell me this was my station. It was evident the old man bore me no ill will. In fact, he was thrilled that I had spoken to him. I can still visualize that smiling face watching me through the window of the train as it pulled away from the station. I've always thought of that incident as confirmation that the attitude of the Japanese people toward Americans took a complete turnaround when WWII was over, thanks to the wisdom and compassion of the United States of America.

I took a skoshi cab to the Tokyo Officers Club to find out a good place to shop for souvenirs for my wife and kids. The club was in what appeared to be an old pre-war hotel that had been renovated. The lobby was packed with officers from the various countries participating in the United Nations police action in Korea. I got in line at the concierge desk behind an Army first lieutenant wearing winter fatigues. Then I realized it wasn't a guy. It was a female officer and from what I could see from my six o'clock position, she looked familiar. I kept trying to get a look at her without being obvious and apparently she sensed it and turned around to face me. I stared at her in surprise and stammered, "Hello, Alexis." It was the nurse from the 8055 MASH. The one who said it was chicken shit for me to request a transfer.

"Hello, captain," she said, and after a cursory look added, "You clean up well." I had on a class-A uniform.

I smiled. "Thank you, ma'am."

"You get your transfer to cozy Tokyo?"

She was a bit sarcastic but I had to laugh. "Not hardly. I'm here on R and R. And you?"

"R and R."

"It's...uh, good to see you, Alexis. This your first time in Tokyo?"

"No. I've been here before."

About that time it was her turn with the concierge. She asked a question and he gave her a note which she quickly read, then walked off without even looking at me. It kind of hurt my feelings. But I figured so it goes.

The concierge gave me the name and address of a department store that sold everything. I thanked him and started for the door when she called out, "Captain?" When I stopped, she said, "I didn't mean to be rude, I just got some very disappointing news and I..."

"That's okay. No offense taken," I said. It was evident that she was upset. "Is there anything I can help you with?"

She hesitated, then nodded. "Yes. Could I buy you a drink?"

"Sure. It's not often I get that kind of an offer. Is there a bar here?"

She nodded and led me to the lounge, which even at mid-afternoon was busy. The Japanese waiter seated us at a small table and she ordered scotch and soda and I had a beer. It was a little early for a martini.

"I hope your bad news wasn't too serious."

She took a deep breath, exhaled, and said, "It was an acute disappointment. My fiancé was supposed to meet me here but it turned out he couldn't make it."

"I'm sorry. Where is he?"

"He's in the Marine Corps...in Korea. He was supposed to get R and R too."

"That's tough."

"We've only been able to see each other once in the last six months and..." her voice trailed off and she lowered her eyes.

I was searching for something to say when the waiter arrived with the drinks. We touched glasses and drank. Then we both dug out cigarettes and I fired them with my Zippo.

"Thanks for coming. I needed a drink but I didn't feel like being hassled by the cowboys."

"You're safe with me. I was never a very good cowboy."

"Somehow I doubt that," she said eyeing me.

"No foolin'. I was able to master the Army's fastest fighter plane at age twenty. But a horse always seemed to know that he could throw me, and inevitably would try...often succeeding."

"That isn't what I meant."

She was wearing a standard Army field uniform the nurses wore in Korea, consisting of olive drab slacks and jacket. It was baggy and shapeless. But she gave me a little smile and I was reminded that she was an attractive girl with glistening auburn hair and a pair of magnificent blue eyes.

"Did you ride a lot on the Tejon Ranch?" She asked.

"No. I lived on Tejon property but I didn't work for the ranch. Did you ride on the XIT?"

She nodded. "Yes. I love riding. I have a beautiful palomino back home. I wish to God I was there."

She rambled on for some time about the ranch and her Texas home and family, and how she used to ride on the big roundups. I could tell she needed to talk, so I nursed my beer and listened. She avoided any more discussion about Korea or the MASH and so did I. We had a second drink and I showed her pictures of my family.

"Your wife is beautiful."

"Thank you. When we met it was love at first sight and it's been that way ever since. It's hell being away from her now, particularly since we had just been separated a whole year and then I get sent to Korea."

"That's terrible. Why did the Air Force do that?"

"Well, I'd like to think it was unintentional. I was away on a top secret project for a year and apparently my personnel records didn't reflect that so when they needed helicopter pilots in Korea, I got tagged."

"I can understand now why you would be resentful about being sent here. Allen and I have only been separated three months and it seems like years."

"He'll make it. The peace talks are back on, ya know."

She smiled. "Thanks, captain. Having someone to listen to your troubles is always an effective way to at least moderate the severity." She dropped her eyes for a moment, then said quietly, "Truth is that Allen's not showing is…well, like the straw that broke the camel's back…I've really been struggling these last couple of months. I counted the days till my R and R. I had it in mind that if I could just be with him for a few days, I could make it through the rest of my commitment in Korea."

"How much time you got left?"

"About three months. Which doesn't sound like much, but I'm at the point where every day is like a year."

"Maybe you should consider a request for transfer, Alexis."

She dropped her eyes again and shook her head. "No…I can't…I just can't." She hesitated, looked up at me and said, "I'm a nurse and that's what I was trained for, but I was never trained to do what I'm doing, or to do it under the conditions that exist at a Korean War MASH.

I struggle every single day to cope and to do what is expected of me. But I do it because it's important and if I don't, others who work under the same adversities will have to do it. We're a team and we work together to save a lot of young men's lives. Like most of the others at the MASH, I hate being there but I'll finish my obligation. And as I said to you before, captain, I can't believe you could do anything in the Korean War any more important than what you're doing...so you also have no other choice."

"When you told me that over in Korea, Alexis, I didn't believe it. But I do now."

She smiled. "Don't tell me my little speech convinced you?"

I returned the smile. "That was a good speech all right, Alexis, but no. I've come to grips with my resentment over being here. And despite the agony of being away from my wife and sons, I too will finish the job. Like you said, I don't have any other choice since I realize now that flying the chopper is the best thing I could do in this war."

We touched glasses and drank. "I'm staying here and Allen and I were going to have dinner here tonight. I have a reservation for two in the dining room. Would you...?"

"I'd like very much to have dinner with you, Alexis. There isn't a guy in Korea who wouldn't trade places with me."

"I doubt that. Not with a down-at-the-mouth nurse crying in her beer over her absent fiancé. The dining room is on the second floor. I'll meet you there in an hour."

She departed and I sat at the cocktail table, sipped the martini and smoked while I thought about having dinner with her. I told myself it was not improper. She was a fellow soldier from Korea in need of companionship and it was evident that our talk had improved her spirits as well as mine. After awhile I made my way up to the dining room. It was large and richly decorated in both Western and Japanese styles. The art and china were quality Japanese, while the tables and chairs were Western with white linen and genuine silverware. There was a dance floor on one side of the room and a large Japanese orchestra playing Western music. The maitre d', dressed in a tux, seated me and I ordered a martini. I glanced around and saw that the place was nearly full of officers: U.S. Army, Air Force and Navy. A few were with ladies, both Western and Japanese. There were also officers from several other countries including a couple of generals. Dozens of black-tied Japanese waiters scurried around between the tables.

I'd been sitting there for awhile enjoying the pleasant atmosphere, when I noticed the ambient sound of conversations decrease. The orchestra was on break so the sudden change was evident. I glanced around and saw the reason. All eyes were on the maitre d' as he escorted a lady into the dining room. She was tall with long glistening hair that fell in waves over her shoulders in striking contrast to a stunning white evening gown that embraced her figure in such a manner as to take your breath away. It had been some time since I'd seen a girl that striking.

Like every guy there, I watched as she made her way through the tables following the maitre d'. I was curious to see what general or colonel was waiting for her. Then suddenly, she was standing in front the table where I sat staring at her. It was Alexis! And Enderton's words echoed in my head: "Wait till you see her out of those baggy Army clothes. She's a knockout." I managed to scramble to my feet and blurted. "Alexis! I uh... didn't recognize you."

"I'm going to take that as a compliment," she said and sat down in the chair the beaming maitre d' was holding.

"Oh yes. You may take it that way," I emphasized. She gave me a warm smile and said, "Thank you, sir. All compliments for an ailing MASH nurse, pining for an absentee fiancé are welcome."

"I'm glad to be of service but you sure don't look ailing in that dress."

She laughed. "I guess I shouldn't have worn it. It was supposed to be a surprise for Allen. But since it cost me a month's pay I just decided, with a little encouragement from two scotches and soda, that I was gonna wear it tonight if for no other reason but my own morale."

"That's a good reason. And it's a beautiful dress worn by a beautiful girl and every red-blooded guy here is happy that you wore it...including me."

"My morale is skyrocketing. Keep talking, captain."

"Okay. That dress would stir up the cowboy in a guy who ain't a cowboy."

"Sorry about that. Maybe I should go and change back into my good ole baggy GIs?"

"You want to see a cowboy cry?"

The waiter appeared at our table and we ordered cocktails.

"As I recall from our long-ago discussion in Korea, you were certain that you should be flying jets. What changed your mind?" she asked.

"You. You said to me, and I quote: 'Quitting just because you resent being here is chicken shit.' And you were right."

"Well, it pleases me if I played a part, but I suspect there is a more to it than that."

"Yes, a little more." I had known since the mission to Ping Do Island that I was not going to submit any more requests for transfer and I would complete my tour of duty in Korea as a helicopter pilot. But I hadn't come right out and said it to anyone. It wasn't a secret; the occasion to discuss it just hadn't come up until now.

I told her how the MASH medevac missions, the water pickups of jet pilots, and the mission to Ping Do Island had caused me to realize that flying helicopters was by far the best thing I could do in the Korean War.

She told me how she got her dress. I listened and tried to keep my thoughts on a platonic level, but it was difficult...and got more difficult as time went by. Ignoring my early warning system, I said, "Would you like to dance?"

"Yes. I would," she replied without hesitation. She was a terrific dancer, smooth and light on her feet. We didn't talk much, just danced. The music was excellent and they played both swing and waltz, and a Japanese version of what was called "jitterbug" in those days. Not many others danced. It seemed like the whole place stopped what they were doing so they could watch us. If I hadn't had a couple drinks, I might have been ill at ease. But I felt fine and it was exciting to be dancing with a girl as beautiful as Alexis.

It was evident from the moment she came into my arms and we started dancing that we should have listened to our warning systems. After our first dance, suddenly it was sizzling chemistry evidenced by the way we clung to each other, moving over the dance floor, oblivious to our surroundings. The orchestra played a series of pieces that were perfect for my style and we danced for some time without a word being spoken, holding each other tightly and moving to the rhythm of the music while emotions burgeoned. At about the time I recognized we were out of control, I was hit on the back by a blow that nearly knocked us both off our feet.

"Kirk! You ole sonovagun! How ya doin'?" bellowed one of my old WWII fighter pilot buddies, who stood with two others in the middle of the dance floor grinning broadly at me.

"I'll tell ya how he's doin'. He's doin' great!" said one of the pilots, ogling Alexis.

"Holy schmoly, is this yer wife?" asked another.

"Great balls of fire!" raved another.

It took me a minute to recover from the shock of being knocked off my pink cloud into the barrage that came from a bunch of half-in-the-bag fighter pilots. I finally managed to gain some composure and make introductions. Alexis was flustered, but she was able to adjust to the situation gracefully. It was good to see my old buddies again, although at that moment I wasn't all that thrilled about it. Later, I realized that their timing, although awkward, couldn't have been better. It put the brakes on a runaway situation that might well have culminated in a disaster.

Our noisy reunion was occurring in the middle of the dance floor, to the displeasure of the whole dining room. So it was decided we should retire to the bar before we got ejected from the establishment. Both generals were glaring at us and the maitre d' was so glad to get rid of us he said never mind the tab I owed for the drinks, and shooed us out the door. If I have this wrong, I apologize, guys, but as I recall it was Captains Jim Poston, Hal Oglesby and Warren Curton. They were squadron-mates from the "Flying Knights" during World War II. We hadn't seen each other since, although I did know the squadron was in Korea flying jets.

The exact progression of the evening after we went to the lounge is a bit fuzzy in my memory but we started with a round of drinks and comments about Alexis.

"Now, what we all wanna know is where did a beautiful round-eye like you come from in this land of jo-sons?"

She laughed. "I'm a nurse at the 8055 MASH."

"In Korea?"

"Yes, in Korea."

"I ain't seen no nurse that looks like you in Korea. You sure yer a nurse?"

"Yes, I'm sure."

"They got any openings for an old beat-up fighter pilot in that outfit?"

"No. But we got helicopter pilots at the MASH, right Richard?"

The cat was out of the bag. I cringed as all eyes focused on me. I knew what was coming. "Yep, we do have helicopter pilots at the 8055 MASH," I confirmed. Incredulous looks from the three fighter pilots.

"What in the hell...uh sorry, princess. What are you saying, Kirk?...You flying them windmills?" asked one of the pilots.

"It's a long story guys," I said as the waiter arrived with the drinks.

"What happened? You get caught with the general's daughter, or somethin'?"

"Not much to tell, guys. I'm flying choppers in the Third Air Rescue Group in Korea and part of that duty is with the 8055 MASH." They all just looked at me.

"Gentlemen, lemme tell you something," said Alexis. "Those chopper pilots save lives on a daily basis, includin' shome of yers."

"Hey, yer right, princess. You are absolutely right! And they ain't a fighter jock in Korea that doshen't know thet," pronounced one of my old buddies.

"Hear! hear!" shouted the pilots in unison.

"It's jus' thet it seems mighty strange ta see ole hot pilot Kirk flyin them things, thash all," said one.

"Yeah, thass hard to believe, awright," agreed another.

"Well, he's flyin'a chopper an doin' a wonnerful job," added Alexis with sparkling eyes and a bit of slur to her words—like the rest of us at about this stage of the celebration.

"Where are you guys assigned and what'a ya flying?" I asked to divert attention.

"Hey, ole buddy, we're over there flyin' jets, F-84s, and tearin' up the countryside. But I gotta tell ya, I'll take a good ole P-38 Lightning any day o' the week, right guys?"

"Right on! She waz the greatest." Everyone cheered again and lifted their drinks.

One of the pilots then launched into a story about struggling home in his shot-up P-38 during WWII. It was interrupted numerous times but eventually got us into one of our old squadron songs:

Beside a Guinea water fall, one hot and humid day.
Beside his battered lightning the young pursuiter lay.
His parachute hung from a very high limb, he was not yet quite dead.
So listen to the very last words the young pursuiter said:
I'm goin to a better land, a better land I know,
where whisky flows from coconut groves, we'll play poker every night.
We'll never have to work at all, just sit around and sing.
We'll have a crew of pretty women, oh death where is thy sting?
Oh death where is thy sting. Oh death where is thy sting-a-ling-ling,
oh death where...is...thy...sting!

"Now if one a' you guys go down beside a Korean waterfall, I'll come'n pick'ya up'n my lil chopper," I announced.

"Yeah, you sure can, ole buddy. You member ole Harry Andrews? He went in'a drink last week an one'a yer birds scooped em' right outta there."

"Yep 'e sure did. But ish hard to believe yer not with us flyin' jets, Kirk. Uh, you like flyin' them heleocapeters?"

"Well, they're a little slow in'a dogfight an they don't have a lot of firepower, but they can out-turn a Zero. Only problem is if ya gotta do a split S, yer in real trouble," I said with a straight face.

There were blank stares for a second or two, then the guffawing exploded. When that finally subsided we touched glasses and tossed off another round of drinks with Alexis hanging right in there with us.

"Yer not gonna believe thish, guys, but they really are fun ta fly," I confided.

The waiter showed up with another bottle of Old Tojo and all glasses were refilled. "Everybody up. Thish toast, by golly, is to our ole buddy Kirk, and hish magnisifent flyin' machine, the heeleocopter!"

"Hear! Hear!" everyone shouted and turned bottoms up.

Again everyone cheered Alexis, who was throwing down the Old Tojo whiskey right with us. "Wha'ever that stuff'iz ish purty good," she slurred with a grin.

"Thish little gal is not only the mosh beautiful nurse I ever seen, she'ze a trooper! We outta make her are offishell mascot and tak'er home wish us." That brought another roar of approval.

"Everybody up!" announced Alexis, pulling herself up and leaning against the table at a slight starboard list. With another chorus of approval and scraping of chairs, all rose. "Ish's my turn ta give'a toast," she declared, a lock of her hair hanging across her forehead and one eye. With the other eye, which was somewhat out of focus, she scanned the table and raised her glass. "Here's ta the greatish bunch'a guys and gals in'na world. Ta the eight oh double nickel MASH!" She tossed off the shot of Old Tojo in one big gulp as the pilots sounded their approval. She stood there a moment with a little crooked smile on her lovely face and a kind of glaze over her beautiful blue eyes. Then she gently pitched forward onto the table and was out like a light.

When I picked her up, she had a smile on her face but she was dead to the world. The guys were all trying to help but were so inebriated they weren't really functioning. In fact, neither was I. But I felt responsible so I got a couple of bellboys to help and we managed to get her up to her room. Then I paid one of the Japanese maids to get her undressed and to bed.

I went back to the bar where the party was still going on full steam, although everybody did miss Alexis. By that time I was in pretty bad shape and knew I was going to crash. So I said so long to my old buddies, checked one last time with the maid who said Alexis was fine and asleep. I got a cab, crashed in the back seat and didn't wake up till we got to the air base.

As those of us who have done that sort of thing on occasion know, you pay the piper. I paid dearly. That Old Tojo had to be as bad as the real General Tojo. I suffered a terrible hangover the next day and poor Alexis was in the same boat, or worse, although I didn't find that out, or see her again, until sometime later at the MASH in Korea.

The Tokyo party left me not only with a terrible hangover, but also with a painful guilty conscience. I had to assume responsibility for what happened to Alexis because I knew she was emotionally distressed that night, and certainly she wasn't a big drinker. Or at least not a drinker that could keep up with a bunch of fighter pilots on R and R. I shouldn't have let things get that much out of control. I should have insisted we have dinner instead of partying until the poor girl passed out. But the conscience problem that really gnawed on me was knowing that if my ole buddies hadn't shown up when they did, I would have had a far more serious problem than a guilty conscience.

It was a fortuitous encounter, with only platonic intentions. But I had to accept that those intentions had been derailed by an intractable monster called human emotions. And that monster had ripped through me—and her—like a runaway chain saw. And I was sure she loved her Marine as much as I loved my wife. So did I just chalk it up to the war?

Yes. That's what I finally decided: the conditions, the alcohol, the timing…all that. But I promised myself that It wouldn't happen again. And it probably wouldn't happen again anyway simply because there wouldn't be another opportunity for a vagabond helicopter pilot running around frozen, war-ravaged Korea.

Chapter 10

Return to Korea

It took me two days to recover from the Tokyo party. When I finally took the electric train back into Tokyo to do some shopping, I didn't go near the Tokyo Officers Club. But I did go to the department store the concierge had recommended and purchased gifts for my wife and kids, and some new canvas, oils and brushes for painting. And all at dirt-cheap prices, if you can imagine anything was ever cheap in Tokyo.

The morning of our scheduled return to Korea, Enderton, Pouhlin, Drake and I met in the dining room for breakfast before catching the bus to Tachikawa and our flight back to K-16.

"If there is anything I really miss in Korea, it's not having a real breakfast," said Drake as he dove into a huge plate of bacon and eggs.

"What I really miss in Korea, Japan, or anywhere else when I'm away from my wife, ain't bacon and eggs, I can tell ya," replied Pouhlin.

"Yeah. Well, I mean beside that," agreed Drake.

"Although not many, there are some advantages we bachelors have," said Enderton, sipping a cup of coffee.

"Then we can assume that you had an enjoyable R and R, Charles?" I asked.

"Oh yes, Richard. That is a valid assumption."

"Anything you would like to share with your envious married buddies?"

He smiled. "I would be pleased to share, but it's an involved story that takes more time than we have this morning. Perhaps on a cold winter's evening back on the Isle of Enchantment."

169

"Isle of Enchantment? Come on, Charles. Our first duty ain't gonna be back to Ch'o Do, is it?" asked Jerry.

"Afraid so, my boy."

"I thought because we were there so long on our last tour that we would get a pass this time around?"

"No such luck, but a couple of you can swap off duty on the South Island."

The South Island was considered the better duty because it didn't get the rough missions the North Island did and the ROK had a small mess hall, which wasn't very good but four-star compared to C-rations and hard tack.

"By the way, has anybody seen George?" asked Enderton. No one had seen George Hayes since that first night at the Tachi Ballroom.

"That's a bit concerning, but then George knows the rules."

"I got a feeling our junior aviator has taken a big bite of the apple," Pouhlin said.

"Yeah, and she's a tempting apple," added Drake.

"You seem all rested and recuperated, Richard," observed Enderton, eyeing me. "You happen to also have an adventure you'd like to share with your teammates?"

I couldn't help smiling.

"Hey, look at that guys! Nobody smiles like that unless he's done something immoral or illegal," declared Pouhlin.

"Is it true what they say about fighter pilots: when they aren't with the one they love, they love the one they're with?" asked Drake.

Drake's little barb struck home, but I couldn't seem to wipe the smile away which made it appear all the worse. Although I could claim that nothing improper occurred during my interlude with Alexis, I knew it would be the subject of great interest and intense interrogation. I also knew that it was too personal to discuss. I finally said, "All I can say, guys, is that you wouldn't believe it anyway," which was the wrong thing to say since it just aroused more curiosity.

"Now that, Richard, is the kind of adventure story I want to hear," said Enderton. "The kind I wouldn't believe anyway."

"I know, Charles. But to answer Jeff, what they say about fighter pilots may still be true. But I'm not a fighter pilot any more. I'm a chopper pilot."

All three sets of eyes zeroed in on me as though I'd just admitted to being a transvestite or something. I guess my sudden claim of being a helicopter pilot was a bit shocking, as they were well aware of my resentment about being in Korea flying choppers. But at least I had diverted their attention.

After a moment Enderton said, "Uh, you find your way to the Ishikawa?"

"What's the Ishikawa?"

"That's one of those places where they wipe out all memory of past loves," explained Pouhlin.

"Well, no. I didn't go there and I still got memory of past loves."

Enderton shifted in his chair and said, "I'm most anxious to hear how this transition from fighter pilot to chopper pilot came about. But however it came, I'm glad to hear it."

"So am I, Charles," I said.

"We should have enough stories of intrigue to last through another full month of winter evenings," added Enderton. "And if my instincts are correct, here comes another story."

Following Enderton's line of sight, we turned and saw George Hayes walking toward our table. It was evident from the look on his face that he, too, had had an R and R adventure to be savored and told on a cold winter's evening. He pulled up a chair and the waiter quickly poured him a cup of coffee. He smiled at us and took a sip.

"Don't tell us, let us guess: you're in love," said Pouhlin.

The smile grew wider. "And I'm gonna get married," he announced.

"Yer what?" blurted Drake.

"I said, me and Kanuri are getting married."

Enderton cleared his throat. "Uh, when is this gonna happen, George?"

"When I come over on my next R and R."

We all exchanged glances and Enderton lit a cigarette.

"You haven't known her very long, George," I finally said.

"Doesn't matter. I love her and she loves me and nothing else matters."

"You gotta get permission first," reminded Pouhlin.

"I know that, Jerry. But there is no reason for the major to disapprove it."

"I think there is, George. You don't really know her," said Drake.

"I know all I need to know."

"Okay guys, we catch the bus at the check-out lobby in an hour, so we better get to hustling," said Enderton and that ended the discussion for the moment. But only for the moment.

The other two pilots and all but one of the medics in our element showed up at the MATS terminal in Tachikawa where we caught another C-124 back to Korea. I didn't know the missing medic and never heard the final story of just what happened to him. The scuttlebutt had it that he, too, had fallen in love with a Japanese girl and went AWOL. That is not a unique story in the business of war.

Even though I'd only been gone a week, it didn't seem quite as cold and dismal in Korea as when I left. It was probably a reflection of my change in attitude about being there flying helicopters, because it was still winter and still freezing cold. But even my drab GI tent at K-16 seemed brighter when I walked in. That was probably because Kim had fired up the potbelly and my clean laundry and a stack of mail lay on my bed.

"You hav'a good time in'a Japan?" welcomed Kim with a big smile.

"I sure did, Kim. It was ichi-bon number one!"

"Awright! Me glad."

"Thanks. Any of my tentmates here?"

"No cappin. You only one. They out on road." He loved mimicking some of the phrases the pilots used.

I laughed. "Okay. One of these days maybe I'll meet them."

"Ah so. You play pachinko in Japan?"

"As a matter of fact I did, but I didn't play very well."

I think there were more pachinko parlors in Tokyo in those days than any other business. They were everywhere and the Japanese played them passionately. For those who don't know, it's similar to a pinball machine except it's played in the vertical position with lots of steel marbles. I hear that it's still a very popular game in Japan.

"I brought you a present, Kim," I said handing him a package. His dark eyes got big as he eagerly accepted the brightly wrapped package.

"Oh sank you, cappin. I open now?"

"Sure, open 'er up."

He gingerly unwrapped the package and when he saw the two-tone bicycle horn I'd got him, he literally jumped up and down like a little boy. The bad news was that he immediately bolted it on his bike and rode back and forth through our camp blowing it until some grouch threatened to smash it he didn't stop.

That day happened to be payday for the houseboys and after Kim collected his stack of dried squid, he came over to the tent and insisted I take some. I had little choice but to take at least one, or hurt his feelings. I wasn't a big dried squid fan, although on a subsequent R and R in Japan I had a squid dish that was quite delightful. A part of the Korean worker's pay was in dried squid as a way to help feed them and they were quite happy with the arrangement.

After Kim left, I eagerly dove into my stack of mail. As I mentioned earlier, mail from home was like an ice cream soda to a kid. We looked forward to getting it, then savored it. You have to remember that in those days you couldn't flip out an international cell phone and call home.

I always picked out and read the letters from my wife first. In this instance, I was still feeling guilt pangs over my interlude with Alexis…and the lingering emotion. But on the long flight back to Korea I had reiterated my pledge that I would not let that happen again.

I eagerly read her love letters and, as always, savored every word. After reading them over a couple times, I turned my attention to the fun little one-page notes from my two sons which always included crayon pictures. The pictures were their version of some of the action in a comic strip that I drew and sent them once a week. It was about the adventures of a character I had named "Two-Gun Kirk." Two-Gun got into a lot of trouble but always persevered because he was a champion of good over evil.

That evening Enderton invited me and Al Lovelady over to his tent for a little after-dinner gab session enhanced by a bottle of brandy and real Cuban cigars that he had somehow acquired while he was in Japan. "Would it be insensitive, Charles, to ask where in the world you managed to get these heavenly things?" asked Lovelady savoring the huge black cigar as we sat around the potbelly in Enderton's tent, smoking and sipping brandy.

Enderton gave us one of his secret smiles and tapped the ashes off his cigar. "As I'm sure you realize, Albert, it's not what you know that counts in life, it's *who* you know. And I happen to know a supply sergeant at the Yokohama U.S. Army depot who, for a price of course, can procure just about anything your heart desires."

Lovelady chuckled. "Well, if he can procure these jewels, I'd like to know him." Lovelady took his religion seriously and lived by a high set of ethics, but he had a weakness for a good cigar.

"I don't care for cigars but watching you smoke one, Ace, is a pleasure in itself," I said.

"Speaking of pleasure, did you enjoy your R and R, Ace?"

"Yes. I, uh, had a great time."

"Although I'm not privy to what that great time includes," put in Enderton, "I suspect that Richard enjoyed an adventure of consequence in the Land of the Rising Sun since he claims we wouldn't believe it even if he told us." Lovelady looked at me with raised eyebrows.

"I found real American peanut butter in the base exchange at Johnson Air Base and purchased six jars. That adventure is gonna totally eliminate C-rations for this kid on my next trip to Ch'o Do Island."

"You can eat peanut butter for breakfast?"

"I can eat it for breakfast, lunch and dinner."

Enderton rolled his eyes. "Okay. But that isn't the adventure I was referring to."

Both sets of eyes were watching with anticipation and I really had no reason not to tell them of my encounter with Alexis and my old squadron-mates. It was a great story and since I had resolved the moral issue, there would be no harm in telling it. But I still couldn't overcome the feeling that it was a very personal thing. And, of course, it would be difficult to tell without giving the wrong impression, so I decided it should remain my secret.

"The truth is, fellows, my big adventure came before I went on R and R and it just sort of jelled while I was in Japan."

I took a sip of brandy, lit a cigarette and explained how my last mission to Ping Do Island had been the final piece of the puzzle that gave me a clear picture and a new outlook on what I was doing as a helicopter pilot in Korea. "That is very good to hear, Ace. I knew you were struggling with it but I also knew that you would find the answer," said Lovelady.

"I suspect there is an interesting piece of that puzzle to remain secret, but that's understandable, as we all have those. And like Albert, I'm pleased you have solved that problem, Richard," said Enderton.

"Thanks, guys. I know why I felt the way I did about being sent to Korea, but I'm thankful that my resentment is over and done. And I have to tell you it sure makes life easier. It's like getting rid of a huge ball and chain."

I went to bed that night feeling pretty good about everything and in a way almost looking forward to my next duty tour on the island. Then sometime around midnight, while I was dreaming about seeing my wife in the sexy nightgown I'd bought her in Tokyo, I was blasted out of my sleeping bag by the air raid siren. It was on a pole outside the tent but sounded like it was six inches from my head.

Stumbling out of a tent in the middle of the night for an air raid alarm was nothing new to me, but in the South Pacific the temperature was about the same in or out of bed and I've spent many nights in a New Guinea slit trench wearing nothing but my shorts. Not so in a freezing Korean winter. Our camp rules for air raids required we put on full winter combat gear, including a steel helmet and a .30-caliber carbine.

You can imagine the confusion, grumbling and cussing that went on with a bunch of groggy pilots trying to accomplish that in pitch blackness. No lights were allowed, so you also had to worry about getting poked in the eye with someone's carbine, or worse, accidentally shot.

I finally got dressed and found a slit trench to crawl into while the siren continued to wail and confusion abounded. "What a bunch of shit!" groaned the guy huddled in the trench next to me. I thought I recognized the voice. "That you, Jeff?"

"What pisses me off is that we have to go through all this and the guy never drops any bombs," Drake growled.

"That's not Bed-Check Charlie's mission," said someone else in the blackness.

"Yeah I know. It's called a harassment raid. But if he don't drop bombs, whatta we doin' out here?"

"Sometimes he does drop a bomb," said the voice. "Here a couple months ago he dropped a bomb and blew up a jeep."

About that time a barrage of anti-aircraft fire started and the night sky was filled with streams of fireballs and exploding fireworks that was like Coney Island on the Forth of July. The fireworks went on for about ten minutes then abruptly stopped.

"Maybe they shot him down," said someone.

"No, the anti-aircraft guys stopped shooting so that our night fighter pilot can go after him," said another voice.

"That's true and sometimes our night fighter shoots him down... or her," said an authoritative voice.

"Whatta ya mean, her?"

"Well, sometimes Bed-Check Charlie is a Bed-Check Suzy."

"You mean the pilot is a woman? How do you know that?"

"The guy that does the casualty disposition stuff told me. Here awhile back the night fighter shot one down and when they found the crashed airplane it was one of those old bi-wing jobs with an open cockpit. The pilot was a little Chinese girl. He said she didn't weigh ninety pounds even in her winter flight gear."

(Subsequently, I did some research on that subject and, sure enough, there were some Chinese women pilots who flew harassment raids over South Korea during the war. They flew an open-cockpit, bi-wing airplane built in Russia called the Polikarpo Po-2. Because of its slow speed, about 90 mph, they were very difficult to shoot down.)

That night no bombs dropped and after a couple of freezing hours the all-clear finally sounded and we crawled back in our sleeping bags. But I lay there for awhile trying to imagine how any pilot could have braved that freezing cold in an open cockpit and flown all the way down to South Korea in the middle of the night. That little Bed-Check Suzy must have been a brave, dedicated and hardy girl.

The next day, Major Woods held a meeting of all personnel and announced that we were now officially the 2157th Air Rescue Squadron of the 3rd Air Rescue Group. To emphasize what a big deal that was, the group commander was going to pay us a visit and our camp had to be spick and span. Even element rotation was postponed for a few days while we all scurried around trying to improve the appearance of the place, which only validated the old axiom that you can't make a silk purse out of a sow's ear.

The colonel and his entourage showed up a couple days later. It was that time of year when you didn't know from one day to the next what the weather was going to do. This day started out springlike, so the major called for class-A uniforms. Then the colonel was delayed and wouldn't have time to inspect our camp, so we all went over to Kimpo Air Base to wait for the colonel and naturally, by the time he got there the weather turned cold and windy. When he finally arrived, we stood out on the ramp and watched his Gooney bird land, taxi up and park. Then he stepped out looking like Caesar surveying his Roman legions.

After the survey, the colonel did say we were doing a great job, praised Major Woods and rambled on about some other stuff, none of which we paid any attention to because we were freezing. He then presented some medals to a couple pilots and medics, crawled back into his airplane and went home. The route back to Japan naturally veered to the north and slightly over the combat zone, which entitled the colonel and his onboard staff to log a combat mission.

• • •

As it happened, Enderton's element didn't have to go back to the island. Instead we were sent to South Korea locations at K-3, K-8 and K-18. My co-pilot, Lieutenant Jim Belyea, medic S/Sgt. John Combs and I were assigned to K-18, an air base on the east coast where a ROK Air Force unit and a U.S. Marine fighter squadron operated. Our primary responsibility was to provide rescue for any of their pilots shot down along the front lines or in enemy territory.

K-18 was luxury compared to island duty. We were quartered in a Quonset hut with a real heating stove. They also had hot-water showers and an indoor privy. The ROK folks ran a mess hall and since they got their supplies from the Americans, the food was acceptable except when they had kimchee. That is a fermented cabbage dish that all Koreans seemed to love. Someone said it was actually pretty good if you could get past the smell, which was about like rotten Limburger cheese. When they served kimchee, I retreated to my peanut butter.

I hadn't spent much time with Belyea as he'd been assigned to other locations up to this point. He was small framed and wiry, and he had a good sense of humor. My medic, Combs, was an easygoing sergeant from Texas. He'd been in Korea for awhile and knew his business. I briefed them on how I wanted us to function on a mission and after a couple of orientation flights in the Sikorsky H-19, we were ready. We used the bigger H-19 at this location because of the possibility of having to fly longer-range missions into enemy territory.

We got our first call on the field phone a couple days later. A Marine fighter pilot had taken some anti-aircraft hits on a ground-support mission and was trying to make it to K-18 for an emergency landing. We kept the alert helicopter parked a short distance from our Quonset, so it only required a couple minutes for me, Belyea and Combs to scramble aboard and crank up. As soon as I was airborne, I punched in dog channel on the radio and called Casino, the air controller for that area, and told him I was airborne.

"Roger, Pedro. The aircraft in trouble is coming down from the X-ray sector toward K-18, but he's got some battle damage and isn't sure he can make it. He might have to eject. Suggest you follow the shoreline north until I get a handle on his intentions."

"Okay, Casino, I got her going full tilt. Let me know when you get me on the scope."

"Roger Wilco."

The air base at K-18 was a short distance from Korea's eastern shoreline, which unlike the west coast, had wide, sandy beaches. I headed up the beach climbing until Casino advised they had radar contact, then I leveled off and continued north. After a few minutes Casino called again and advised they had lost contact with the MAYDAY aircraft but suggested I continue north.

"Check and see how far it is to the MLR," I said to Belyea over the intercom. I was flying at about a thousand feet, but if we had to cross into North Korea over the MLR I would prefer to gain more altitude.

"It's not very far," Belyea replied after a quick glance at the map.

"Casino, this is Pedro. Do you anticipate an MLR crossing?" I asked.

"We're still out of contact with the MAYDAY aircraft, Pedro. Stand by."

"Roger, Casino. Request a fighter cap if a crossing is imminent."

"I'm workin' on it, Pedro." The agreement our helicopter rescue unit had with joint operations control, required a fighter CAP to cover us when we penetrated enemy territory for an MLR pickup.

A few minutes later Belyea said, "MLR about five miles dead ahead."

"Okay, I'm gonna start climbing. Keep an eye out for ground fire."

"You goin' in without a CAP?"

"Only if I have no other choice."

I had just put the Sikorsky into a climb when I received a transmission: "Pedro, this is Casino. We've regained contact with the emergency aircraft. He's clear of the MLR and headed for K-18 with some control problems. He may not make it, so you better head back this way. Take a heading of one seven zero degrees."

"Roger, Casino, one seven zero degrees."

I took up the new heading and pulled in full power. "Check the hoist, we may have to make a water pickup," I instructed our medic over the intercom.

"Roger, capt'n. I've already checked it and she's ready to roll."

A few minutes later: "Pedro, from Casino. Looks like the emergency aircraft is gonna make it to K-18. He's got the field in sight."

Having gone through many emergency situations myself in WWII, I could relate to the tension and concern the Marine fighter pilot would be going through at about this time: struggling to keep the battle-damaged aircraft flying, hoping he can make it but knowing that the aircraft might go out of control at any moment.

Then a few minutes later: "Pedro, from Casino, be advised the emergency aircraft has successfully landed at K-18. Thanks for your help. You can come on home."

It was gut wrenching to be involved in a rescue attempt where the pilot in trouble didn't make it. And conversely, it was always uplifting when he did, particularly when I was directly involved. In a sense it was disappointing that we didn't get to participate on this mission. That may sound strange, but after all you go through to get into position to save someone's life, you want to do it. You want to accomplish the mission and experience the satisfaction that comes with it. But this was one of those missions that turned out well even if we didn't participate, other than to be there just in case. But even if we didn't directly participate, you can imagine how much of a morale booster it was to the pilot in trouble just knowing that we were there.

That evening at the mess hall I happen to sit next to one of the Casino operators who said to me, "Were you the chopper pilot this morning when that Marine fighter made an emergency landing?"

"We are guilty," I replied, since the other two members of my crew were sitting there with me.

"You know who the pilot was?"

"No."

"Ted Williams."

"Ted Williams, the baseball player?" croaked the medic.

"The same."

"I didn't know guys like him flew combat missions," said Belyea. Not many of them did. But one who did was Ted Williams. One of the greatest baseball players ever, he was a Marine fighter pilot who flew 49 combat missions in Korea. He was also one of those who made it without our assistance, so we didn't save his life. But we were there in case and I'm sure he felt as good about it as we did.

A couple days after the Ted Williams mission, we had a sunny, springlike day on the east coast of Korea so I decided to paint a landscape. It had been so cold that most of my painting had been in the tent working on my Varga-wife painting. Belyea was writing letters and agreed to cover the alert phone and come get me if we got a mission call. I promised not to go far.

I walked across the airfield a couple hundred yards to where a bunch of ROK P-51 Mustangs were parked beside an old shack of some kind. I thought it would make a great painting: the sleek, silver Mustang with the red-and-blue ROK insignia against the weathered grays of the old building. So I set up my folding easel and was just getting into a preliminary sketch when a truck came out onto the field and a bunch of South Korean pilots in flight gear climbed out. "And so it goes," I muttered to myself as the subject of my painting was about to fly away.

I hurried with the sketch, but a few minutes later the pilots were in the P-51s and Rolls-Royce engines were cracking with that distinctive, beautiful sound they make. I gave up on the sketch, fired a cigarette and sat down on my little folding canvas seat to watch as they taxied toward the takeoff end of the runway. Each of the flight of P-51s pulled into takeoff position one after the other, revved the engine until it sang, then roared off. It brought back some warm memories.

When the last pilot in the formation revved his engine it began to pop and backfire, which meant he had fouled it during taxi or he had a bad engine. I watched curiously to see what he was going to do. He revved it to high RPMs to clear the engine, but it kept cutting out, which meant he probably had fouled plugs or a bad mag, so he would have to abort the takeoff.

He didn't. He poured on the coal and roared off down the runway. I held my breath but he kept on going and pulled her off the ground. He got up about 100 feet and I thought he might make it when the engine quit cold. Then it abruptly started again and the sudden surge of engine torque turned his flight direction almost 90 degrees. Now he was headed directly for the operations buildings on the air base at about 30 feet above the ground. The engine quit again and there was no way he could miss crashing into the buildings.

But he didn't crash. At the last second the engine roared again and he pulled up just in time to abort a crash but his wing clipped about ten feet off the flagpole!

As I was watching the whole episode it reminded me of an old-time Laurel and Hardy comedy movie. I was certain that he would crash for sure now with a chunk of his wing missing and the engine cutting in and out.

But he didn't. He somehow managed to keep the Mustang flying until he'd circled the field and came back in for a landing. With the engine still sputtering and coughing, he landed and taxied back to the spot where he had been next to the old shack, shut it down, climbed out and walked off.

A few minutes later a jeep drove up and an American captain got out and began to examine the damage to the Mustang's wing. My curiosity got the best of me and I walked over to also have a look. The captain explained that he was the American maintenance officer for the ROK squadron.

"The Koreans are pretty good pilots and they fly some rough missions, but they do have a couple problems," he admitted.

"Well, I'm an old fighter pilot myself and I can tell you that guy did some mighty fancy flying to get out of that alive," I said.

He laughed. "Yeah, he sure did. But it's their pride that sometimes gets them in trouble."

"How is that?"

"It's important for them not to lose respect so they resist any kind of an abort. In this case it was bad because he should have aborted that flight in the first place. On the plus side, in combat they'll fly through hell or high water to complete the mission."

"Can't fuss with the plus side," I said.

"The problem I have as their maintenance supervisor is that they don't communicate all that well. Look at this entry he wrote on the Form One," said the captain handing me the form. Each aircraft has a Form One, which is where all fights are recorded and includes any comments or squawks about the airplane. I looked at the form. In the maintenance squawk section the ROK pilot had written: "Airplane sick."

I laughed and said, "Well, maybe he's just following that old saying of KISS." (Keep it simple, stupid.)

The captain grinned. "Maybe so."

Our springlike weather ended that night and another winter storm moved in so it was back to freezing temperatures and icicles. I decided to give up trying to paint out of doors until the real spring arrived. Then a couple days later it cleared and we got an unusual request from JOC. A seaman on a cargo ship in the Sea of Japan had been severely injured in an onboard accident and needed quick surgery to save his life.

That kind of call today would be routine for an emergency medical service helicopter and nearly all ships now have an onboard helipad. In those days they didn't, and landing on one was a real trick because of all the obstacles, rigging, wires, etc. Not to mention the little problem of finding a ship in the middle of the ocean without any navigational aids.

The JOC commander said to me over the alert phone: "It's your call, captain. We don't have any strikes going on right now, so if you want to give it a go it's okay with us. But be advised we don't have a Dumbo or another chopper in that area, so you will be without backup."

At that time of year the Sea of Japan didn't have floating ice cubes on it like the Yellow Sea, but the water was still plenty cold so it would be risky flying out that far. If I had to ditch we would be in serious trouble.

"How far out is the ship?" I asked over the field phone.

"He's about fifty miles east of your location."

"Can you get a Dumbo headed our way?" I asked.

"Yeah. I can request one, but it will take some time."

"Okay, get the Dumbo going and we'll give it a shot."

"I'll get 'em launched."

"You got any ideas how I can find the ship?"

"Yeah. They'll make some black smoke when they get word that you're coming. They say you should be able to spot it for miles. Unfortunately they don't have your radio frequencies so you won't be able to contact them...unless you happen to know Morse code?"

"I'll have you know I could take and receive fifteen words a minute of Morse code when I was in pilot cadet training. The bad news is that all I can remember now is A and N."

All pilots knew A: dit dah, and N: dah dit in Morse code. It was the signal used by all low-frequency radio range stations which in those days was the primary radio aid for air navigation. When you put dit dah and dah dit together, it makes a steady hum. It's what we called flying "on the beam." But the ship wasn't a radio range, it would just have a telegrapher sending Morse code.

"Pedro, I guess you won't have any communications then with the ship. You will have to do pilotage [visual navigation]."

"Is there a place I can land on the ship once I find it?"

"I don't have a clue. You'll have to play that by ear."

"All right. Tell them we're on our way. Start putting out smoke."

"Roger Wilco. Good luck, Pedro."

We put on our exposure suits and took off a few minutes later. I wasn't comfortable about flying out that far over water without backup, but I figured it was worth the risk if we could save the seaman's life. I climbed up to 5,000 feet which allowed me to see farther over the horizon to spot the ship and at the same time keep radio contact with Casino. When I called Casino and told him where I was going he replied, "Pedro,

I can't paint a surface ship on radar that far out, so you're on your own."

"Casino, I figured that. But if I suddenly dive off your radar screen, you can tell Dumbo where to come looking."

"Is there a Dumbo in the area?"

"No. But JOC's got one coming."

"Okay. Give me a call if you get in trouble."

"You'll be the first to know."

It's an insecure feeling to fly high in a helicopter without instruments and without a parachute, and worse to be out of sight of land, particularly when you really don't know where you're going.

"I don't like this feeling at all," groaned Belyea over the intercom.

"Relax, Jim. Navy pilots do this all the time," I said.

"That's why I ain't in the Navy."

The truth was I didn't like the situation any more than he did. But as it turned out we spotted smoke on the horizon a short time later and flew directly to the ship without incident. Now came the problem of how to pick up the patient. It was a pretty good-sized ship, but as I suspected, it was covered with rigging, cables, hatches and cargo booms. There was just no way to get our hoist cable down through all that clutter to pick up the patient.

"How we gonna get him?" asked Belyea, as I hovered over the ship.

I could see that some of the ship's crew had brought the patient up on deck in a litter. But it was evident from the way they were looking up at us that they didn't have an answer to that question either.

"I'm gonna hover down under that cargo boom and land on the deck," I said.

Belyea looked across the cockpit at me as though I'd lost my mind.

I instructed him to watch for obstacles on his side of the helicopter and the medic to do the same for the tail rotor. "Sound off if I get too close. Okay, here we go," I said and started my approach. It would be a tight squeeze, but I was sure I could make it, provided a sudden gust of wind didn't interfere. I dropped down to a hover over the water and edged up toward the ship. Fortunately the captain of the ship realized I needed a steady course. I had to hover up under a big cargo boom until I was over the deck, then drop down onto a space between a hatch cover and a bulkhead.

"The tail rotor is awful close to that hatch cover, capt'n" warned the medic as I eased in under the boom. Now that I was committed I began to have doubts, and I could see by the expression on their faces that the ship's crew also had doubts as they watched me from every quarter. I wouldn't doubt that it was the first helicopter most of them had ever seen.

"Look out for that cable!" shrieked Belyea.

"I see it."

"Another one on the left!"

"Okay. Where is the hatch cover?"

"You're still over it. Move forward another five feet."

If flying high was uncomfortable, this was much worse. I felt as though I had trapped myself in a maze of obstacles that were all closing in on me and the rotor wash, swirling around between the bulkheads and rigging, made precise control difficult.

"Clear of the hatch cover!" advised the medic.

That was what I wanted to hear. Now I could attempt to set the helicopter down. The sea was fairly calm but I still had to compensate for some rolling and pitching of the deck and the buffeting rotor wash. I had never landed on a ship before, but I sensed that once I touched down I had to stay down because a bounce in these tight quarters would be disastrous. The rotor blades would strike objects and shower the ship with broken pieces like a daisy cutter (fragmentation bomb). I spiked the landing wheels and chopped the throttle. The Sikorsky rocked a little but held her position. I had done it!

"Good job, capt'n!" blurted the medic. And I did feel pretty good about it until I glanced out and saw how tight a squeeze it was and suddenly realized I'd only won half the battle: I still had to get out of there!

The medic jumped out and helped get the patient loaded into the helicopter while Belyea and I both fired up cigarettes. I kept the rotors turning but with down collective the blades were in flat pitch so we were stable on the deck. "You got it figured how we're gonna get out of here?" asked Belyea, glancing out at all the obstacles that surrounded us.

I didn't want him to know of my concern so I managed a grin and said, "Hey, Jim boy, have confidence. We're goin' out the same way we came in."

It only took a couple of minutes to load the patient and the medic was back on board the helicopter. "Okay, capt'n. We got him aboard and we're ready to go. He's in bad shape so we need to get him to the nearest MASH as quickly as possible."

"All right, let's do it. Same drill, guys, only there isn't room to turn around so we gotta do it backwards," I said with as much confidence as I could muster.

One of the ship's crew, whom I took to be an officer, came up beside the helicopter, shouted his thanks and gave me a thumbs-up. I waved, ground out the cigarette and cranked in power. Combs kept the cabin door open so he could lean out and guide me, shouting instructions, while Belyea shouted warnings from his side. Backing up a helicopter is not all that difficult, but it is when you're surrounded with booms, hatches, bulkheads, cables and swirling rotor wash.

We made it, flew back to shore and got the patient to the MASH in time to save his life. The nearest MASH to us at that time was the 8076. (That was Dr. Otto Apel's MASH. He is the author of an excellent book titled *A MASH Surgeon in Korea*.)

I believe the helicopter pilots who flew in Korea strived to apply common sense and professionalism in evaluating the risk of their missions. But I have to admit that sometimes we would stretch a little when we knew the stakes were high and someone would live or die by our judgment.

Chapter 11

Life and Love at the MASH

O ther than concern that at any daylight moment you could get called to fly into the front lines to pick up a downed pilot and get your tail shot off, duty at K-18 was one of the more desirable of our helicopter rescue locations in Korea. They had the best facilities and relatively good chow. But I was glad to go back to the MASH for my next assignment. Pulling wounded off the battlefield was satisfying. And just being around the MASH folks was enjoyable, particularly Hawkeye, who always brightened your day with some kind of humor or something.

On the down side I couldn't suppress an apprehension about seeing Alexis again. I reminded myself that I had resolved that issue. It was simply a matter of keeping it in perspective and acting my age. After all, I was a 29-year-old, happily married man with a family. And she was a young girl who was in love with and engaged to a Marine. So in reality, it had just been one of those happenstance things that occurs in wartime and she had probably forgotten about it anyway...so I told myself.

The pilot crew for the MASH this time was Enderton, George Hayes, Lieutenant Brian Moore and me. Pouhlin and Drake were assigned to K-8 and our others to K-2. I had met Moore at K-16 during our last element change, but this was our first duty together. Like Hayes, he was one of the younger pilots.

Moore was personable, but a bit emotional at times. He would probably be classified as handsome, being tall and slender with a full head of wavy blond hair, which he ran his hand through constantly. I assumed it was a nervous habit.

Element change at K-18 was done by Gooney bird to K-16, then if there was a Sikorsky H-19 available we would be flown to the MASH. If not, it was the freezing ride in a GI truck. Fortunately this time, it was a 30-minute ride in the Sikorsky.

The 8055 was still camped up the valley north of Seoul on the banks of the frozen Imjin Gang River. There hadn't been a major change in the MLR, so it hadn't been necessary for them to move. It was the longest period the 8055 had been at one location since the war started. The peace talks at Kaesong, North Korea, were still going on, but so was the war and therefore the slaughter, providing the MASH with lots of business. Some of the more vicious and bloody battles of the Korean War, like Pork Chop Hill and Old Baldy, came in the spring of that year, 1953.

"Richard, me lad, welcome back to your home away from home," said Hawkeye when I met him in the compound at the 8055 shortly after we arrived.

"Thank you, sir, it's good to be back. Meet George Hayes." After greeting and shaking hands, Hawkeye said, "You any relation to Frank Hayes of Poughkeepsie?"

Hayes shook his head and said, "Where is that?"

"You never heard of Poughkeepsie?" More head shaking. "You ever heard of Smith Brothers cough drops?"

"I think so."

"Well, Poughkeepsie is where the Smith Brothers make their cough drops. It's a town up the river from my little home town called New York City." Hawkeye's eyes always sparkled when he was doing one of his things. He had a uncanny capacity to come up with some kind of wit, or story or something, no matter what the situation. And it wasn't that he worked at it. It just came naturally. Hayes looked at him as though he wasn't sure what he was saying.

"Frank Hayes was an intern at Bellevue General the same time I was there. He was related to the Smith Brothers." Hayes sort of smiled.

Hawkeye returned the smile and said, "Gotta go work on some body parts. Come on over for the cocktail hour tonight, guys. We're having it in our new O Club. Oh, and you bring the cocktails, we're fresh out."

"You got an O Club now?" I asked.

"Hey, wait till you see it. It's got more class than the Top of the Mark." (That was the day's famous night spot on the top floor of the Mark Hopkins Hotel in San Francisco.)

After Hawkeye left, Hayes looked at me and said, "That guy is a surgeon?"

"Probably one of the best in Korea." Hayes shook his head again.

That evening after sundown, Enderton came up with a bottle of gin and the four of us walked over to the new O Club, which to our surprise was a new Quonset hut.

"How do you suppose they managed to get that?" wondered Moore.

"That took some doing and I'd bet Hawkeye negotiated the deal," said Enderton.

It was a small Quonset, but adequate, with a potbelly in the center and a homemade bar at one end. The doctors had constructed the bar and a poker table out of the wood from a large shipping crate. The nurses had painted the bar and table and made some bright window curtains out of dyed surgical sheets. GI beds and mattresses covered with GI blankets served as sofas, and there were some folding camp chairs, and even a couple of homemade lamps. All in all it was kind of homey and at least offered a place to go when off duty other than a one-quarter share of a pyramidal tent.

When the four of us walked in, Hawkeye, Michael Johnson and Alice Smith were standing at the bar. "Welcome, welcome, fellow travelers, who I trust come bearing spiritual gifts, most specifically, liquid spirits," said Hawkeye.

Enderton held up the bottle of gin and Johnson snatched it from his grasp. "Charles, my boy, you are particularly welcome," he said and quickly went behind the bar and brought out some glasses.

"Hi, fellows, good to see you again," said Alice. She was still overweight, but was always up, with a way of making you feel good with her beaming smile.

"Alice, love. Did you miss me?" said Enderton putting his arm around her.

"Oh terribly, Charles."

"That's my girl. Meet George Hayes, he's one of our infamous Tiger element members."

"But he's no relation to the Smith Brothers of Poughkeepsie," said Hawkeye.

"He'll grow on you, George," said Alice. "Welcome to the MASH."

"Ditto from me, George," said Michael. "And step up to the bar. Garson is pouring and since you're the new kid on the block, you get first call. Gin straight up or straight down?"

"Thanks, captain. Do you have any mixer?" asked Hayes.

Hawkeye answered, "I want you to know, George, this is a first-class joint. We have genuine U.S. Army grapefruit juice that comes in shiny tin cans, or we got genuine Korean H_2O containing lots of little critters to flavor the gin. Also notice that Garson is pouring into genuine crystal in this ichi-bon number-one Quonset on the banks of the beautiful Imjin Gang River."

"Yeah, we noticed. How did you manage to get a Quonset, Hawk?" asked Enderton.

"Ah yes. That was a trick that I wish I could take credit for, but I must confess that it was our own little Roxanne who came through on that with flying colors."

"Roxanne got the Quonset?" blurted Moore.

Hawkeye glanced at Moore with a look that suggested he'd said something he wished he hadn't, which was unusual for him. I had met Lieutenant Roxanne Cooper during my first tour at the MASH, but I didn't know her all that well. She was a pretty girl although second to Alexis. From what Enderton had told me she was a good nurse but a bit of a free spirit. Moore was single and had it bad for her. Their romance ran hot and cold depending on what she had going at the time. She was sort of a female version of the WWII fighter pilots: when not with the one she loved, she loved the one she was with.

After Hawkeye's declaration, everyone knew, of course, how Roxanne got the Quonset. Obviously distressed, Brian ran his hand through his hair and looked at Alice as though to say, Tell me it isn't so. Alice looked away and said, "Come on, Mike, get to pouring." We all joined in urging Johnson to hurry up with the drinks, but he couldn't find the can opener. Finally it was done and we all held up our drinks and toasted our new commander in chief, Dwight D. Eisenhower. He had promised to end the Korean War and bring us all home.

Then the Quonset door opened and in walked Alexis and Roxanne, who were friends despite the difference in their philosophies about life, love and sex. Since it was still winter and cold, they were dressed in regulation female winter clothes which were ill-fitting and not very flattering. However, it's hard to disguise a pretty girl, no matter what she is wearing, and of course, I had seen Alexis in a dress that would make men do back flips. But it was our eye contact that was anything but disguised. It was instant reply of the night in Tokyo and I could see my conscientiously conceived resolution going down in flames.

When Roxanne and Moore's eyes met, you couldn't tell if they were going to embrace or slug each other. After an awkward moment Roxanne turned on a smile and said, "Hi Brian." He looked flustered, ran his hand through his hair, and muttered, "Hello Roxanne."

Alexis and I just looked at each other with expressions on our faces akin to when you get caught with your hand in the cookie jar. Finally, we exchanged hellos then turned stone silent. I stood there like a wooden Indian trying to think of something to say when Hawkeye shattered the scene with: "I know, I know, you girls just couldn't bear to be away from me." He said, grabbed a girl in each arm and walked them up to the bar. Roxanne assured him that he was absolutely right. His charm and charisma rendered her putty in his hands.

Johnson, who had assumed the role of bartender, fixed them a drink while Hawkeye rambled on. Then we all had another toast. This time Alice called it in honor of the 8055 mess sergeant who had gotten into the denatured alcohol and had to be shipped out in a strait jacket. But Alice claimed he was a good guy despite the awful food he fixed.

Roxanne told Hawkeye he should go to bed because he'd been up most of the night and day with some difficult surgeries. Hawkeye was quick to reply, "Ah so! I know a proposition when I hear one, Roxanne." She laughed and claimed she was just interested in his welfare. He claimed charity begins at home...in bed.

"Your problem, Hawkeye, is that you burn the candle at both ends," declared Alice.

"I do! I do! Me and Edna St. Vincent Millay:

'My candle burns at both ends

It will not last the night

But ah my foes, and oh, my friends—

It gives a lovely light!'"

"Hawk, that was inspiring," said Johnson. "Ya know, I once had it in mind to be a poet. Can you imagine that?"

We all stood at the bar talking and bantering for awhile then a couple more doctors and nurses came in and the group sort of broke up and paired off in separate conversations. Roxanne and Moore drifted off to one corner of the Quonset, leaned against the metal wall and looked at each other. Alice, Hawkeye and Enderton engaged in some kind of psychological discussion while Johnson poured drinks for the new arrivals. That left Alexis and me. We looked at each other for another awkward moment, then she said, "I thought I had resolved what I was going to say to you, but now the cat's got my tongue."

I smiled. "That's about what I was going to say." She returned the smile. She had even white teeth except one in the front was chipped. She told me that night in Tokyo that it was from being bucked off a horse. "And since the cat let go my tongue, I want to apologize for that night in Tokyo, Alexis."

"You have nothing to apologize for, Richard. It is I who should apologize." She paused then added, "I want to tell you, although you may not believe it, I've never behaved like that before in my entire life."

"Well, I don't think you did anything all that bad."

She shook her head. "It was bad...very bad. I'm ashamed just to think about it. But I paid dearly. I thought I was going to die I was so ill the next day."

"You had a legitimate reason to hang one on, Alexis. I didn't. Besides, I should have known better because I know those crazy fighter pilot buddies of mine and how they party when they get a day off from the business of war."

"They were a fun group and from what I can remember I had a great time...until...well, you know. But they were all gentlemen...as you were, Richard. But I was not a lady. I was so absorbed in my own emotional distress that I acted with little consideration of the consequences to myself or anyone else. I still find it disgusting to believe I did that. My only excuse is that I didn't intend to...uh...act that way. I mean, wearing that dress...and...well, you know."

"I was a willing participant, Alexis. Remember? But I didn't have an excuse. At least you had a reason. And then you just got caught up in the party and drank too much."

"That was bad enough, but my behavior before I drank too much was even worse."

I knew what she meant. Our emotions had gone into runaway mode there on the dance floor before the fighter pilots' arrival put on the brakes. "It was the circumstances," I proclaimed. "And as it turned out, we have nothing to be ashamed of."

"And logic tells me that is where we should leave it," she said. I nodded and we fell silent. Then she added, "But getting your emotions to agree with logic isn't always that easy."

A timely interruption by the others ended the conversation. They came to get our opinion on the question whether Hayes should or should not marry the Japanese girl, Kanuri, and if so, how could he get Major Woods' permission.

I stood there pretending to listen to the discussion while the battle of my emotions raged. I could not suppress a physical excitement at seeing Alexis again and at the same time I was distressed to realize how little control I had over my emotions. And the look in her eyes told me that she had the same problem. How could I feel like this? Could I suddenly fall in love with a girl I hardly knew? No, of course not. I was in love with my wife. It had to be the old bullshit about what war does to you, etc. Yeah, well, that's bullshit!...or was it?

"Isn't that right, Richard?" interrupted a voice.

"What?"

"Sometimes Richard drifts off into his own little world," said Enderton with a grin.

"That's...uh, true," I muttered.

"Was a Zero on your tail?"

"Not this time, Charles."

"Okay. Here is the question. Alice agrees with George that if two people are truly in love, nothing else matters so they should go for it. What's your take?"

It took a moment to refocus my thoughts, then I said, "Well, I'm a romantic. But, uh...you have to make sure it's true love before you take that step," I said with another high-voltage eye exchange with Alexis.

"I, too, am a romantic," claimed Enderton. "But marriage is a serious business and shouldn't be entered into lightly, so my vote is to wait till they know each other better."

"How am I gonna get to know her better when I only get to see her one week out of every eight weeks?" groaned Hayes.

"That's the whole point, George. You're fighting a war and don't have time right now. So wait till you finish your tour and ask for an assignment to Japan. Then you can get to know her."

"I don't want to wait that long."

"Yer gonna have to wait anyway. You can't bring her over here and the war ain't gonna suddenly stop. Not for awhile anyway. Meanwhile, write letters—you can find out a lot about someone through their writing," advised Enderton.

"That's great except that she doesn't write or read English. But she does speak it pretty well and she wants to learn to read and write it, too."

The discussion continued for awhile with everyone giving Hayes their opinion and advice. Then suddenly another voice said, "Why do you want to complicate a beautiful relationship with marriage, George?"

It was Roxanne. She and Moore had walked up to where the group was gathered. Hayes was at a loss for words for a moment, then recovered and said, "Because I love her."

"What's that got to do with it?"

"It has everything to do with it, Roxanne," spoke up Alexis, who suddenly voiced an opinion.

Roxanne laughed. "Alexis and I have had this discussion a million times."

"And we still disagree."

"Yes, but I think the armor is tarnishing," said Roxanne, looking at Alexis meaningfully then turning and looking directly at me. I took a big gulp of my drink.

Alexis looked stricken for a moment. Recovering, she said, "Yes, I have to admit that. But tarnished or not, I still vote for marriage." Hayes looked triumphant. Roxanne reached across and warmly squeezed Alexis's arm as though to let her know they were still friends despite their disagreement on that subject. I was standing there looking distracted and wondering if Alexis had told Roxanne about Tokyo or was she just guessing? It was evident by the look she gave me that in either case she knew there was something going on between Alexis and me.

"Brian and I are gonna go look at the railroad bridge in the moonlight. See ya later," said Roxanne, taking his arm. Moore's look of distress turned to a smile. Everybody knew there was no moon that night.

By some kind of telepathic agreement, Alexis and I avoided each other as the discussions continued until the gin was gone. Then we all walked over to the mess tent and had dinner. It was worse than usual and Alice claimed it was because they had shipped out the mess sergeant, whom she apparently had a crush on.

• • •

The commies began an offensive the next morning on one of the nearby hills called "Old Baldy." It turned out to be a major battle and cost a bunch of lives. When it was all over, the MLR was pretty much where it had been and nothing had changed, but it did keep us busy with both choppers flying in the wounded from sunup to sundown. And it kept the surgeons, nurses, corpsmen and everyone else at the MASH working around the clock. Alexis and I continued to avoid each other. Moore's romance was curtailed, and all discussions on life, love, and Hayes' marriage were discontinued—at least for awhile.

Finally the commies backed off their attack and things quieted down. Many historians refer to that last year of the Korean War as "The Battle of the Hills." It was kind of like the trench warfare of World War I where every once in a while one side would advance a few yards then the other side would take it back, while thousands were slaughtered.

A few days after the Old Baldy conflict, a British Infantry outfit that was camped up the river a short distance extended an invitation to all the officers and nurses at the MASH to attend a dining in. It was a timely invitation as everyone had been doing double duty and was ready for some relaxation. We four pilots and most of the MASH crew went except those on duty. We drove up the valley to their camp in several jeeps and were royally received by our British hosts.

They had erected a large tent for the occasion and decorated the interior. I couldn't imagine where they got it, but it was almost like a circus tent. In the center was a large homemade heating stove that looked like it might have been the boilers out of a steam locomotive. I didn't find out where they got that either. Red-and-white parachutes hung across the ceiling of the tent providing a festive ambiance. There were several homemade tables covered with parachute nylon and real china plates and silverware. While the British can be a bit conservative, they are also very imaginative and even had three musicians playing—a saxophonist, a clarinetist and a drummer working on a steel fuel drum. They made great music, sporadically accompanied by the sound of distant artillery since we were within a few hundred yards of the MLR.

There were about fifteen in our group who were escorted into the tent by a young British leftenant in full dress uniform. He took us directly to a homemade bar and introduced each of us to the commander, who was a big fellow with a wide smile and a beautiful handlebar mustache. He made a great welcome speech: "I say, good of you to come! It's our pleasure to have such honored guests as you chaps and ladies of the MASH. All of us in Korea know of your great work. Step right up to the bar and we'll have a toast of greeting straight away."

The bartender, another young leftenant, announced that he had British gin or British gin, and we could have it straight or with British quinine water. And another surprise, they had real cocktail glasses.

"I say, ole fellow, let's not dilute good British gin with accoutrements. We MASH types like our liquor straight, right guys and gals?" said Hawkeye.

"Not exactly," spoke up Roxanne. "I'd like my British gin accoutered with some of that British quinine water."

"Hear hear," echoed a couple of the other nurses.

"Pantywaists," chirped Hawkeye.

The young bartender's eyes zeroed in on Roxanne, who looked really nice in her class-A nurse's uniform. The locomotive heating stove made it warm enough in the tent so that we could discard our heavy parkas. "Gin and quinine coming up, ma'am," he announced.

While our drink orders were being filled, the rest of the group of British officers crowded around and were introduced by their commander. They were all young, handsome fellows who had been in Korea for some time and were hungry just for the sight of a women, particularly pretty young women like Alexis and Roxanne. Actually though, all the nurses looked nice and were quickly surrounded by the British officers, and shortly thereafter were dancing with them. The dance floor was plain ole Korean dirt, so about all they could do was walk around in circles, but the musicians played nice waltzes and just to have a woman in their arms for a few minutes was thrilling for the young officers.

We chopper pilots and the MASH doctors sort of stood there at the homemade bar drinking and talking with the Brits, who waited their turn to dance. I'm sure they enjoyed our company, but I'm just as sure they preferred the nurses' company.

One of the officers talking with us was a member of a unit that did covert intelligence work with the ROK. They were called "Donkeys," and they slipped behind the enemy lines at night to get intelligence, slit sleeping men's throats, contaminate water supplies, spike guns, and generally raise hell. He told us this story:

"We had this one chap, Wingate, who managed to find a hole in the perimeter fence that protected a gook compound. He used it night after night to slip in and raise bloody hell, then slip out. One night ole Wingate finishes his devilment and comes back out through the little secret hole. To his surprise the gooks had found it and were waiting for him."

"Well, what happened?" asked someone.

"Oh, they did to ole Wingate what he'd been doing to them—they slit his throat." The storyteller shook his head. "Bloody good joke on ole Wingate, eh?"

Although by now most of us were feeling the effects of the gin, there was an obvious sudden silence among our group. The storyteller noticed and explained: "It's how we handle it, chaps. It's how we tolerate the agony of losing a friend in this kind of rotten work. You can't let it get to you or you're really in trouble. So we have to keep a stiff upper lip and all that sort of thing." Someone proposed a toast to Wingate and we all raised our glasses and drank.

When the orchestra took a break, the dancers all gathered around the bar for a drink and a cigarette. Lighters popped out on the end of long arms from the eager group of Brits who surrounded the ladies. Hawkeye then told a hilarious story about a British doctor, then insisted I tell my favorite WWII joke. I'd had enough gin to accommodate:

"There was this Navy pilot who prided himself on always doing everything exactly right. So he takes off from the carrier one day and goes out on a combat patrol leading a flight of four fighters. They run into a flock of Japanese Zeros and are so outnumbered they are all shot down except him. He's able to escape, but his plane is riddled, the canopy shot away and all instrument are inoperative. He's wounded and bleeding all over the cockpit but he keeps flying and manages to find the carrier and through superior skill makes a successful landing. He jumps out of the crippled fighter, runs up to the captain of the carrier and says: 'Captain! Captain! I made it! I made it because I did everything right!' The captain said, 'Ah so...but you make one little mistake.'"

Everyone laughed, then one of the Brits reciprocated with a joke about an American in a British pub. That somehow precipitated our breaking into song:

> Twas a cold winter's evening, the guests were all leaving, ole Riley was closing the bar.
> When he turned round and said to the lady in red, 'Get out, you can't stay where you are.'
> She shed a sad tear in her bucket of beer as she thought of the cold night ahead.
> When a gentleman dapper stepped out of the crapper and these are the words that he said:
> 'Her mother never told her the things a young girl should know.
> About the ways of military men and how they come and go.
> She lost her youth and beauty and life has dealt her a scar.
> So think of your mothers and sisters, boys....and let her sleep under the bar.'

As the sound of song echoed through the tent, I noticed out of the corner of my eye that one of the red-and-white parachutes had fallen down onto the locomotive heating stove and was on fire. I was expecting the Brits to go put it out, but they didn't seem so inclined as they harmonized on another song. Enderton and I made simultaneous decisions: we ran over and pulled the burning parachute off the stove and stomped it out while the singing continued. We got the fire out at about the time the song ended. Then they all cheered our firefighting efforts and the commander said, "I say, jolly good show, chaps!"

Enderton looked at me and grinned. "Ya gotta admit, these Brits are cool under fire." I agreed and we left the smoldering parachute and rejoined the party.

Enderton and I elbowed our way up to the bar and when we finally got there I found myself face to face with Alexis just as the music started again. "Dare we?" she said in that wonderful voice of hers. My security system went berserk with warning shots bouncing off the inside of my skull like .50-caliber slugs. I ignored it all and said, "We shouldn't, but let's do it anyway."

It was an instant replay of our previous encounters. The chemistry bubbled and brewed just as it had before, only more so. And neither of us made any attempt to conceal our feelings. We just clung to each other wordlessly, hardly moving in what was more of a passionate embrace than a dance. After awhile a Brit cut in and it took all the willpower I possessed to release Alexis and step away. Our eyes met for an instant and the exchange was like a 5000-volt short circuit. When I got back to the bar, Enderton handed me my drink that he'd been babysitting and said, "There may be something to this myth about the mesmerizing effect fighter pilots have on women."

I took a big slug of gin and muttered, "I'm not a fighter pilot any more, remember?"

"Maybe she doesn't know that."

"She does."

"Well, whatever it is, you got it and I wish I had it. As you know, I'm an Alexis watcher and I've not observed her like that before. How did it happen?"

"I met her in Tokyo...by accident."

"Ah so. Then you, my boy, have succeeded where all the rest of us have failed miserably."

"It's not like that, Charles."

"Oh? Then my eyes must be deceiving me."

"Seriously. We just...It was a platonic thing that sort of got out of hand and..."

"Hey, Richard. I gave up on Alexis long ago. Oh, I still dream a little on occasion but that's all it is. So don't sweat it."

I shook my head. "No...we're not...I haven't even kissed her."

"With the kind of stuff going on that I just saw, you don't need to kiss her."

"I know…I know, Charles. But what I don't know is what the hell to do about it."

He looked at me strangely. "That doesn't compute, Kemo-Sabe."

"I solve one damn problem and walk right into another that's worse than the first one."

"Yeah, well it's a problem a lot of us would like to have."

"I can't…I'm married and I love my wife."

"Of course. But you're not with the one you love and this is war and all that jazz," Enderton counseled.

"What about her Marine? She says she's in love with him and they're gonna get married."

"Then I'm right, it's that fighter pilot's irresistible charm. And remember, she's entitled to a little war exemption and all that jazz, too."

"All I know is that she and I got a thing going and neither of us seems to be able to turn it off."

"Well, okay. Maybe this thing you got going is something more than just war jazz?"

"Don't even say that, Charles."

"Hmmmm. Maybe we better have another drink."

As I turned toward the bar someone bumped me. It was Moore and he was headed for the dance area with fire in his eyes. One glance at Roxanne told me why. She was dancing with a handsome British officer who was holding her in a vice grip and she wasn't resisting.

"More trouble coming," I said to Enderton.

"Yeah, I see it," he replied, handed me his empty glass and headed after Moore. He didn't make it in time.

Moore grabbed the Brit by the neck and jerked him away from Roxanne, who fell face down onto the ground. He then picked her up and started brushing the dirt off. The Brit stood there looking at Moore as if to say, What's your problem? Roxanne gazed at Moore for a moment, then laughed, flung her arms around his neck and kissed him. A big cheer went up and everybody went back to what they were doing.

Enderton came back to the bar grumbling. "Christ! Some times I feel like a mother hen with a bunch of errant chicks!" About that time the British commander twisted his handlebar mustache, walked over to what looked like a piece of angle iron hanging on the tent pole and beat on it with another piece of angle iron. "I say, ladies and gentlemen, dinner is served!"

Everyone took seats from the selection of folding chairs, wooden boxes, etc. The dinner was then served by mess personnel in dress uniform. It was one of the grandest affairs I've ever attended, considering the conditions under which it was held. I can't remember what was served, only that it was delicious and the camaraderie outstanding. We toasted lots of folks, beginning with the queen, of course. There were some speeches, some jokes and Moore even apologized to the handsome Brit he had jealously manhandled over Roxanne.

After a long and wonderful dinner, we drank some more, sang some more and danced some more. I suspect it was primarily circumstances that kept Alexis and me apart for the remainder of that evening. She was, of course in great demand as a dance partner and when not dancing, she was surrounded by the Brits. We did exchange a couple high-voltage glances, which we both knew only poured fuel on the fire.

Moore and Roxanne disappeared shortly after dinner and sometime in the early morning hours the musicians finally collapsed and the party was over. Although one jeep of MASH folks ended up at a battalion CP somewhere on the MLR, and another landed in Uijongbu, we all eventually found out way back to the 8055 MASH. It was a grand evening and one of those events in life that you never forget.

It was all quiet on the western front the day after the British party, which was fortunate because there were lots of serious hangovers, including all four of us pilots. We stayed in our sacks most of the day. I spent much of that time thinking about my Alexis dilemma, which resulted in more confusion and no solutions.

I felt better the following morning and after breakfast decided to clear my troubled thoughts and do an outdoor painting. It was a beautiful day and I had wanted to paint a picture of the bombed-out Imjin Gang River railroad bridge since I first saw it, but it had been too cold or we were too busy. After making a deal with Enderton that if I saw choppers taking off I would quickly return, I grabbed my painting gear and followed the trail down to the bridge, which was only a short distance from the MASH.

The river was still frozen but the sun was bright and the contrast between the gray, broken slabs of concrete and twisted, steel rails against a cobalt sky made a great composition. As though I was afraid it would suddenly turn cold again before I could get it done, I hurriedly put up my easel and launched into the painting.

After about an hour of intense painting, I put down my brush and fired a cigarette. When I stepped back a few feet to view my progress, I saw someone coming down the trail. I figured it was probably Jon to tell me we had business and I had to return. A few minutes later he walked up to where I stood, only it wasn't Jon. It was Alexis. Our eyes met for a silent moment then she said quietly, "Sorry. I didn't mean to disrupt your concentration."

"It's okay. I needed a break anyway."

Because it was so warm she wore just GI work slacks and a jacket. Her eyes seemed to reflect the vivid blue of the clear sky and her beautiful auburn hair gleamed in the bright sun. She stepped closer and looked at the painting. "That's good, Richard. Have you been painting long?"

"Since I was a boy. I wanted to be an artist."

"It looks like you have done quite well."

"I mean a real artist."

She looked at me curiously.

"The war, marriage, a family...another war...but I have no complaints," I said.

"When I saw you walking down here I thought it might be a good time for us to talk. But it took awhile to get up the courage to come. I finally decided that since the sun is shining and we're not under the influence...."

"Good rationale," I agreed with a smile.

She returned the smile and said, "I don't know how to say this other than..."

"Just say what's on your mind, Alexis."

"Yes...all right. I thought I had resolved my quandary about our relationship, Richard...until the other night at the British party. Now I'm right back where I started."

"I'm having the same problem."

We stared at each other for a moment then looked back to the painting. She said, "I've always been able to control my emotions, within reason anyway. In fact, there was a time when I had began to worry about myself. I was so involved in my training and subsequent nursing, that I had little interest in men. Then I met Allen and it was as though the floodgates opened and I discovered how wonderful meaningful emotion can be."

She turned and looked at me. I nodded for her to continue because I didn't know what to say. "Now, I'm in a sea of uncertainty that I don't understand. As you know, we settled on a reasonable excuse for that night in Tokyo. But after what happened at the British party, I don't think we can we use that excuse, do you?"

I knew this conversation was going to occur, and I had spent hours thinking about it. About what I would say...about what I must say, regardless of emotional influences. But now that it was time to say it, my thought process went into a flat spin. I finally recovered and sort of mumbled, "I'm, uh, having trouble with what I want to say, Alexis."

She gave me a little smile and said, "Take your own advice, Richard. Just say what's on your mind."

I nodded. Hesitated. Then the words just came out. And I was pleased with what I said because I knew it was right: "We are just plain ole humans, Alexis, with plain ole human needs and desires, and war plays hell with those emotions. So, we can't really judge what our true feelings are for each other. But even if we could, there is nothing we can do about it anyway, because we're both committed to others."

She looked at me with those beautiful blue eyes for a long moment then said, "I believe that is true, Richard, even though it hurts."

"Yes...I know."

After a silent moment she stepped across to me and I took her into my arms. We clung to each other for awhile, then kissed tenderly there on the frozen bank of the Imjin Gang River, with the roar from a flight of jet fighters echoing off the twisted wreckage of the bombed-out railroad bridge.

After a time, she pulled away, looked at me lovingly for a moment, then turned and walked back down the trail. I watched her until she disappeared into the olive-drab shapes of the MASH tent city. I felt a sharp jab of regret as I watched Alexis walk away from the Imjin Gang River Bridge that day. I wanted to run after her, but I knew I couldn't. We had settled it with honor and deep affection. It was the last time I would ever see her. Fate stepped in the next day when Alexis and the head nurse went to a meeting of medical personnel in Seoul. Our element rotated before they returned to the MASH.

Chapter 12

Night Mission

The night before the Tiger element rotated from the MASH to our next assignment, I flew what was probably my most memorable mission in Korea. It all began that morning at breakfast with a discussion about flying the helicopter at night.

"Well I don't think the chopper cares if it's day or night when it flies, right?" said Hawkeye.

"That's correct. It doesn't care. But I do. I can't see where I'm goin' up in those canyons at night," I said.

"Aw to heck with the canyons! Why can't you fly up there like those night fighter guys do? The gooks can't see ya at night."

"But how ya gonna find the pickup spot?"

"Details, details," said Johnson.

"I know. It's easy—turn on your landing light!" said Hawkeye with a big grin.

"Great idea, Hawk," agreed Johnson.

"Yeah, but even if Igor Sikorsky had thought of that and put a landing light on his chopper, every gook on the MLR would be shooting at me when I turned it on," I countered.

"Well, as Georgie Patton used to say, No guts, no glory... Or was it Dugout-Doug said that?" Hawkeye asked.

"No. It was Audie Murphy," Johnson replied.

"Well if Audie can do it, Richard can do it. Right, Richard?"

That evening we had a little element change happy hour. For some reason the Quonset O Club was closed, so we had it in our tent and the place was packed. I was the pilot on alert that afternoon and had to wait for darkness before joining the festivities. I held out until the bombed-out railroad bridge was no longer visible through the Plexiglas door window. I had a little help in that the Plexiglas was so faded you couldn't see through it anyway.

As I worked my way through the crowd toward the bar, which was on our map table, I heard the alert field phone ring. Enderton happened to be standing next to it, so he answered. I glanced over and saw him talking and shaking his head, finally hanging up. I shrugged it off and went back to what I was doing: mixing some gin with a little canned grapefruit juice. Then I heard the phone again.

This time I saw Enderton speak for a moment then frowning, glanced at me and motioned for me to come over. I picked up my drink and made my way back over to where he was. "What's goin' on?"

"I don't know what to think. Some lieutenant at the aid station in G sector called and says one of his men is bad wounded and he knows we got somebody brave enough to fly after dark to save a man's life."

"What did you tell him?"

"I told him it wasn't a matter of bravery; we can't fly at night because we can't see where we're going, so it's against regulations. But the guy insisted there had to be someone here who would do it."

Hawkeye! I said to myself. He'd been joking that morning because he knew why we couldn't fly at night. But then knowing how he was, it sounded like a challenge he might concoct. I glanced around the tent and, sure enough, he wasn't there, which was unusual for Hawk. He was usually the first one to a party. I smiled to myself. I would call his bluff. "If he calls again, tell him your bravest helicopter pilot is on his way."

Enderton looked at me skeptically. "What?"

"We're being had, Charles. Just leave it to me," I assured him.

"Okay. It's your game, but you know the orders on night flying."

"I know, but just go along with me, okay?"

He shrugged and turned back to the nurse he'd been talking to. A couple minutes later the field phone rang again. I picked it up. Sure enough this guy identified himself as a lieutenant at pickup station 30 in the G sector. "You got to come get him!" he pleaded. "He's bad hit in the stomach and an ambulance ride from here will kill him for sure."

"Okay, I'll come get him," I replied, grinning to myself at how well ole Hawkeye had coached this guy, whoever he was, on how to challenge me. I had seen some of Hawkeye's fun and games and he could really lay one on when he put his mind to it.

"Thank you, captain. You will save this man's life for sure. You know where number 30 spot is?"

"I know where it is, but how am I gonna see it at night?"

"Well, can't you turn on your landing light?"

I almost laughed. "No. I don't have a landing light and besides every gook in North Korea would shoot at me."

"Okay. How about if we get some trucks and jeeps and turn on the headlights when we hear you coming?"

Ole Hawk had thought of all the details. "Say, uh, won't you take some fire from your North Korean friends when they see the truck lights?" I asked, grinning to myself.

"Well, if you remember, we're kinda down in a little saddle-like place on the ridge and if we keep the lights pointed down I don't think the gooks will see it."

"Oh, yeah. Good thinking," I said, chuckling silently. Then I saw Hawkeye come through the tent door. He had a nurse on his arm and it was pretty evident that whatever he'd been doing, it wasn't playing tricks on me.

"Are you really serious, lieutenant?" I suddenly croaked into the field phone.

There was a momentary silence on the other end of the line. "I don't understand," he replied in a cold voice.

"Well...I mean you really have a patient?"

Another silence. "I don't know what your problem is, fella, but just what the hell do you think we've been talking about?"

I suddenly felt like I'd been kicked in the stomach. "I'm sorry," I muttered. "Sorry." Here I'd thought it was a joke and it wasn't. It was real. And now it was a problem: my problem.

"Are you gonna come and get this man or are you gonna let him die?" snapped the voice on the other end of the field phone.

"Yeah. I'm gonna come and get him," I heard myself say. I had no choice. There was no way I could back out of this thing now, regardless of orders or the consequences. "I'll be there as soon as I can make it. When you hear the chopper coming, turn on the truck lights," I instructed and hung up the phone.

Enderton was busy talking to the nurse, so I slipped out the door without anyone seeing me. There was no point in discussing it with him anyway. He could only repeat the orders of no night flying and since I had made up my mind to go there was no point in putting him on the spot. But as I began to think about what I was attempting, it occurred to me that it couldn't be done...not alone anyway. There was no way I could fly the helicopter without being able to see the instruments, or at least the tachometer. Thy rotor RPM is thy staff of life, without which thou shall surely perish...and thou cannot see the rotor tach at night!

I walked down to the medics' tent. They were also having a party and wanted me to join. I begged off and told them my problem and asked for a volunteer to go with me...someone to hold a flashlight on the tachometer. They looked at me as though I might have already had a bit much to drink, but one of them volunteered anyway. I suspect he'd had a belt or two, but not so much that he couldn't hold a flashlight. I wish I could remember his name. He was a brave young man to do what he did. He grabbed his medical kit and a flashlight and we headed for the helicopter.

I guess everybody was busy that night partying or whatever because I was able to start the engine, warm it up and lift off before anyone even knew what was going on. Then they all came pouring out of their tents in time to see us lift up from the helipad and disappear into the Korean blackness in the direction of the MLR.

In addition to his being brave enough to go, the medic had to fly without a seat belt so that he could move forward in the back seat far enough to hold the flashlight on the tachometer. We had covered the lens with surgical tape so that only a tiny beam of light shined out to spot the tach. That kept the glare from giving me vertigo, which would have meant certain disaster.

I had never flown a helicopter at night so it was scary at first. But like Hawkeye had said, the H-5 didn't seem to mind that it was flying in the dark. I climbed up to an altitude above the tops of the ridges so that I wouldn't plow into one in the darkness. Bear in mind the helicopter I was flying had no instruments for this type of flying and no lighting of any kind.

There was no moon but fortunately it was a clear night so I could see the dark outline of the horizon and the star-studded sky above. Below the horizon was just a big black hole. Once I leveled off above the ridges and put friction on the collective to hold power, I began to feel more comfortable. I then set throttle friction so it would hold constant RPM and I concentrated on flying by the sound of the rotors.

"Okay, you can switch off the flashlight, but be ready to snap it on again if I holler," I instructed the medic over the intercom.

After awhile my eyes got accustomed to the darkness and I was able to see the outline of the ridges below and pick out the contour of the Imjin Gang River from the reflection of starlight off the ice.

I knew which canyons were friendly in that sector, but there was no way I could identify or fly them in the darkness. But I had been to number 30 in the G sector earlier that day on a patient pickup so I was familiar with the spot. The challenge was to find it or get close enough for the lieutenant to hear me coming. He would then turn on the truck lights and hopefully I could see where to land. Of course the North Koreans and the Chinese would also hear me coming. But with no lights on the chopper they couldn't see me...could they?

I remembered that the canyon leading to that spot intersected the river at a sharp bend, so I stayed over it, navigating by starlight and watched for the bend. The Sikorsky was purring like a contented kitten and my eyes were adjusting well to the darkness.

"You okay back there?" I asked my medic.

"I'm fine, sir. But I wish I'd thought to bring my parka."

"That makes two of us," I replied.

It had been another springlike day so I too had forgotten to put on my parka and now the temperature was nose-diving. But that was the least of my worries. A few minutes later I was able to see the bend in the river, but when I turned north it was pretty much a guessing game from there on. Identifying the correct canyon was impossible since it was just black shapes in a sea of more black. Within minutes I had become so disoriented I had no idea which way to turn. I was just wandering around turning this way and that, probably in circles and probably over North Korea. The only good news was that nobody was shooting at me. Or if they were I didn't know it. It was getting colder in the chopper by the minute and even in the darkness I could see my breath making white mist, yet I could feel beads of perspiration popping out on my forehead.

"If you see anything, sound off," I said in desperation to the medic.

"Yes sir. But I can't see nothin, capt'n."

Neither could I. So now what? All I could do was hope to stumble onto spot number 30 as I wandered over the countryside, no doubt flying in and out of North Korean territory, which made it was only a matter a time till I flew over an anti-aircraft battery and they shot us down.

Okay. I'd given it a college try and now it was time to get the hell out of there before I got us both killed. I hated to give up, but I had no choice. "Shine the light on the compass," I instructed the medic. Igor had put a magnetic compass on his H-5 helicopter.

"Where is it, capt'n?"

"Up on the canopy."

He shined the light around until he finally found the compass. I took a quick look and banked around to a south heading which would take us back to the MASH. Then just as he turned off the flashlight, truck lights snapped on in the blackness below and directly ahead. It was such a surprise I couldn't believe it for a minute.

"Capt'n! There it is!" shouted the medic.

"I see it," I replied as I went down on the collective and back on the cyclic in one swift movement. "Put the light on the tach, quick!"

He quickly zeroed in on the tach. With the truck lights for reference I wasn't worried now about vertigo, but I sure didn't want to lose my RPM. I knew the wind was light so I made a beautiful steep approach right down to spot number 30. There was only one hitch: I flew right through the top of a tree. Fortunately, I flew through the part with small branches so there was little damage to the chopper. But the irony was that I knew the tree was there, as I had said to someone earlier that it might well be the only tree left standing on the Korean battlefield.

When the Sikorsky's wheels touched down on the good earth at the aid station, I quickly pulled the clutch engagement lever. I had to stop the rotor blades so I could leave the pilot's seat to assess the damage. I kept the engine running at idle because I didn't want to take a chance on it not starting. The medic had already leaped out as several GIs in battle dress appeared in the truck lights carrying the patient on a litter. As soon as the rotor had wound down sufficiently, I opened the cockpit door and was met by a battle-weary first lieutenant dressed in full combat gear. He had a dirty face and there were dark circles under his eyes. "Thanks, captain. I know you broke the rules and took a risk but you've saved the life of a fine soldier. And...I'm sorry for what I said earlier."

I nodded as I climbed down out of the helicopter. "I had it coming, lieutenant," I said as I glanced over the H-5 to see if I could see any visual damage from my spatial dispute with the tree.

"I thought you were going to crash for sure when you hit that tree," the lieutenant muttered.

"It didn't bother me because I never saw it. How close are the gooks?" I asked, relieved that I could see no serious damage on the bird.

"Just over that ridge," he said pointing to a dark shape off in the darkness. "We heard you up there a couple times and it sounded like you flew right over their positions. I don't know why they didn't open fire."

"The patient's on board, sir. We're ready to go," said my medic climbing back into the helicopter.

"Thanks again, captain. I owe you one," said the lieutenant, offering his hand. We shook hands briefly and I crawled back into the pilot's seat of the chopper, strapped myself in and flipped the rotor engagement lever. As I waited for the rotor blades to gather momentum, I told myself that I should be in pretty good shape now. I would simply crank on full power and climb straight up above the ridges, out and away from the enemy positions, then turn south and head for the 8055. Within seconds the rotor was up to full RPM and I was ready to go. I glanced out through the front canopy. The lieutenant and his men were all standing around the chopper, with the rotor wash buffeting their winter parkas. Their smudged faces reflected the pale headlights of the trucks that were parked around the helicopter.

"You ready back there?" I said to the medic.

"Yes sir, I'm ready."

"Okay. Put the flashlight on the tach and we're outta here."

When he adjusted the spot of light on the tach, I cranked in full RPM and pulled pitch. The 450 horses in the Pratt and Whitney engine barked loudly into the Korean night and the Sikorsky leaped off the ground and climbed skyward like a homesick angel.

Then all hell broke loose. Lines of fireballs sprouted from the blackness everywhere and it was obvious they were all aimed at me. There was no point in trying to take evasive action, the stuff was in all quadrants. And I suddenly realized why. When I'd climbed up from the landing spot at full power, there was a stream of fire shooting out of my exhaust stack at least six feet long! The gooks could see it for miles: it made a perfect target!

I could hear the sound of lead and steel piercing the Sikorsky: Ping! Pow! Plunk! Then the controls began to feel strange...and at the same time she began to shake badly. I could almost feel the helicopter beginning to disintegrate around me. She was slowing down as though all was lost. The sound of the rotors was diminishing...RPM was decreasing...RPM! I was losing my RPM!

"The flashlight!" I shouted as I quickly lowered the collective. The beam from the flashlight stabbed the tach and my heart stopped. The RPM was below the red line! I slammed the collective to the floor and was thrown violently up in my seat against the shoulder straps. The poor medic and the flashlight went flying across the cockpit as the Sikorsky dropped earthward like a rock.

But then all helicopters drop like rocks when you slam the collective down; it's like suddenly removing your wings. I was pretty sure at that point that recovering my RPM before the bird struck the cold, hard, Korean earth was another long shot. But it did recover. I couldn't see the tachometer because we'd lost the flashlight, but I heard that big rotor begin to sing and I knew I'd made it. I pulled in some collective to stop the rapid descent and had her level again when the next episode of the drama occurred. The North Koreans suddenly stopped firing and, just as suddenly, I was flying in the bottom of an inkwell. From a sea of red-and-white glare to pitch blackness. It was vertigo time in spades!

Somehow I managed to keep the helicopter level, at least long enough for my eyes to readjust and pick up the reflecting starlight to give me reference. Surprisingly, the H-5 seemed to be functioning normally. The medic recovered the flashlight and I checked all the gauges and everything looked okay. I couldn't believe it, because I was certain we'd taken a lot of hits. I could only conclude that in my anxiety to get away from the ground fire I had held too much collective for too long and simply bled off my RPM. One thing about the ole Sikorsky H-5, it would let you know when it didn't like what you were doing: it would shake like a hound dog out of water.

The rest of the flight went without incident. I found the river and followed it to the valley where the MASH was and we landed there a few minutes later in a flurry of activity. The lieutenant had called and told Captain Enderton that we were on our way and the whole MASH turned out to meet us.

The patient was critically wounded and we had gotten him there in the nick of time. After they operated, he hovered on the edge for several days, but he recovered. I never knew his name, but we rarely knew the names of the thousands of men whose lives we saved with the helicopter in the Korean War.

"You crazy bastard!" were the first words I heard that night when I stepped down out of the chopper. It was Enderton, but he was grinning and a little flush-faced.

"You got any gin left?" I asked.

"Yeah, we still got some. And you're gonna need it. You're in deep kimchee, ya know."

"I figured that. Do they know at HQ?"

"Not yet, but when they find out there will be hell to pay. What possessed you to do it?" he asked his words slightly slurred.

About that time Hawkeye walked up and put his arm around my shoulder. "Ya see, Richard, I knew you could go up there and save people's lives with your landing light."

I smiled and looked at Enderton. "I rest my case."

Despite an awful gin hangover the next morning, I went out to the helipad to inspect the battle damage on the H-5 and found not a single bullet hole. I couldn't believe it. I could have sworn I heard bullets striking everywhere. Obviously they hadn't. Despite all that fire the commies had put up, they hadn't touched me. That gave me some hope that maybe I wouldn't be in quite as much trouble for violating orders.

Sure enough, Enderton told me that since there was no damage, he wasn't gonna say anything. So it looked like I was off the hook.

I wasn't off the hook, but that's another story that comes a little later.

Chapter 13

The Geisha House

In the normal course of rotation, our elements would go from R and R to the North Korean islands, then to the MASH, then to one of the various fighter/bomber bases, then to home base alert duty and back to Japan for a week of R and R. Because a couple of bad winter storms upset that schedule in the early months of 1953, we were out of sync. To get back into the proper schedule, Enderton's element pulled another tour of home base alert at K-16 after we left the MASH.

Normally K-16 was pretty good duty because our mess hall did a fair job, we had a hot shower now, and there was a small military PX in Seoul that sold a few luxuries. Other than to go to the PX, however, there wasn't much of a reason to go into Seoul, unless you enjoyed seeing the terrible destruction and desperate, miserable living conditions war had brought to that once-beautiful city.

As if there wasn't enough misery already, the spurt of warm weather brought an early thaw and the Haun River quickly went over its banks and flooded all the lowlands, including our camp which became a sea of mud and muddy water. Then, of course, it froze again a few days later and we had frozen mud and frozen muddy water.

On the plus side of the ledger, Hayes got a letter from Kanuri, written in English. You never saw a guy so happy. He ran around the camp showing it to everybody. It was pretty scratchy and some of the words were hard to decipher, but it was close proximity to English anyway. "Ya see, that proves she wants to do all she can to make sure we can communicate and stuff," he explained to Enderton, me, Pouhlin and Drake that evening as we sat around the potbelly in Enderton's tent.

We had shut the potbellies down, but then came the freeze and we had to fire them back up again.

"Yeah, that's good, George," agreed Enderton. We also agreed.

He looked at Enderton and said, "Okay then. How about you asking Major Woods if he will approve my request to get married and we can have an almost-spring wedding next week when we go to Japan on R and R?"

"Whoa! Hold the phone, George! You gotta speak for yourself on that situation."

"Yeah and there is a lot more to it than just getting the CO's approval, George," advised Pouhlin. "That request gotta go through command and that takes months."

"Spoilsport," muttered Drake.

Pouhlin shrugged. "Well he might as well know the truth of what's facing him."

"It takes months to get an approval? How do you know that?"

"Because I know a guy who wanted to marry a Korean girl and by the time he finally got it approved the girl had married somebody else," said Pouhlin, turned and winked at me.

"Aw, yer full of it, Jerry," said Hayes.

"Well, if you're really gonna do this thing, George, one thing *is* for sure: you better get your tail in gear and ask Major Woods," said Enderton.

Hayes declared he was sure enough going to do it the very next day.

As it turned out Major Woods had gone to Japan that morning to a meeting at group headquarters, so Hayes couldn't see him. Before the major returned, we got our orders for R and R and while we were flying to Japan, Major Woods was flying back—we passed him somewhere over the Sea of Japan. Hayes' disappointment was displaced, however, by his excitement at getting to see Kanuri and he literally ran out of the terminal at Tachikawa the moment we landed.

The four of us stayed at Johnson Air Base again and enjoyed the great food and quarters. None of us could believe that instead of going on R and R, Moore had volunteered to go back to the MASH and fly missions so he could be with Roxanne. The other two pilots in Enderton's element headed out to their "ranches," as did some of the medics.

Since it was almost spring in Japan too, we were able to do some sightseeing including a trip to Mt. Fuji, which was a fascinating experience. I also shopped in Tokyo again and found more inexpensive gifts for my wife and kids. I didn't run into Alexis or any of my old fighter pilot buddies on this R and R, but I did have a unique, fascinating experience at a Japanese geisha house.

Enderton roared off in his MG the day after we got there and I didn't see him again till the day before our scheduled return to Korea. I found him that morning at his usual place drinking coffee and smoking a cigarette in the O Club dining room.

"You look rested and recuperated, Charles. Did you have a memorable experience?" I asked, sitting down at the table beside him.

He grinned. "Oh yes. I always do in the Land of the Rising Sun. And you?"

"Yes. Most relaxing," I admitted.

"Any more accidental meetings with beautiful nurses?"

I shook my head. "Not this time."

"How is that going?"

"It's settled. You could say that we put it to bed when I was at the MASH this last time, but that would be misleading," I said with a grin. "In a way that was the more serious of my Korean War problems, and emotionally the toughest one to solve. But I'm consoled by the fact that we solved it in an uncompromising manner that preserved our honor and the deep affection between us."

Enderton raised his eyebrows. "Congratulations. I sure wouldn't have put any money on that outcome."

"Neither would I."

"Well, we all have to deal with these complications in life on occasion. Yours truly included."

"You have a complication, Charles?"

"Oh, yes... I...uh...Richard, how about a special touch of Japanese culture for your last night of R and R?"

"What do you have in mind?"

"A special place that I guarantee you will enjoy."

"What kind of culture?"

"Just leave the details to me."

I hesitated.

"Trust me."

I nodded, "Okay, Charles."

We drove out of the air base in his MG about five o'clock that evening and headed for Tokyo. He was pressing the season with the top down, but I had on a winter blouse so it was tolerable and I had an exhilarating ride through Tokyo and out into the outskirts of the city. I was getting a bit numb, however, when he finally turned into a side street with two- and three-story wooden structures. A short drive later he pulled up to a masonry wall with a wooden gate. The gate opened almost immediately and we drove into a driveway where several other cars were parked. A Japanese man appeared and gestured for us to follow him. I looked at Enderton skeptically.

He grinned. "You're gonna love it. Don't worry about a thing."

"One question. You have been here before?"

"Oh yes."

The guide escorted us down a stone walk that wound through a garden where Japanese lanterns reflected multicolored lights over a variety of trees, shrubs and flowers. The pathway crossed over a meandering fish pond and terminated at a large, ornately carved wooden door. It swung open as we approached and a mature Japanese woman appeared in a brightly colored kimono. She bowed and said in English, "Welcome back, Capt'n Enderton. It good to see you agin."

Enderton returned the bow. "Thank you, Mama-san. Good to be here again."

Once inside, two similarly dressed young Japanese girls appeared and moved silently up beside us.

"This his first time, Mama-san," Enderton explained to the older woman as he slipped his shoes off and handed them to one of the girls.

"Ah so," she replied, with a gold-laced smile.

"It's their custom. They don't wear shoes indoors," Enderton explained to me.

After I removed my shoes and gave them to one of the pretty girls, we put on a pair of cloth slippers and were led down a spotless corridor to a room where we entered through a wood-and-paper sliding door. The interior was lighted by electric lanterns and the walls were covered with oriental murals of dragons, castles and samurai warriors. The only furniture was an ornately carved dividing screen beside a low, polished wooden table on a colorful, fabric floor mat. Again out of nowhere, it seemed, the two girls who had taken our shoes reappeared. Standing before us, they each held bright, embroidered silk kimonos. "Now they are gonna trade you a clean, sweet-smelling kimono for that stinky ole uniform, and when you get it back it will be freshly cleaned and pressed."

By this time I had guessed that Enderton's special place was a high-class geisha house of some kind. "Charles, I've had enough temptation here of late. Am I gonna have to face some more here?"

Enderton smiled. "Not the kind you have in mind. What we're going to enjoy here, Richard, is a cultural experience in delightful entertainment, good drink and outstanding gastronomy. Now they do have a selection of other pleasures if you so choose, but I have already ordered the cultural option."

I looked at him suspiciously. "I trust that you're a man of your word?"

"That is a valid assumption, my friend. Now, peel off your clothes, but keep your cigarettes," he said and began to undress.

I glanced at the Japanese girls. Their heads were bowed, revealing the festooned decorations in their glistening black hair. I couldn't help but notice that they were pretty young girls with shapely figures and creamy, flawless skin.

"They won't look at you," Enderton advised. When in Rome, I said to myself, and undressed. After the exchange was made and we had on the kimonos, the girls disappeared with our uniforms.

"You look great in that kimono, Richard. Now come on over here and let's get into the proper posture so I can give you a synopsis of the sociological and cultural significance of the Japanese geisha." Enderton said, moving across and sitting cross-legged at the table. I followed suit and managed to get my legs under the table just as the sliding door opened and two new Japanese girls appeared. They both carried decorated trays holding a small porcelain bottle, a tiny teacup and a steaming towel.

These girls wore traditional, floor-length, long-sleeved Japanese kimonos. Their glistening black hair was swept up into ornamented buns. Their movements were quick and efficient, yet with a quiet, delicate poise. Kneeling silently beside us, they offered the steaming towels.

"This is just a quick clean-up for now. We'll get the...uh, full treatment later," Enderton explained, wiping his hands and face with the hot towel. "Come on, wipe up," he urged.

After the towel exercise, Enderton said, "Now they're going to pour us a drink in those little china cups. It's called sake. Ever taste it?"

"No. It's a white wine, isn't it?"

"It's actually a beer made from rice, but it does taste more like a wine. They serve it hot."

The girls removed the used towels, then filled the tiny cups from the bottles. Enderton picked up his cup and said, "Here's to culture," and drank the contents in one gulp. I picked up mine and tasted it. I was pleasantly surprised. "Not bad," I admitted.

"Ah yes. It warms the belly and stirs the imagination," he said as the girl attending him refilled his cup. The small cups only held one big gulp. I finished it and my girl quickly refilled it. "Are these geisha girls?" I asked.

"Not exactly, although they are a part of the geisha team that will tend us tonight. You see, the geisha is a professional entertainer of men and that includes a variety of entertainment functions."

"But aren't they really just prostitutes?"

"Not so. The legitimate Japanese geisha is not a whore. She is a classy lady who is not only beautiful, but also knows how to entertain men—how to carry on a conversation, dance, sing and play instruments. This geisha house is sort of a westernized version of the Japanese original, but it offers all the amenities of the traditional with some added features for western travelers."

"That's a surprise. I thought a geisha house was just a high-class whorehouse. Do these girls speak English?"

"This set doesn't talk much. They just pour the sake until we signal uncle."

"How many sets of girls are there?"

He smiled. "Several."

"Okay, Charles. You're Red Leader tonight." We touched cups and tossed off another gulp.

We smoked cigarettes, chatted, and drank sake while the girls dutifully filled the cups and smiled. After consuming a couple bottles, I was feeling the effects and so was Enderton. "Richard, I gotta admit that I had an ulterior motive in inviting you here tonight. Oh, I knew you would enjoy the experience, but I also wanted the ambience in which to confess my li'l complication and solicit your advice." I looked at him suspiciously. "That confession about solving your quandary was right impressive, ya know. I'd like to get your take on mine."

"Well, I'm at your service, Charles. But I sure can't guarantee my advice, specially after a couple bottles of sake."

He got a big smile on his handsome face and said, "I'm havin' a boat built here'n Japan an when it's finished, I'm gonna sail around the world."

I looked at him. "Sail around the world?"

"Yeah. In a Tahiti ketch."

"What's a Tahiti ketch?"

"The greatest li'l sailboat you ever saw. You can go anywhere in one an' you don't need fuel, jus' the sail. The Japanese are great ship builders."

"Tha's quite a revelation. I would never have suspected that bein' an aviator, you would want to become a swabbie."

"It's a dream I've had since I was a li'l boy, an the time is comin' to do it. As my favorite poet, Louisa May Alcott, would say, 'I am not afraid of storms, cuz I have learned how to sail my ship.' Learnin' the technique of actual sailin' is the easy part."

"I don't know much of anything 'bout sailing, so I can't give you any advice on that," I admitted.

"That isn't what I need the advice on. My li'l complication is the selection of a first mate."

"You got a first mate?"

"Not 'zackly. But I need one cause it will take years to complete my journey, so it's an important selection. I have to confess that I selected one here awhile back, but it didn't work out so good."

I downed a cup of the sake and waited for him to continue. "My selection of a first mate was Alexis."

"Alexis?" I sort of croaked.

"Thas the one. As you know, I've had a thing for that girl since I first met her. How some ever, despite my best efforts I've made no headway. Like I toll you at the British party, you got what turns her on. I don't. Thas that. An' I want you to know, Richard, I'm not jealous. Besides, it's academic now anyhow, so lemme tell you my dilemma, okay?"

I nodded.

"To choose Alexis for my first mate was no doubt a pipe dream. But my second choice of a first mate is not a pipe dream."

"Ah so," I said, with relief that he was minimizing his disappointment over Alexis.

"Yes sir. Shez real an' she is lovely an' she is interested in me an' she'll sail anywhere I wanna go."

"Now thas the kind of first mate to choose."

He smiled and said, "Yeah, I think so," paused and turned serious. "But there's a problem. An' thas what I would like your opinion on, Richard."

"I'll give it my best shot."

"She's the Japanese boatbuilder's daughter."

It took a moment to collect my thoughts, particularly since we were now on our third bottle of sake. "From your description of her qualifications, she sounds like an ideal first mate."

He nodded. "I know an I've told myself that but..."

I knew what Enderton's problem was. It had come out several times when we were discussing Hayes and Kanuri. "The bridge too far thing?" I said.

"Yeah. I guess so. I honestly believe it's a tough road to mix cultures at this point'n time an would probably end up badly. But I gotta tell ya, I truly enjoy bein' with this girl. An' when we're together it's...well, it's jus' great. I go there when I'm on R and R an stay with her in a neat li'l place right on'a water in the village where my boat is bein' built. An every minute we're together is wonerful." We both took shots of the sake.

"Charles, like I said, it sounds like she has all the qualities of what you want in'a first mate. But I'm gonna give you the same advice you gave George. Give it some time. You ain't goin nowhere till this war is over an' you can't sail yer boat round the world till it gets built an you get out of the Air Force. So you don't need a first mate fer awhile, right?"

He nodded. "Thas all true and it's probably a pretty good piece of my own advice. Ya see, I figured you would know all this stuff about women, bein' as how yer a fighter pilot that beautiful women like Alexis fall all over."

"Naw, she didn't fall all over me till I got to be a chopper pilot."

"Hey! Yer right!" We both laughed and tossed off another shot of sake.

About that time the young girls disappeared and the mama-san we met at the front door appeared and sat down beside us. "We honored to hav'a you come again to our house, Capt'n Enderton, and welcome to you, Capt'n Kirkland," she said smiling. I hav'a all number-one geisha for you tonight." She then gave her hands two quick claps and five lovely girls, all in different-colored kimonos, moved silently through the sliding door and into the room, their sparkling brocade dresses rustling softly as they formed a line before us.

"You get first choice, Capt'n Kirkland," said Enderton with a wave of his hand.

"What for am I choosing?" I asked, surveying the beautiful girls. They stood silently watching me with shy, demure expressions on their dark-eyed, doll-like faces.

"The one you choose will serve an' entertain you fer the next portion of the evening," explained Charles. "She will prepare yer dinner an' serve it, then entertain you. You won't believe her talents."

"Yeah, I'm sure. I thought you said no temptations?"

"Remember, this is the cultural presentation." I rolled my eyes at him. He laughed.

The girls were all beautiful but I noticed one particularly delicate little flower who couldn't have been five feet tall. Her face was like that of an exquisite doll with flawless features and skin that looked like velvet. Her eyes were coal black and sparkled like that had tiny bits of quicksilver sprinkled in them. "Awright. I choose the lovely lady on the left end."

Enderton nodded. "You got good taste, my friend. Isn't she delightful? My choice is the lady on'a other end. I have the feeling she can cook a great sukiyaki."

The mama-san got to her feet, clapped her hands again and she and the girls quietly disappeared through the sliding door. "Now prepare yerself for a grand experience in gastronomic delight," declared Enderton.

Moments later, the two selected geishas reappeared. They had changed their clothes into less formal kimonos and brought with them more sake and an array of cooking materials which they quickly set up on another table that was brought into the room. Working swiftly and efficiently, they alternately poured sake and prepared dinner over a charcoal-fired hibachi.

"They're great li'l chiefs. Oh, the sauces an' vegetables are prepared in'a regular kitchen. But they'll do the final preparation an' cookin' right here before you. Look at that! You see how she did that? An jus' wait till you taste it," exclaimed Enderton, his cheeks beginning to turn a warm pink from the effects of the sake. And I could feel my face getting a bit flushed also. The sake had a kick, particularly on an empty stomach.

"I assume they don't join in the eating part of the show?"

"You assume correct. They are trained servers." Charles was right. They prepared and served in several courses a unique and excellent Japanese dinner consisting of exotic appetizers made of both raw and cooked fish in tasty sauces, delicate soups, and beef, pork and chicken dishes with a variety of fresh vegetables.

The girl I had chosen had pronounced her name to me at the outset, but otherwise spoke little. She demonstrated great perception in sensing my slightest desire during the course of the meal. All the dishes were served in small china bowls using wooden chopsticks. Fortunately both Charles and I knew how to use them. When the dinner was completed, the girls quickly whisked away the cooking equipment and dishes and we got up, stretched our legs and smoked a cigarette.

"Wasn't that an excellent dinner an'a fun experience? Thas the way they are trained an the best is yet to come." I looked at Enderton. "Now don't jump to conclusions," he cautioned.

Dressed in elaborate theatrical attire, the two girls reappeared about 20 minutes later. They wore sparkling gowns of bright brocade, and their faces were painted with vivid, high-intensity paint to appear as colored masks. Their hair, in convoluted folds, was swept up and held in place by decorative combs. The petite geishas appeared unreal, as if they were finely made, exquisitely painted mannequins.

We sat cross-legged facing the dividing screen where they performed an animated oriental dance, taking turns dancing and playing a small string instrument. The dancer twisted her body and rotated her head in a series of exotic movements that seemed disjointed, yet each move or gesture was in rhythmic harmony with the sound of the string instrument played by the other geisha. They made several presentations, similar in style, but varied enough to be entertaining. At the conclusion of each performance, we would clap and cheer and they would bow in quiet recognition.

When the girls had taken their last bow and retired from the room, Enderton said, "They're not the top dancers an' musicians of Japanese theater fame, but they're pretty damn talented an' it gives you a slice of their culture."

"A pretty good slice I'd say."

"Right on, and now yer gonna get another slice. You'll love it."

"What am I gonna love?"

"The bath. Japanese style."

"How do they do that?"

Sounding casual, Enderton said, "Oh, in their traditional way."

Before I could phrase my next question, the sliding door opened again and the girls stepped through. All of their makeup had been removed and now they wore regular kimonos. My geisha walked up to me and smiled, her teeth showing white in a small delicate mouth. Her dark eyes reflected those little specks of dancing quicksilver. She then reached out, took my hand in hers and led me out through the wood-and-fabric sliding door.

"Good night," said Enderton with a smile.

Before his "good night" registered, the girl had led me to a room with wooden walls, kind of like a sauna. There was a large, sunken, tile-lined bathtub on one side that was full of steaming water. It was almost big enough to swim in.

I suppose I was mellow enough from the food and drink to just accept what came next as part of the procedure. She slipped off my kimono, keeping hers on, sat me down on a wooded stool and dumped a bucket of warm water over me. Then she proceeded to scrub me with a big sponge full of soap. After washing off the soap with another bucket of water she motioned for me to get into the sunken tub. She was quite professional about the whole thing, but when I stuck my toe in the water it was far too hot. She insisted, however, and little at a time I got down into the scalding water. She smiled and said "stay," as you might instruct your hound dog. Then she departed the room. After awhile I couldn't have gotten out of the tub if I tried.

When she finally came back, I knew how a Maine lobster must feel when he's getting cooked. I was surprised at how strong she was for a little girl. She hauled me out of the tub, rubbed me down with a towel, put the kimono back on me and led me down a hall to a bare room, except for a sleeping mattress on the floor.

That was the exciting finish to the story. Enderton had told it straight: she tucked me in, turned off the light and departed. I remember waking up the next morning after one of the best night's sleep I've ever had.

"The only complaint I have about this place is they don't serve coffee," said Enderton the next morning as the two of us, dressed in kimonos, sat cross-legged on a floor mat, drinking hot tea and smoking cigarettes. "I have trouble getting my motor goin' in the morning without my coffee."

I glanced out at the beautiful garden, visible through an open window, and said, "I have absolutely no complaints."

Enderton looked across at me. "Then I can assume you enjoyed yourself last night?"

"That's an understatement. I had no idea that a geisha house was anything like this."

"Well, the traditional geisha house is somewhat different. As I said, this one has been westernized a bit. I've been to both and frankly, I like this version better."

"I'm not familiar with the traditional, but I suspect I'm with you."

A short time later two lovely girls delivered our freshly cleaned and pressed uniforms. Then the mama-san showed up and we visited a bit and paid the bill. I don't remember the price, but I do remember it was reasonable. I sometimes wonder if such a place still exists in Japan and what the price would be now. Probably enough to really buy the Brooklyn Bridge.

Chapter 14

The Painting of Sosa Ri

We had to hustle some, but we made it from the geisha house to Tachikawa in time for our flight back to Korea, which was scheduled for 1300 hours. Everyone was there except George Hayes. "Has anyone seen him?" asked Enderton anxiously as we stood in the MATS passenger terminal waiting for them to call our flight.

No one had seen him. "Do any of you know where the girl lives?" asked Enderton.

"You mean Kanuri?" said one of the medics.

"Yes, her."

"Yeah. She lives with one of the other girls that work at the Tachi Ballroom."

"Where?"

"In a broken-down apartment not far from the ballroom."

The ops clerk yelled out that our flight was ready to board. "Richard, cover for me. I'm going after him and we'll catch the next flight to Seoul."

"If you can't find him today, you better come on back, Charles," I cautioned.

"Okay. Kirkland's in charge of the element guys," he said and hurried out the terminal door. Fortunately our flight got delayed so we were late leaving Tachi and didn't get to K-16 until late that evening so no one noticed we were short a couple pilots.

I saw Bill Ryan in the mess tent the next morning and he asked me where Enderton was as he hadn't seen him. I waffled it, saying I thought he and Hayes had gone to the PX in Seoul.

"When he gets back tell him I want to brief your element this afternoon. You guys are scheduled to leave in the morning for the islands."

"Yeah, I know. Uh, I'll tell him."

I didn't get the full story of what happened until some time later, but Enderton and Hayes did show up later that morning, saving us all from a court-martial. The gist of it was that Enderton found George there at the broken-down apartment with Kanuri. Hayes had just decided he wasn't going back to Korea. Enderton told him he was going back one way or another. I guess he decided to go peacefully.

The next day we rotated elements. Enderton, Hayes, Moore and I went to Ch'o Do. Belyea and Drake went to the South Island, and Pouhlin and the other pilots went to fighter bases down in the southern sector.

It was evident that spring was coming because the ice on the Yellow Sea, which had almost reached the island from the mainland during our last tour, had all but disappeared. The days were warmer but it was still cold, particularly at night, and the Yellow Sea was still so cold we had to wear the uncomfortable exposure suits during the day.

Nothing had changed at our camp on Ch'O Do Island except there were pieces of a wrecked H-19 helicopter scattered all around our front yard. One of the pilots in the element before us had come back from a mission with some ground fire damage. Since the weather was good, they decided to do the repairs right there so a repair crew was flown up from K-16 in another H-19. They did the repairs, but damage to the tail-rotor controls was not detected so when the pilot took off on a test hop, the chopper went into an out-of-control spin. The pilot fought it for awhile but finally dropped the collective and slammed into the ground, turning it over. The rotor blades, going full speed, struck the ground and hurled parts and pieces all over the place. The good news was that no one was hurt. It was a problem for Ace Lovelady, however, because he was now short another helicopter.

It was still necessary to have our Korean stove going. But after sundown, when we went off alert, we peeled off the exposure suits and were able sit around in just our flight jackets rather than the heavy winter parkas we wore constantly during our last tour. As was the custom, everybody fixed whatever he wanted for dinner. While the others heated C-rations on top of the stove, I dug out my peanut butter and fixed a sandwich with Japanese crackers, chasing it with a Toddy. That was a canned chocolate-milk drink you could buy in the Seoul PX. It was made of condensed milk and tasted a little chalky, but it was tolerable.

I hadn't had a chance to talk to Enderton in private so I wasn't sure just how it was between him and Hayes. I knew that they had gone to see Major Woods before we left K-16, to ask for permission for Hayes to get married. But I hadn't yet found out how that came out. Apparently not well, because Hayes was very quiet. And I could tell by the way Moore was sulking that he too was in a bad mood. I guessed that something had happened between him and Roxanne.

We went to bed that night in a rather tense atmosphere. I was restless, but finally got to sleep somewhere around midnight. I hadn't been asleep more than a few minutes when the air raid siren started squalling. It was on a pole up the hill from our tent area and was triggered by the Kodak guys up in the radar station on top of the ridge. Since there was no one around to police us, we didn't bother putting on helmets, carbines or combat gear. But it was freezing now, so we had to put on our winter parkas, then went outside and stood around talking and smoking with the medics and our mechanic.

After awhile Enderton called the guys at Kodak on the field phone and asked them what was going on. They confirmed there was unidentified aircraft in the area. He had just come out of the tent to tell us it was for real when the fireworks started. The sky suddenly lit up with bright flashes and explosions all around us.

We dropped our cigarettes and made a dive for the bomb shelter, which was a cave dug into the side of the ridge just up slope from our camp. It wasn't dug to hold seven people, but we all crammed into it because it appeared that either bombs were being dropped on us or they were lobbing shells from the North Korean shore batteries on the mainland.

We stayed crammed up in that freezing cave all night long. Occasionally there would be a lull and about the time we thought it was over—boom! boom!—it would come again. It was a miserable experience that I thought would never end. When they sounded the all clear, it was almost daylight. We dragged our frozen bodies to the tent and crashed in our sacks. I was asleep in two minutes and slept for all of 30 minutes when the field phone shrieked and it was Kodak with a MAYDAY call.

If you have ever tried to get into an exposure suit when you're so groggy you can't see where your legs are supposed to go, you'll know how it was that morning in early spring of 1953 in North Korea. But we flew the mission and picked up an Air Force pilot who had been shot up on an early morning bombing mission. He had been hit over North Korea, but managed to glide out over the water before ejecting. It was a mission that could have been a disaster because of our lack of sleep, but fortunately it turned out to be textbook perfect. When we got back to our camp after the mission, we all crashed and slept the rest of the day. Fortunately there were no more MAYDAY calls.

It had turned cold again and storm clouds moved in over the island, so we sat around the 55-gallon fuel-drum stove and talked about the mission and smoked cigarettes. The guys at Kodak told us that an enemy bomber did drop some bombs, but what had kept us in the cave all night was a duel between the UN artillery there on the island and the commie artillery on the mainland.

I guess the satisfaction of a successful mission and a good sleep put us all in a better mood and both Moore and Hayes loosened up and began talking about their respective love problems.

"I'm sorry I let you guys down by almost going AWOL," Hayes confessed. "But you can count on that not happening again."

"It's history, George," said Enderton.

"Well, if it weren't for you, Charles, I'd be in deep kimchee, and I really appreciate you covering for me, Richard."

"You'd do the same for me, George. How did you make out with the major?" I asked.

He shook his head. "I don't know, because all he said is that he would look into it. He wasn't even sure what the regulations were. But he also asked how long I'd known Kanuri and when I told him, he frowned."

"Aw, that doesn't mean anything, George," said Moore.

"What do you think, Charles?" asked Hayes.

Enderton glanced at me and shifted on his homemade stool. "You'll get a fair shake from Major Woods," he finally said.

"But do you think he'll give me permission to get married?"

Enderton hesitated. "Yeah...I believe he will. But I don't think it will be until you get to know her a little better." He said, then looked at me and winked.

Hayes nodded slowly. "I want to marry her now and she wants to marry me, but if that's what the major says, we'll wait." We all said that was a good decision.

"Yeah...I wish Roxanne wanted to get married," Moore sort of mumbled, almost to himself.

"You asked her to marry you?" asked Hayes.

"Yeah."

"Well, what did she say?" I asked.

Brian took a deep breath. "She thinks she loves me but she's not ready to get married. I don't know what to do. I know she's a little...uh, free spirited, but I really love her." He lit another cigarette off the butt of the one he was smoking and took a couple of puffs. "I'm like putty in her hands. You won't believe what I did this last time I was up there."

We looked at each other and Hayes said, "What'd you do?"

He hesitated. "I shouldn't tell this...don't let it go any farther, guys, okay?" We nodded. "She wanted to go on a combat mission, so I took her."

"Jesus Christ, Brian!" blurted Enderton. "You flew Roxanne in a chopper on a mission into the front lines?"

"Yeah, and I damn near got us both killed."

"Does anybody know about it?"

"Only my medic and he's a good troop. He won't squeal. I talked him into letting her take his place on the mission. I mean she's a nurse and could do that part of it. But when we got up there and I started to land at the pickup spot, it came under fire from chink troops. I managed to do a quick-pedal turn and get out without getting shot down, but only by the hair of my chinny-chin-chin."

"You take any hits?" asked Enderton.

"Fortunately no. But that was just pure luck because they had me boxed and were pouring it on. I could hear the damn automatic rifles firing. But we did get the patient out later that day after our troops flushed out the chink patrol."

Enderton shook his head. "Christ, what we do for love!"

"Tell me about it," moaned Moore. "But you wouldn't believe that Roxanne. She loved it. Her eyes were sparkling the whole damn time, even when they were shooting at us."

"You're kidding! She wasn't scared?" asked Hayes.

"If she was, she didn't show it. That girl's got balls...uh, you know what I mean."

"Brian, I gotta tell you, that was irresponsible and stupid," growled Enderton.

"I know Charles. I know. But like you said, what we do for love."

"You sure nobody else knows about it?"

"I'm sure. When I got back near the MASH, I dropped down and flew up the bottom of the river until I was opposite the helipad, then popped up and landed quickly. Roxanne got out and disappeared before anyone knew we were there."

After we had asked more questions and hashed it over for awhile someone said, "I wonder if she's the first nurse to ever go on a combat mission?"

"Not exactly," I said, which drew curious looks.

"A buddy of mine was the pilot of a night fighter in WWII, the P-61. It was called the Black Widow. He knew a nurse who was in an advance medical unit when we were stationed in New Guinea. He not only took her with him on a combat missions, he did it several times and once she was with him when he shot down a Japanese bomber on a night mission."

"Holy cow!" exclaimed Hayes.

"Okay," said Moore. "So I'm not the only guy to succumb to the power of woman."

"Anyone ever find out about your friend?" asked George.

"Not that I know of."

"You ever meet the nurse?" asked Moore.

"No, but I guess she was something like Roxanne. They were gonna get married after the war."

"Did they?"

"No. He was killed. Fortunately she wasn't with him on that mission."

It was quiet for a moment, then the field phone shrieked. It was Kodak and they warned us that they expected more boom-boom shortly. So we each quickly fixed whatever our dinner was going to be. Mine was the same: peanut butter, Japanese crackers and Toddy. Kodak was right—it started again before we could eat our dinner, so we had a candlelight picnic in our quaint bomb-shelter cave. It only lasted till about midnight, however, so we did get to bed at a reasonable hour.

The next day a message came through that we were going to have a VIP visitor: a real live Air Force general. That was a surprise because we didn't get many top brass visitors on Ch'O Do Island. Apparently the general wanted to see at first hand a genuine behind-enemy-lines operation.

"That's all we need is some big brass weeney coming up here to tell us what we're doin' wrong," grumbled Enderton.

"I'm surprised they would even venture up here," I observed.

"They don't very often. But every now and then they come, stay a few minutes, then get to hell back to Japan and award themselves a citation for courageous duty behind enemy lines. But this is the first general that's ventured up here. This should be interesting. Maybe he'll inspect our crashed helicopter and give us a lecture on accident prevention."

"That's easy," said Hayes. "Don't let the helicopters go where somebody can shoot at 'em."

A couple days later an Army landing ship nosed up to the Sosa Ri dock and up the hill came the general and a couple of his lieutenants in a jeep. They were dressed to kill, so as to speak: full combat gear, polished combat boots, steel helmets, side arms, and all the whistles and bells. They went up to the radar station first, then drove down to our little hideout.

After a cursory look at the wrecked helicopter, the general and his two sidekicks marched into our cruddy tent. He was a little guy but he wore a huge silver star on his epaulets. After glancing around he said to his aides, "Like I told the men at Kodak, it's a bit primitive but the type of thing you expect in a behind-the-lines combat operation. You see how resourceful these boys are?"

The two pasty-faced, bright-eyed lieutenants snapped in unison, "Yes, sir!"

"It's like I keep telling those guys who squall that we need this and we need that up here on the firing line. You want to keep these operations lean and mean. You don't need a lot of unnecessary junk. Right, men? This is a behind-the-lines quick-response crew that saves our airmen's lives by their swift action. And if they are attacked by the enemy they have to bug out in a hurry. And they don't need or want a lot of baggage. And look at that! Just look at that stove. That's good ole American ingenuity. And that's exactly what I been telling 'em," said the general, addressing us as we sort of stood at attention beside the 55-gallon fuel drum with sand in the bottom that we used for a heating stove.

The general then waved his arms some more and said, "And look around, gentlemen. Look at all the resourcefulness here: homemade chairs and tables and stuff. They have made this place combat compatible and they're doing a great job up here in the combat zone. You have my congratulations, men," said the general, glancing at us, then at his wristwatch. "Okay. I don't want to interfere with this combat operation any longer, so let's get on out of here and let these men do their job. Keep up the good work and by the way, is there anything you need?"

It was on the tip of my tongue to say: Yeah. How about a shower or a decent privy or maybe a real stove to cook on and boil our drinking water? But before I could get it out, one of the lieutenants blurted, "I got an idea, general! Why don't we get them a shuffleboard? They could set it up right over there between the cots and when they're waiting for a MAYDAY call they could play shuffleboard."

"Yeah, great idea," said the other bright eye.

Even the general sort of rolled his eyes and said, "Well, you men let us know if there is anything you need...Okay, let's move!" he barked just like John Wayne, and strode out of the tent in his polished combat boots.

As we watched them drive off down the hill, Hayes said, "Well, he was complimentary of our creativity."

"Yeah. And he didn't say a damn word about the wrecked helicopter. I was expecting a lecture on that for sure," said Enderton.

"But...a shuffleboard?" croaked Moore.

I shook my head in disgust at not only the general's oblivion to the things we obviously needed, but at my own lack of mettle for not speaking up. "Well, we all stood here like dummies and didn't say a damn word."

"Yeah, but I already know from past experience, you'd be wasting your breath," replied Enderton. "Those guys have a blueprint in their minds as to how things are suppose to run and you ain't gonna change it."

"I know, Charles, that was evident from the outset. But it still riles me that I just stood there and didn't open my damn mouth."

"I hear ya, but there's something intimidating about a general. You just have trouble speaking up," said Enderton.

"I though he was pretty complimentary," said Hayes.

"Well, at least he had the balls to come up here," I conceded.

A benefit that came out of the general's visit was that he went off and left his jeep. We couldn't figure out why, unless he just forgot it.

Anyway, we sort of inherited it. Actually there wasn't any place to go except down to the boat dock or up to the village, where we weren't supposed to go anyway since it was inhabited by North Koreans. But it was comforting to know that we now had a jeep.

The next day was clear and we flew a long unsuccessful mission to the outer limits of our range looking for the pilot of a photo reconnaissance who had bailed out. It was almost hopeless from the start because the water was still so cold in the Yellow Sea he wouldn't have lasted long anyway. But we had to try, and we did, landing back at Ch'o Do with nothing but fumes in our gas tanks.

The following day, Ace Lovelady flew up in another H-19 with a couple of mechanics to salvage usable parts from the wrecked chopper in our front yard. While his crew worked on the helicopter, he volunteered to go on alert so I could take the jeep and go do some painting.

"Don't go into the village, Ace," he warned.

"Yeah, I know. They are North Koreans."

"And pirates."

"Pirates?"

"Yep. Before the war that village was the hideout for a band of pirates who used to raid the mainland."

"I'd heard that, but considered it scuttlebutt," said Enderton.

"Nope. I've read the intelligence reports on it. Those old decrepit-looking sanpans down there in the harbor have high-powered marine engines and they are armed to the teeth. Our intelligence guys use them now for raids on the mainland."

"With the pirates?"

"Who better to know how and where?"

"So now they're on our team?"

"That's right, but there's still some questionable folks in the village, thus the orders to stay out of it."

"You convinced me, Ace. I'll paint somewhere other than the village."

Armed with my .45, paint box and folding easel, I drove off down the road in our inherited jeep. The roads on the island weren't much more than trails and they went every which way, so after wandering awhile I ended up on a hill that overlooked the Sosa Ri village and the small bay where the pirates boats were tied up. Since I wasn't in the village I wasn't breaking the rules and it was a picturesque scene.

Sosa Ri was a typical North Korean fishing village with a couple dozen houses stacked at varying levels along the shore of a small bay. They all looked weathered and austere. Some had dilapidated wooden roofs and others were plain ole grass and sod. Several lazy columns of smoke drifted up from what looked like outdoor fire pits. A number of fishing boats of various sizes and the pirates' sanpans were scattered along the beach.

The major structure in the village was apparently a combination temple and schoolhouse. It was a two-story wooden building with slitted windows and those curled oriental beams. It looked out of place. But it was a great focal point for a painting since it was the only structure that looked freshly painted and it was a bright orange. I dove into the painting and had been working on it for about an hour when I heard something that drew my attention. I turned around and there beside the jeep peering at me were two shaggy-headed little boys dressed in ragged peasant clothing. They were probably six or seven years old, about the age of my sons.

At first they startled me and of course my mind was on the pirate thing Lovelady had spoken about. I reached for my .45, then one of the boys smiled. I couldn't help but smile, and put my .45 back in its holster.

"Hello," I said. Then they both smiled broadly and said something I couldn't understand.

"I'm painting a picture," I said pointing at the canvas. They looked at me, then at the picture and inched forward slightly. I realized they spoke no English so I pointed again at the painting and said, "So sar ee," moving my finger from the painting and pointing at the village down the hill. Then I waved my hand indicating they should come closer and look. "Come...look," I encouraged.

Cautiously they moved up a bit and peered at the painting with big dark eyes. Then one spoke excitedly and pointed. I deciphered that he'd sure enough called it Sosa Ri. The other boy laughed and pointed, also repeating the name of their village. I felt kind of pleased that they recognized it. But it occurred to me that they might not be alone, so I wanted to terminate the painting and get out of there. I dug into my jacket pocket and offered them each a C-ration fruit bar. They obviously knew what that was and didn't hesitate to accept it. I quickly packed my gear back in the jeep, started it and waved good by. They stood there eating the fruit bars and waved as I went off down the hill in the jeep.

I wished later that I hadn't been so cautious and that I'd finished the painting there on the hill. But I had completed enough of it that I was able to finish from memory and some aerial photos I subsequently took from the helicopter. It's my favorite of the painting I did in Korea and whenever I look at it now, a half-century later, I think of those two little North Korean boys. I now have grandchildren about their ages.

Chapter 15

Spring of '53

During the last days of our island tour of duty, the weather was terrible with freezing rain and clouds so there was no flying and we were getting tent fever badly. Then it turned spring like again and Kodak called and advised that Dumbo was in the area with some goodies for us. We all ran outside and contacted them on the handy talkie radio.

"Hey, guys, how ya doin'?" came the voice over the radio as they flew the SA-16 Grumman Albatross low over our camp. The big yellow stripe around her fuselage with the black letters RESCUE was plainly visible as the amphibian roared past.

"We are glad to see ya, Dumbo! Is the war still goin' on?" asked Enderton.

"Far as we know it is. We been grounded too. But the weather guru claims that spring is just around the corner," said the voice from the amphibian.

"I hope he's right. Ya got some mail and goodies for us?"

"No mail, it got delayed. But we have a whole crate of eggs for you."

"You got a crate of real eggs?" Enderton barked incredulously.

"Believe it or not, we do." We all cheered. It was a rarity to get real eggs in Korea, specially at Ch'o Do. "Okay, we're coming around on our drop pass now."

We watched anxiously as the SA-16 banked around and started its low pass over our camp. When it was overhead we saw the side door open and a crewman toss out the crate of eggs. The parachute popped open and glided gently down. The crate of eggs took a different trajectory: it reminded me of my dive-bombing days in the South Pacific when I rarely hit the target. The crate arched across our camp and struck the outcropping of rocks just above our bomb-shelter cave with a big, juicy splat! The parachute glided down and landed right at our feet. They had forgotten to attach it to the crate of eggs!

I think the statute of limitations has run out on a court-martial for actions committed during the Korean War, so I'll confess what we did. We drew our .45s in classic John Wayne style and blazed away at the Slobber Albert as it flew off toward K-16. We didn't hit it, of course, as the .45 handgun has a very limited range, but it sure made us feel better. Also on the plus side, we managed to salvage enough remains from the smashed eggs to make a couple of bites of scrambled eggs for each of us. I mixed my share with some peanut butter and that helped disguise the Korean dirt that got mixed in.

It did look like spring had finally sprung as the good weather held and we rotated to K-16 a couple days later. As usual, the first order was to head for the shower. I remember my WWII CO, Gerald Johnson, always demanded the camp crew build the shower as one of the first things they did when we moved into a new camp. Unless you have experienced going without a shower for two or three weeks, you don't realize how it affects your morale.

Kim greeted me enthusiastically, took my dirty laundry and handed me a clean towel. After I stood in the shower my allotted time, I came back to the tent and he told me about the accident he'd had with his bicycle: "I coming fast down'a big hill and a'suddenly this cart is appearing. I put on'a brake but only stop after crash into cart. Bicycle is bad broke and Kim is broke too," he said with a grin.

I laughed. "Well, you look okay. What about your bicycle?"

"Oh, is all okay now. Major Lovelady, he fix it up good."

"Well, you want to keep an eye out for carts from now on Kim," I counseled.

"Ah so. And no go down big hill no more," he said with another big smile.

Two of my tentmates, who were in other elements, were also in camp and I met them for the first time. I don't recall their names because I don't think we crossed paths but once or twice during the whole time I was in the squadron. But that was just the way it was. We were traveling gypsies whose paths crossed only on occasion.

That next morning I met Major Woods walking across the compound and he asked me if I had a few minutes to spare. Since we weren't leaving for the MASH till later in the day, I said sure and we walked on over to his office.

"So how are you doing, Richard?" he asked after we were seated in the corner of his Quonset hut office.

"I'm doing fine, major," I replied.

"Well, I was wondering because your...uh, application for transfer hasn't come across my desk."

"It...uh, must have gotten lost somewhere," I said with the hint of a smile.

He looked at me curiously for a moment. "Well, things do get lost around here. You want another form?"

"Well, I don't think I'll have time to fill it out right now. We're getting ready to go to the MASH and I got a lot of stuff to do before we leave."

"Oh...okay," said the major with a knowing smile. I returned the smile.

"So you just got back from the islands, how did it go?" he said, picking up the pack of cigarettes on his desk and offering me one.

"It went all right," I said accepting a cigarette, which he lit with his Zippo. (I don't know that I ever saw another kind of lighter in either WWII or Korea. I quit smoking when the jury came in there in the late '50s, but I still have that same Zippo that I used in both wars in my memento case.)

After we had our cigarettes fired, the major leaned back in his chair and said, "I understand the general declared everything at the islands is on target. Any comment?"

"Who am I to dispute the good general?"

"I'd like your opinion."

"Okay. The crews are doing a good job up there, major. A damn good job, despite a lot of unnecessary adversity."

"You mean the living conditions?"

"That's right. And it wouldn't take all that much to make a big difference in the way we live up there."

"I'm aware of that, but the word from above is that we should keep our austere, quick-bug-out posture at our behind-the-lines operations."

"I think we could improve our living conditions without compromising our operational posture."

Woods nodded. "I've only been there for a quick visit. But I'm going again as soon as I can arrange it and personally make an assessment. But my guess is that sustenance is the biggest complaint and I don't know there is anything we can do about that."

"Sustenance is only one of the problems."

"But it's always a major one." He paused and chuckled. "Reminds me of the Colonel Schinz episode. You've heard that story, haven't you?"

"No. Who is he?"

"Well, Colonel Schinz is a fighter pilot who was shot down in a dogfight over MiG Alley here last summer. He squawked MAYDAY and his flight buddies heard him, but somehow he got separated from them. He'd lost his engine but he managed to glide out to the Yellow Sea and eject over one of those little islands. He lucked out and landed in his parachute right on the island. Fortunately for him, it was small enough to be uninhabited. He wasn't all that worried because he knew his buddies had heard his MAYDAY call and would call rescue to pick him up. But when our guys went up there, they couldn't find him because he wasn't where his buddies reported. They searched for several days and couldn't find him so he was listed as missing in action. The colonel, on his little island, didn't know that and was expecting to be rescued within a day or two at most. So he set up camp there under a big tree and waited to be rescued. The next day he was sitting under his tree when a little baby bird came fluttering down. It had fallen out of its nest.

The colonel climbed up the tree and put the baby bird back in its nest. A few days later, he climbed back up the tree, got the baby bird and ate him."

It was a great story that I subsequently read in some official Air Force reports. The colonel actually remained on the island for several weeks and managed to survive until a passing UN aircraft spotted his SOS signals stamped out in the sand and he was finally rescued.

"Anyway," said Woods with a grin. "I am going to look into what we can do to improve living conditions on the islands and still remain, uh...mobile."

"It would be a big morale booster, major."

"On another subject, have you met this Japanese girl that Lieutenant Hayes wants to marry?" he asked.

"Yes sir, I've met her."

"What's your opinion?"

I shook my head. "That's a tough call."

"Enderton thinks he's jumping into marriage without knowing the girl."

I worked to suppress my smile and said, "I, uh...can't help but agree. He probably should get to know her better."

The major nodded and we sat smoking silently for a moment. "I married a girl I hardly knew during World War II. But I lucked out—it was the best decision I ever made. The only problem is that now it's pure hell to be away from her," the said in a low voice, glancing at the picture on his desk.

"I was single in WWII and I can tell you war is a lot tougher on a married man," I said.

"Amen," replied the major.

"Well...thanks for your input, Richard," he said, getting up and extending his hand. "I'm...uh, glad your application for transfer got lost."

I nodded. "Me too."

We were scheduled to leave for the MASH that afternoon, but for some reason it got delayed till the following day so after dinner about a half dozen of us got together for a poker game. Someone came up with a bottle of bourbon and Ace Lovelady showed up with a handful of cigars. I don't recall whose tent we were in, but I do remember two of the players were new pilots who had only recently arrived in Korea and hadn't started their tour yet. Naturally they were curious.

"You guys going to the MASH tomorrow to do front-line medevac. Is that rough duty?" asked one of the pilots as we sat around in makeshift chairs with the cigar smoke boiling up in clouds around the dangling overhead light.

"It can be rough duty," muttered Enderton, studying his cards through squinting eyes. "I'll take two." Cards were dealt to the players who sat around a wooden homemade table covered with an olive-drab GI blanket, which has been standard for gambling on in the U.S. Army/Air Force forever.

"You take any enemy fire up there?"

"On occasion."

"Open with ten won." (Won was Korean money.)

"Sometimes we get a few mortar shells."

"See ya, and up ya ten."

"And once in a while a chink patrol sneaks across the MLR and tosses a grenade or two."

"They do?"

"Pot's right, cards to the gamblers."

"What?"

"They throw hand grenades in your camp?"

A nod.

"They ever do that around here?"

"Oh, now and then."

"Anybody beat two kings?"

Some time, some more bourbon, and a lot of smoke later, the tent was quiet while one of the players debated whether to call or fold. The tent door squeaked open. We all turned and looked to see who it was. All we saw was a hand grenade on the end of an arm that tossed it into the tent, then shut the door. We stared at the grenade as it bounced across the wooden floor and rolled up to within a couple feet of where we sat. It was sizzling.

The scramble to evacuate the premises was probably akin to the running of the bulls in Spain. Chairs, cards, money and pilots spewed in all directions as we scrambled in a mad dash to get out of the tent. Some literally dove through the door, their bodies landing on the Korean earth outside with groans and moans and a few choice superlatives.

When the hand grenade went off, it was like a small firecracker "pop!" But nothing happened. The grenade was still lying there on the floor of the tent, smoking. Of course no one stopped to consider that a hand grenade doesn't sizzle or smoke. As we subsequently discovered, it was a real grenade, but with the powder removed and a firecracker substituted. Enderton would have been the prime suspect for planning the prank since he'd been pouring it on the two new pilots about chinks and hand grenades and stuff. But I knew it wasn't him because he nearly broke his neck getting out of the tent the same as all of us. So who was the culprit?

If we had been at the MASH, a dollar would get you ten that it was Hawkeye. He was infamous for pranks. Whoever it was that night at K-16 would have come to bodily harm if we had caught him. And it took awhile before we began to see the humorous side of it. But still no one would own up. In fact, we never did find out who the prankster was. (At least I didn't until a half century later when I tracked down Jerry Pouhlin to get his input for this book. He finally admitted that he was the culprit. But as I told him: of all the Korean tricks and jokes long forgotten, that one is still vividly remembered.)

The afternoon after the hand grenade incident, Enderton, Moore, Drake and I, plus our medics, were trucked up the valley to the MASH. It wasn't too bad a trip because the roads were in pretty good shape and it you could almost feel spring in the air. The 8055 MASH was en-camped at the same place there on the bank of the Imjin Gang River. Although the MLR had pretty well stabilized along the 38th parallel, the Battle of the Hills was still going on. Sometimes there were lulls in the fighting, then there would be a prolonged, bloody attack and counterattack, which gave us and the MASH plenty of business—all while the peace talks continued.

It was late morning when we arrived at the MASH and relieved Captain Bob Ferry's element. We visited for a few minutes then they crawled on the truck for the ride down the valley to K-16. They were just getting ready to leave when Moore came running up and yelled to hold the truck. Then he said to me, "Major Woods just called and ordered you back to K-16."

"What for?" I asked.

"He didn't say. Just that you're to return to K-16 on the truck."

"Did Enderton talk to him?"

"No. He's off somewhere with Hawkeye. I took the call."

"Damn."

"The major said to make sure you got on the truck," repeated Moore.

"Come on, Kirkland, if you're goin' with us, snap it up!" shouted Ferry.

"Okay. Let me get my B-4 bag," I said and ran up to the tent and got on the field phone. But I couldn't get a line to K-16, so I reluctantly grabbed my bag and got back on the truck that I had just gotten off.

It was late afternoon when we arrived at K-16 and after the long ride up to the MASH and back again, I was in no mood to meet with the CO. But as much as anything, I was curious, so I threw my B-4 bag in the tent and went over to Woods' office.

When I entered his office, he handed me a piece of paper and said, "Sorry about the inconvenience, Richard, but I need to get this settled before it becomes an issue that will cause both of us unwanted problems. Read this."

I sat down on a folding chair in front of the wooden table he used as a desk and looked at the paper. It was a recommendation for the Distinguished Service Cross for one Captain Richard C. Kirkland AO-749566, for conspicuous bravery in the face of the enemy while saving the life of a wounded United States soldier. It had been submitted by the lieutenant at pickup spot 30 in sector G. The DSC is a very high honor for valor and second only to the Congressional Medal of Honor. I just sat there looking at it.

"You're to be commended, Richard, for saving the man's life under those circumstances," said Woods. I didn't know what to say. "But the next guy who breaks the rules and tries to do that might not be as skilled…or as lucky. Would you agree?"

I still didn't know what to say although in all honesty I had to admit: "It was mostly luck, major."

"That would be my guess."

I nodded.

"There is an old military axiom that only a hair separates a citation for valor from a court-martial. In this case I could easily approve either. That was a hell of a mission and you saved a man's life. But if I approve a decoration, I'm condoning breaking the night-flying order, which you and I both know is a good rule. The new choppers coming out of the Sikorsky factory now have lights and instruments and before long we will be flying night missions routinely. But the birds we're using now for medevac are simply not equipped for night operations."

I nodded again.

"As you know, we're doing important work here in Korea. We're establishing a revolutionary new system of lifesaving medevac on the battlefield and rescue of combat aircrews. I can't afford to have helicopters wrecked and pilots and medics killed trying to win medals."

"I didn't do it to win a medal, Major Woods."

"I know you didn't."

It was quiet for a moment as the distinctive sound of a Gooney bird, taking off on the airstrip at K-16, filled the tent. When the sound had died away, Woods leaned back in his beat-up chair and said, "How is my buddy Hawkeye doin'? He get any good ones on you lately?"

I looked at Woods and smiled. "Well, sorta…but he didn't realize it."

"He is a character. Well, get Al Lovelady to fly you back up there and give Hawkeye my regards," he said, dropping the recommendation for my DSC in the trash box beside his cluttered desk.

I didn't get the medal. But I didn't get a court-martial either. As I've thought about it over the years, I think it all came out pretty well. I had a lot of exciting and emotional experiences in Korea as well as World War II, but the night mission at the 8055 MASH was certainly one of the most memorable and satisfying. There is something special about saving someone's life when you know there was no other way it could have been done.

Chapter 16

Chopper Missing

ce Lovelady flew me back to the MASH late that afternoon after my meeting with Major Woods. He would always take the opportunity to get in a little flying when he could get away from his duties as maintenance officer. When I walked into the tent at the MASH I was the center of attention. "So what was that all about?" was Enderton's opening question.

"Oh, nothing of consequence. What say we head for the mess tent?"

"Come on, Richard, what's goin' on?" insisted Drake.

"Nothing important."

"It's your duty as a member of the Tiger element to share with your fellow tigers," said Enderton.

I smiled. "Look guys, it's not a big deal and you already know anyway."

"What do we already know?"

"Don't fly the helicopter after dark."

Looks of uncertainty. "How did he find out?" Enderton asked.

I told them the story, adding: "And that's a Tiger secret. Okay, fellows?"

They all thought I should get the medal but they also could understand the CO's point. So we agreed on a pact of secrecy about the mission and walked over to the mess tent for dinner.

"Hey guys!" shouted Hawkeye who was sitting with Johnson and a couple nurses at one of the tables. "Come and join us." The four of us got whatever it was they were serving for dinner and joined them.

"The wandering gypsys return. Where were you this time?" asked Johnson.

"The Isle of Enchantment," said Drake.

"Then you must have had some enchanting adventures. Tell us one," said Hawkeye.

"They were all too enchanting to describe, Hawk," said Enderton.

"Come now, favor our dull lives with a story of excitement and adventure. Like an air-to-air battle between your trusty chopper and the Red Baron of North Korea, or should I say the Red Gook of North Korea."

We laughed and Enderton said, "Hey, one of our chopper pilots did tangle with a MiG back in the early days of the war."

"You're kidding?" said Johnson.

"No. He was out over the Yellow Sea on a MAYDAY call and a MiG made a firing pass at him. He managed to evade the MiG's fire by making quick turns right down on the deck. I guess the MiG made several firing runs then gave up and went home."

"Wow! I bet that chopper pilot had to change his pants when he got home," said someone.

"Hi guys," said Alice Smith, who sat down at our table. "It's good to see your smiling faces again."

"That's the Tiger element trademark, smiley faces," said Enderton.

"Now that's what I like to hear, a positive attitude," said Alice, with her usual cheerful voice and smile.

"So all is well in your little slice of the Imjin Gang River valley paradise?" I asked.

"Richard, me lad, if it were any better, we couldn't stand it," replied Johnson.

"Well I could," grumbled one of the other surgeons at the table.

"Now, Arthur, remember, positive attitude, stiff upper lip and all that sort of thing," said Hawkeye. "Guys, meet Arthur. He's our resident expert on hemorrhagic fever." Arthur nodded. He was a big man with a friendly face, but it was evident he didn't share Johnson's casual attitude toward hemorrhagic fever, whatever that was.

"We've had another outbreak," explained Alice.

"Damn!' said Drake. "Is it bad?"

"Well, we don't know yet, we've only had a few cases," replied Arthur.

"What's hemorrhagic fever?" I had to ask.

"It's a fever we don't quite understand," replied Arthur.

"You catch it and you start bleeding right through your skin until you're dead. Isn't that the way it works?" asked Drake.

"Well, in the worst cases, but it's not always fatal. It was almost an epidemic here in Korea during the early days of the war, but seems to have died out, until these recent cases popped up."

"Then there's a cure?"

"We're working on it."

"What causes it?"

"We don't know exactly. There are some theories about where it comes from but we don't have a firm grasp of it yet," added Arthur.

"Diane, come on over and meet the chopper pilots," said Alice to a nurse walking past our table with dinner tray in hand. She was tall and thin with short blond hair. She looked efficient. She sort of smiled and sat down next to Alice. Alice introduced her around then added, "Diane just joined us here a couple weeks ago. She replaced Alexis." She glanced across at me and added, "She went home to get married to the Marine."

My reaction to the news was something of a dichotomy: I experienced a sharp jolt of disappointment that I would never see her again, yet at the same time I was genuinely pleased at her good fortune...not to mention grateful for my exoneration.

"I thought she had a couple more months to go on her tour," said Enderton.

"She did. But since Diane arrived early, the chief nurse let her go home early. She was ready to go home, Charles. And it worked out real well because her fiancé also got his going-home orders so they are gonna get married now back in the States."

Enderton looked at me and said, "What's that old saying? All's well that ends well?" It did end well. Alexis got her Marine, whom I'm confident she loved. I got an honorable and warm memory, and Enderton got a cleared deck for his decision on a first mate. Not all war stories turn out that well.

A couple of the other surgeons arrived and there was some more talk about the outbreak of hemorrhagic fever. While that was going on, Enderton got up and left though he hadn't finished his dinner. Shortly after that Moore asked Alice where Roxanne was. She hesitated, then admitted that she was on a three-day pass in Seoul. Then the new nurse Diane, who apparently wasn't aware of Moore's relationship with Roxanne, let the cat out of the bag that an Air Force colonel had picked her up in a staff car. So Brian didn't finish his dinner either.

It wasn't officially spring yet, but the day after our arrival at the MASH it was warm enough to turn off the potbelly and even sit out in front of our tent with our shirts off. Johnson reminded us that it was still only April, so this was just a teaser and there would be more cold weather. But I guess the commies sat out in front of their tents too because there was no action on the MLR.

I remember the day well because it was not only warm and beautiful, it turned out to be quite eventful, even though we didn't fly a single combat mission. The main event was Roxanne's return from Seoul with the colonel. I didn't get to see the action because it happened over in the nurses' area. But it was an exciting event in that Moore knocked the colonel flat on his back with a haymaker. However, the colonel got up and slugged Moore and knocked him on his ass too. In the exchange Moore got a couple broken teeth, and the colonel got a broken hand. So I guess you could call it a draw. Apparently the colonel decided that discretion was the best part of valor and elected not to press charges. The MASH dentist fixed Brian's teeth, and one of the surgeons put a cast on the colonel's hand. As usual, Roxanne forgave Moore and he forgave her and they were back in love again. Enderton chewed Moore out royally and gave him a long lecture about controlling his emotions. But I doubt it sunk in because Moore was really in love with Roxanne and just couldn't control his jealousy.

The chief nurse was really pissed and transferred Roxanne back to Japan for reassignment. That action evidently kicked up a confrontation with the MASH commander. He didn't want to let her go until he had a replacement. So the colonel and the chief nurse squared off. The chief nurse must have won the battle because a couple days later Roxanne got her shipping orders. Moore was devastated. He alternated between sulking on his sack and ranting that the chief nurse was a bitch and had no justification to transfer Roxanne, and he was going to file a complaint with the Inspector General.

"In the first place, Brian, it's your own damn fault that she got transferred and you're lucky you didn't get a court-martial yourself," growled Enderton.

"Not really, the son of a bitch wouldn't dare bring charges because he's married."

"Ah so….the twist in the plot," said Drake.

"Well then why the hell is Roxanne messing with him if he's married?" snapped Enderton.

Moore dropped his eyes and ran his hand through his hair as he always did when he was nervous. Silence in the tent. "She can't help the way she is, Charles," he said softly.

"Yeah…I guess not."

"She's a good person and a good nurse. She…just likes to have fun, that's all."

"Yeah."

"I love her and she loves me."

A nod.

"And one of these days we're gonna get married."

Another nod.

"She'll be stationed somewhere in Japan and I'll get to see her when I go on R and R."

"Meanwhile, don't complicate things, okay?"

Hesitation. "Yeah…Okay, Charles."

The next morning Al Lovelady flew up in an H-5 to bring a part for one of our ships. Moore talked him into letting him fly Roxanne down to Seoul, where she was catching a flight to Japan. Lovelady wasn't crazy about doing it but he knew about Moore and Roxanne so he agreed. It turned out to be kind of a neat affair at the MASH. Everyone knew about what had happened and although some didn't approve of Roxanne's behavior, they all knew she was a dedicated nurse and a sweet girl that you couldn't help but like. So most of the MASH turned out to see her off.

It was almost as though she and Moore were going on their honeymoon. Everybody gathered around the chopper there at the helipad and someone even tied a ribbon on the door handle. Roxanne looked great in her class-A uniform and Moore was beaming. Everybody hugged and kissed and finally when Moore pulled pitch and lifted off, everybody cheered and waved as the chopper flew off over the bombed-out railroad bridge and on down the Imjin Gang River valley toward Seoul. It all worked out. Lovelady filled in on the alert schedule that day and spent the night with us. Moore flew back the next morning and Lovelady returned to K-16.

A couple days after Roxanne's departure, I was awakened by the field phone at the crack of dawn. Enderton was first on the flight schedule so I rolled over in my sleeping bag with the intention of going back to sleep. I was vaguely aware that he took the information on the pickup and left the tent. A few minutes later I heard the chopper rev up and take off and shortly thereafter I was back with the sandman in a deep sleep.

Some time later the sandman was displaced by Drake shaking me. "Richard! wake up! Enderton's missing!" It took a moment for the news to register, then I sat up quickly. "What?"

"He's been gone nearly two hours and his pickup spot is only a twenty-minute flight," said Drake, standing next to my cot.

"Did he get the patient?" I croaked.

"Yeah. He picked him up over an hour ago and headed back then, just disappeared."

"He's gotta be down somewhere," put in Moore.

"Was he under fire?" I scrambled out of my sleeping bag and grabbed my clothes.

"There wasn't any at the pickup spot, but there's a big firefight on one of those hills nearby," explained Jeff.

"Show me," I said, pulling my pants on and moving barefoot over to the map table.

Drake identified the pickup spot and where the firefight was going on and I could see that it looked bad. Enderton's egress route would have taken him right through the area now under fire. "Is the other ship ready to go?" I barked, as I pulled on my boots and coat and grabbed my .45.

"It's ready," said Brian.

"Okay. Call squadron operations and JOC and give them the info. I'm out of here," I said and banged out through the tent door on a dead run.

"You want a medic?" Drake shouted after me.

"No!" I shouted back and ran across the compound and out to the helipad. If I had to pick up Enderton, his medic and a patient, I would be at max load so I shouldn't take a medic now.

It was still freezing at night, but such a relief from the bitter cold we'd had all winter that I hardly noticed. The Sikorsky H-5 started on the first crank and within a couple minutes I had the rotors turning and was strapped into the seat and ready to go. As soon as I saw a rise on the oil and cylinder head temperature gauges, I pulled pitch and headed out across the MASH compound toward the MLR.

I abandoned our usual procedure of flying down in the bottom of the canyons to avoid ground fire. I climbed above the ridges and took a direct course to the area where Enderton probably got in trouble. As I skimmed along the ridgeline I scanned the area below, but it was difficult to see because the sun was still low on the eastern horizon, casting long, dark shadows over the craggy ridges and canyons. As I approached the sector where the firefight was going on, I could see the smoke from artillery fire boiling up in the distance. The adjacent canyon was probably my best bet, so I held my altitude and headed toward it. I couldn't see any anti-aircraft fire coming my way, but I sensed ground fire, which you can't see until it hits you. Then, of course, it's too late.

As soon as I was over the ridge, I lowered the collective and dove for the bottom of the canyon, leveling off just above the rocks and brush. Skimming along, I flew up the canyon toward the firefight where Enderton would be if he was shot down. I could only hope he'd been able to land or autorotate without a serious crash...and hopefully the commies hadn't captured him.

I snaked up the canyon, turning and banking with the contour of the convoluted ridges until I came around a bend and directly into a maelstrom of fire and smoke. I had blundered into the thick of the assault. I kicked rudder pedal violently, spun the chopper around and dove back down the canyon. It's one of the neat things you can do with the whirlybird you can't do with a fixed-wing aircraft. There was no evidence I'd taken hits, as the bird seemed to be flying normally as I hurtled back down the canyon. If Enderton had flown through that same firestorm he had no doubt taken hits and would be in one of the canyons nearby.

I stayed low until clear of the area then pulled in collective and climbed up the ridge so I could get into the next canyon, which would be the most likely place he'd go. Sure enough, the moment I skimmed over the ridge I saw Enderton's chopper dead ahead and my insides knotted. The H-5 was lying on its side in the bottom of the canyon with the rotor blades twisted like pretzels and intertwined with the strewn wreckage. He had probably flown into the firefight canyon just as the attack started, took hits that had damaged the H-5, then managed to fly out this far before losing control and crashing...and it didn't appear to be a survivable crash.

My worst fears seemed to be confirmed as I approached the crash site. There was no sign of survivors. I set the bird down nearby, quickly shut the rotors down, jumped out and ran over to the wreckage. To my relief and surprise, there were no bodies in what remained of the helicopter. I did see blood here and there but no Enderton, no medic and no patient. After a closer look at the cabin of the Sikorsky, I realized that despite its mutilated appearance, it was possible that both occupants could have survived the crash. And so could the patient if he'd been in the port-side carrying pod, which was still intact. The starboard pod was smashed to bits. There was no visible evidence of a struggle and the surrounding area was void of habitation of any kind. So what happened to them?

There were only two rational possibilities: either a commie patrol had found them alive and taken them prisoner, or one of our patrols had found them and taken them to an aid station. In either case, the best thing I could do was fly back to the MASH and get on the field phone. I ran back to the chopper, quickly started it, engaged the rotors and headed down the valley toward the MASH.

Moore heard me coming and was at the helipad when I landed. The instant I chopped throttle and disengaged the rotor, he ran up and pulled the pilot's door open. "They're okay!" he shouted.

I nodded, then just sat there in the pilot's seat while I waited for the required two-minute engine cool down...and my emotions to settle. It was another of those gut-wrenching experiences in the business of war. I had lost friends several times in WWII, but I got a reprieve this time. It was a turn of good fortune, but it takes a while for that awful feeling to go away before you can proceed on course. I guess Moore knew that. He backed away from the chopper and stood there waiting for me. When I finally cut the engine and crawled out, he said, "One of our patrols found them and took them to an aid station. They're beat up, but nothing real serious."

"That's awful good news, Brian."

"Sure is. You okay?"

"Yeah."

"Uh, you want some breakfast?"

"Well, maybe a cup of coffee."

"Come on, I'll walk over there with you."

Enderton, his medic and the patient were brought back to the 8055 MASH in an ambulance later that day. They had taken some lumps in the crash, but nothing life-threatening. Hawkeye and Johnson patched them up temporarily, and Major Woods called on the land line saying he was sending an H-19 the next morning to bring them back to K-16 for additional medical attention at the 121st Army Evac Hospital in Seoul.

I broke out a bottle of Jack Daniel's I'd been saving for just such an occasion and we had a ripping happy hour that night in the 8055 Quonset O Club. Hawkeye, Johnson and several of the others surgeons and nurses came over. After he'd had a couple drinks, Enderton's lumps felt better and he was ready to tell us his story.

"Look at it this way, Charles—you only got four more to crash and you'll earn your chopper acehood," said a grinning Hawkeye.

"I don't think I'm gonna make it Hawk," replied Enderton.

"Aw, don't give up so soon, Charles. The way things are going at the peace talks, you'll probably have another couple years to get your quota of five," added Johnson, taking a big shot of the Jack.

"Well, Mike, it isn't the crashing that bothers me. It's that godawful sudden stoppage when you hit the good Korean earth," said Enderton, adjusting the sling on his arm.

"When I first saw that pile of wreckage laying in the bottom of the canyon, I would'a bet the ranch there were no survivors," I had to admit.

Enderton nodded. "When that baby let go and we fell out of the airspace, I would have bet the same."

"Were you pretty bad shot up?" I asked.

"Not that I realized. Hell, I'd picked up the patient and was heading back cozy as you please, when all of a sudden the bird just seemed to come apart. I slammed the collective down but I was too low to get into full autorotation before we plowed into the ground."

One of the more serious flight problems the helicopter pilots faced in medevac mission on the battlefields of Korea was the one Enderton had encountered. Flying low in the canyons compromised our autorotation capability. And Wilbur Wright had it correct: the helicopter falls to earth with deathly violence, especially when it doesn't have sufficient altitude or speed to go into autorotation.

Enderton continued, "After we hit, those big ole rotor blades just kept right on goin' around, beating the helicopter into the ground something awful, ripping off parts and pieces and spewing them in all directions. Christ, I thought it would never stop. When it finally did and I realized I wasn't dead, I looked out through the broken canopy and all I could see was these two huge eyeballs staring at me.

The chopper was lying on its side and the external carrying pod on the port side was sticking up in the air, almost inverted. The patient, a Frenchman, who spoke no English, was still strapped in, although the pod cover had been ripped off. He was just hanging up there staring at me with those big eyes as if to say, What in Christ's name is going on here? The poor bastard had a broken back, but when we lifted him out of the pod I swear he tried to get up and run off."

"He broke his back in the crash?" asked someone.

"No. He had that when I picked him up at the aid station. Fortunately they had loaded him into the left pod. If he'd been in the right pod...well, it was smashed to bits in the crash."

"And so goes the luck of the Irish...French in this case," said someone else.

The next morning Enderton and the medic were flown back to K-16 and I took command of the Tiger element. As he was boarding the H-19, Enderton turned to me and said, "Ya know, Richard, sometimes ole Mr. Fate plays the hand pretty well. You're ready and able to ramrod this act, and I'm in need of some time to get my act back together."

"Your act is okay, Charles. And I have no doubt you and your first mate, whoever she may be, will sail that Tahiti ketch off into the sunset."

He grinned. "Think so?"

"I know so."

"Don't take any wooden won," he said and crawled into the helicopter.

Unfortunately, I never saw Charles Enderton again after that day and I never heard for sure if he chose the boatbuilder's daughter as his first mate. But if I were a betting man, which I am, I'd bet he did.

Chapter 17

Mission Accomplished

From the time Enderton left the element till the peace talks at Pan Mun Jom finally ended the fighting in Korea on July 27, 1953, the hill battles continued to rage with some of the most vicious fighting of the entire three years. The air war also intensified those last few months and on one single day U.S. Navy pilots flew a record of 538 offensive missions. Over MiG Alley, Air Force pilots fought Russian and Chinese pilots right up to the last day, producing a score of American jet aces.

I commanded the Tiger element during that final deadly phase of the war, but not much changed in our gypsy lives or in the way we did our business. We continued to provide battle-taxi service for the MASH and pickup service for the Air Force, Navy, Marines, ROK and other UN pilots and crews shot down over North Korea or the Yellow Sea.

On the final day of the war, we still had a sign over our tent door that read: "You ditch and call, we bitch and haul, anytime, rain or shine." We also still had our 55-gallon fuel-drum stove on Ch'o Do Island and I was still surviving on peanut butter, crackers and cans of Toddy—except when the Dumbo crew dropped us fresh fruit or some other goodie.

Speaking of the crews that flew the SA-16 Amphibians, they did a great job in Korea, and even if we did shoot at one that time they dropped the crate of eggs without a parachute, we appreciated their efforts and help. They were the bright spot of our day when they flew over our island camp and it was comforting to know they were usually on station somewhere in the combat zone to help when we needed them.

In the late spring of '53 an SA-16 made a landing in the Yellow Sea under rough sea conditions to pickup one of my element's crews that had crashed. An H-19 flown by Jim Belyea, his co-pilot and medic went down on a mission just south of the island and a Dumbo answered his MAYDAY call. And if the Amphibian hadn't responded when it did, we would have lost them because the chopper at Ch'o Do, which would normally have responded to his emergency, was off on another mission.

On my last tour at Ch'o Do Island, just before the cease-fire, I had the opportunity to do a series of paintings of native life, including one of the smaller villages we called Sosa Ri number two. That was just before they evacuated all the islanders who wanted to live in South Korea, which most did. It was a humanitarian thing to prevent reprisals from the North Koreans who took back control of the area in accordance with the peace-treaty terms. I don't know which side the pirates ended up on.

Duty on the islands was high risk under difficult living conditions, but it was also a humbling experience that gave me perspective on more than just the war. And we saved a bunch of pilots' lives that would have been lost in WWII. On one of our missions at Ch'o Do during those final days, we picked up a young fighter pilot out of the Yellow Sea who had gotten all shot up over MiG Alley and had to eject from his disabled Saber jet. I'll always remember what he said after we pulled him out of the water and into the chopper: "Can you get me back to K-16 in time for the afternoon mission?" His name was Captain Joseph McConnell, Jr. We got him back in time for the afternoon mission and he went on to became America's leading jet ace and remains so to this day.

The helicopters of the Third Air Rescue Group were given credit for picking up 846 pilots and aircrew from behind enemy lines during the Korean War. Add to that 8,373 soldiers and airmen we snatched from the battlefields and air-taxied to the front-line MASH. Quite a feat for a handful of taxi drivers.

At my final MASH tour, Hawkeye was still keeping up morale at the double-nickel MASH with his constant good humor and positive attitude. It just seemed that no matter how bad things got, he always managed to smile or crack a joke. I can't remember of ever seeing him depressed. They exaggerated some in the movie and TV series, of course, but the part about his quick wit and good humor was right on target. And keep in mind while he was doing all those antics, Dr. Sam Gilfand was also performing his share of duty and then some. He was an outstanding surgeon, as well as a super person.

I remember an incident during one of those hill battles when we were inundated with wounded. I had put on a gown and mask and was helping out in the OR, which we would sometimes do between medevac flights. Suddenly one of the MASH medics had an appendicitis attack and it was determined to be an emergency. When they carried him into the OR, Hawkeye had just completed a long and complicated surgery on a critically wounded GI. It seemed that he always got the worst cases. I guess that was because he could save a life even when it was all but hopeless. "Okay we gotta take care of our own, so it's time out for a quick appendectomy," he said, standing there in his blood-splattered gown holding a scalpel. "Richard, time me."

"Go!" I said and glanced at my watch. His incision was swift and accurate and within a few minutes the procedure was complete and he held up his scalpel and said, "Time!" The orderlies lifted the litter off the operating table and carried the medic into post-op while another group brought in the next badly wounded patient. I don't remember how long it took Hawkeye to take out the medic's appendix that day, but it was some kind of record and Diane, the nurse who took Alexis' place, told me that she'd never seen a better or more accurate procedure.

Speaking of Alexis, Alice told me during my last MASH tour that she had gotten a letter from Alexis saying that she and her Marine fiancé did make it home and were happily married. She asked Mary to be sure and tell me. I was pleased to hear it. Unfortunately, those kinds of situations don't usually turn out that well in the business of war.

One of those that didn't was the love affair between Moore and Roxanne. Just before the war ended, he went on R and R to Japan to see Roxanne, but she'd taken up with another Air Force colonel. I don't think it was the same one from Seoul. At any rate, they had another big squabble and they didn't have time to patch it up before Moore was shipped back to the States. It was a tragedy in a sense because I was around them enough to know that Moore was genuinely in love and I think Roxanne was in love with him too—as much as she could be with any one guy. But it was a volatile relationship because Brian was jealous and men were attracted to Roxanne like flies to honey. And being a bit of a free spirit, she just couldn't resist the attention, particularly when Moore wasn't around. I did see him at a USAF helicopter pilots' reunion in the states a number of years later and he was happily married and had a family. But he admitted, after a couple drinks, that he could never quite forget Roxanne. And so it goes in love and war.

I lost track of George Hayes after I left Korea so I don't know what happened with his romance with the little Japanese girl, Kanuri. I remember that when the war was over Major Woods was still waffling on his approval for them to get married. It was one of those things you just can't get a handle on. I know Hayes was in love, and I believe that Kanuri was in love with him. Being a natural born romantic, I believe that love can conquer all...well, almost all.

I lost track of Jeff Drake, but I talk on the telephone often with my good friend Ace Lovelady. I tracked down Jerry Pouhlin living the life of Riley in Florida, and he helped me with some memory for this book. Jerry told me he heard that Charles Enderton did go around the world in his Tahiti ketch, but I was never able to catch up with him.

So how did we do in the Forgotten War? To my way of thinking it was "Mission Accomplished," and then some. Although I arrived in Korea with a terrible resentment over being sent there, I came home feeling just the opposite—with a keen sense of pride in the USAF Air Rescue Service and my part in that unprecedented lifesaving effort. I elected to remain in the USAF and was fortunate to have played a supervisory role in the establishment of a worldwide helicopter rescue system.

I'm proud to have been one of a handful of pilots who brought the helicopter out of the novelty category and into the mainstream of aviation that Leonardo Da Vinci, Igor Sikorsky and all the other pioneers prophesied it would, particularly in life saving. The Korean helicopter experience not only ushered in a new set of battle tactics for the military, it established a whole new system for getting critical patients to medical aid in both the military and the civilian worlds.

After I retired from the USAF, I was involved in helicopters for another 30 years and had occasion to fly patients to hospitals where I landed in the parking lot or in the street. In one instance in Chicago in 1967, my landing on the front steps of the University of Chicago Hospital was considered so sensational it was on the front page of the *Chicago Tribune* the next day. Today, there are few hospitals that don't have a heliport. That all originated from MASH Angel in Korea.

True, it was one of the deadliest wars in history, and true we raged back and forth across Korea like a yo-yo killing and destroying. And after all that, we ended up right back where we started: North Korea and South Korea a divided nation at the 38th parallel. The two armies are still poised at the MLR and the United States still has nearly 40,000 troops in South Korea.

But that's the bad news. The good news is that South Korea, thanks to the United States, our UN partners, and all the brave men who died there, is a modern democratic republic that holds free elections and is one of the economic giants of the world. By comparison, I think we all know about the tragedy of North Korea. When I visited Seoul here a few years back, I couldn't believe my eyes. Where there had been nothing but rubble and devastation, I saw a magnificent, modern city. I think I counted a half-dozen beautiful bridges crossing the Haun River where there had been only a wobbly pontoon bridge when I left Korea in 1953.

As I told an audience recently in Washington D.C., at one of the events at the 50-year Korean War Commemoration, I'm proud to have been a part of making that happen and to have played a role in the unprecedented performance of the MASH Angel team. Together we cut the wartime mortality rate of World War II in half and brought about one of the most significant improvements in battlefield morale in the history of warfare.

During one of our recent conversations, my old buddy and fellow helicopter driver, Al Lovelady, said to me, "Ya know, Ace, it was tough in Korea, but by golly, we got the job done."

"Yeah, we did Ace. And the motto of the Korean War Commemoration has it right: "Freedom Isn't Free.""

EPILOGUE

During the half century that followed my Korean War experience, I saw the primitive "Chopper" we used in Korea transformed into a technological marvel that now flies around the clock saving lives. Today's helicopter performs emergency air evacuation and air rescue by snatching victims from raging flood waters, burning buildings, mountain tops, earthquake sites, accident sites, ship wrecks and many other life threatening situations including one of the greatest humanitarian efforts in American history: Hurricane Katrina, where over 70,000 lives were saved by helicopters.

Having taken a lesson from the life saving performance of Korean War helicopters, U.S. military requirements for the Viet Nam War precipitated the development of a second generation helicopter with advanced technology and turbine power. This new breed of whirlybird was utilized in various combat and rescue applications in Viet Nam that are legendary.

With this experience in hand, designers and manufacturers in the post Viet Nam era began to produce even more efficient and better performing helicopters that were operationally and economically feasible to be utilized for civil emergency medical operations.

In 1967, I flew my pregnant wife to the University Of Chicago Hospital in the middle of the night in a helicopter and landed on the front steps. My son was born a short time later. The next morning the front page of the Chicago Tribune blared: HELICOPTER BEATS STORK! It was sensational and was carried in newspapers across the nation.

However, acceptance of helicopter civil emergency medical evacuation came slowly. But in the 1970's, programs began to develop in major metropolitan centers, sponsored by hospitals and trauma centers. These programs providing quick point to point transportation of accident victims in congested urban areas and for inter hospital transfers. These programs have grown in number and maturity and have spread into rural communities also.

The rural emergency medical operations have demonstrated the life saving capability the helicopter provides as a quick response air ambulance, or air rescue vehicle that does not require an airport and can land almost anywhere to pick up a patient, accident victim, or medical emergency of any type and fly the patient directly to a hospital.

Today, these programs are in operation around the world. There are 310 air medical service providers utilizing over 840 helicopters in the United States alone and they have a remarkable record of saving lives, particularly in rural operations where long distances and limited medical facilities are involved.

Before the rural programs were initiated, victims of roadside accidents or critical illness could wait hours for emergency assistance, then have additional hours of road travel which often meant the difference between life and death.

The rural helicopter emergency medical programs are operated by private enterprise companies across America. They provide a highly effective rapid response on a round the clock basis by channeling the emergency calls through a central state-of-the-art dispatch center that is strategically located.

Trained dispatchers utilize the latest electronics and computerized systems to dispatch the nearest helicopter on the most efficient and acceptable weather route. Satellite tracking provides route and mission management as the helicopters respond to multiple calls across their areas.

To provide the highest possible degree of safety, air crew and maintenance personnel are experienced, highly trained, and standardized. All maintenance is performed under strictly controlled conditions and in accordance with the manufactures and federal maintenance requirements.

Since the helicopter must respond at all hours, fly to and land in all types of weather and terrain conditions, a high degree of pilot skill is required. This is assured through continuing training and procedure checks in the latest technology flight simulators. Medical crews who must also have a high degree of skill and experience and receive continuing training on procedures they must know to handle the various medical challenges they face on a daily basis.

These angels of mercy do not take off and land at paved airports or drive down wide highways. They operate into and out of cluttered areas between power lines and trees, in backyards, corn fields, mountain tops, road sides, or wherever else is necessary to save a patient's life. Yet, because of their skill, training, technology, and effective mission management, they do it and save lives, day and night. The proof of their capability is in the results: They save thousands of lives annually that would otherwise have been lost since there was no other way they could have been saved.

Recently, I visited one of the rural operations: The Air Evac Lifeteam, an independent provider at West Plains Mo. As I watched the dispatchers responding to calls, initiating electronic surveillance and dispatching the helicopter crews, my thoughts went back to those primitive days of long ago in Korea. It is deeply satisfying to have been a part of that pioneering effort. But it is even more satisfying to see the heritage of that effort in today's emergency medical MASH ANGELS.

The helicopter emergency medical crews do their lifesaving around the clock in both urban and rural America. Fortunately, Hurricane lifesaving only comes rarely. But it came dramatically with Hurricane Katrina on August 29, 2005.

The performance of civil and military helicopters and crews who responded to that call performed one of the greatest humanitarian efforts in American history, adding another gold star to the legacy of the MASH ANGELS.

After the hurricane struck, tens of thousands of people were homeless, clinging to roof tops or wreckage in a 90,000 square mile area. Nearly 600 helicopters responded from every corner of the country: They came from emergency medical operators, law enforcement, private owners, and news media, off shore oil companies, utility companies, exploration, forestry, U.S Coast Guard, U.S. Navy, U.S. Air Force, U.S. Army and National Guard units throughout America.

Those helicopters snatched survivors under severely adverse conditions of swirling waters, entangled wreckage, hanging electrical wires, fallen trees, and billowing smoke from raging fires. Those equipped with night vision goggles continued the life saving even after dark. When they couldn't land on the tops of flooded buildings and houses, they hovered around the entangled power lines and trees, or used their rescue hoists to lift survivors from the water, roof tops or floating wreckage.

The larger helicopters carried 10,000 pound sand bags to fill holes in the dikes. Others evacuated survivors from the collection points to safety out of the flooded area.

THE VAST MAJORITY OF SURVIVORS AT KATRINA COULD NOT HAVE BEEN SAVED BY ANY OTHER MEANS THAN BY HELICOPTER because of the conditions and because it had to be done swiftly and effectively before lives were lost. And despite the adversity of high risk operating conditions, not a single life was lost by helicopter accident during the entire operation. This remarkable performance by helicopters at Katrina may well be the greatest humanitarian effort in American history.

Igor Sikorsky, father of the American helicopter, said to me in December of 1955: "The helicopter concept is wholly rational and I envision it will bring into the world a whole new means of saving lives."

If Igor were here today, he would join me in saying: "Congratulations to America's MASH ANGELS. Keep up the great work!"

Richard C. Kirkland
Vienna, Virginia
August, 2009